REFERENCE GUIDES IN LITERATURE

NUMBER 11

Ronald Gottesman, *Editor*
Joseph Katz, *Consulting Editor*

Eudora Welty:
A Reference Guide

Victor H. Thompson

G. K. HALL & CO., 70 LINCOLN STREET, BOSTON, MASS.

Copyright © 1976 by Victor H. Thompson

Library of Congress Cataloging in Publication Data

Thompson, Victor H
    Eudora Welty : a reference guide.

    (Reference guides in literature ; no. 11)
    Includes index.
    1. Welty, Eudora, 1909-   --Bibliography. I. Title.
Z8964.86.T48   [PS3545.E6]   016.813'5'2   76-1983
ISBN 0-8161-7801-1

This publication is printed on permanent/durable acid-free paper
MANUFACTURED IN THE UNITED STATES OF AMERICA

Contents

Introduction

When Eudora Welty published A Curtain of Green in 1941, she gained the attention of the literary world, and, in the years since then, her writings have inspired a wide, though largely uncoordinated critical response. Much has been written, but because of the lack of comprehensive bibliographies, few scholars seem to have a panoramic view of the criticism. It is the purpose of this annotated bibliography to create such a perspective. In attempting to be as comprehensive as possible, I have consolidated the information contained in earlier selective lists and have added many new entries. Of the earlier lists, I am most indebted to Seymour Gross' "Eudora Welty: A Bibliography of Criticism and Comment" (1960.B5), which contains not only articles in scholarly journals, but also textbook explications and newspaper articles, and to Noel Polk's "A Eudora Welty Checklist" (1973.B56).

I have annotated the entries listed by Gross and Polk, as well as those listed in the MLA International Bibliography (1941-1973), the Mississippi Quarterly Annual Checklist, Articles on American Literature Appearing in Current Periodicals, Book Review Digest, and numerous shorter bibliographies. I have also annotated explications in textbooks from Langden Burns' "A Cross-Referenced Index of Short Fiction and Author Listing" (1970.B22; 1971.B10), and the entire collection of short story anthologies in the Library of Congress. Finally, I have annotated the Welty newspaper files of the Mississippi Department of Archives and History, and the reviews of Losing Battles, One Time, One Place, and The Optimist's Daughter held by Random House. Those few items I could not locate I have marked with an asterisk and identified the original source reference. Those newspaper entries I could see only in xeroxed form sometimes lack page number(s) but are otherwise complete.

The only works consciously excluded were brief biographical sketches which simply repeated the known facts of Welty's life, redundant articles in newspapers, extremely trivial or brief reviews, and those writings by Welty which did not bear directly on her fiction. What remains allows the reader to create a fairly coherent account of Welty's personal and professional activities over the past thirty-four years and to gain a complete perspective on the critical reception of her writings.

INTRODUCTION

The entries are of three types: bibliographical, biographical, and critical. In addition to the bibliographies of Gross and Polk, the bibliographical entries include all known lists of critical works, as well as all specialized bibliographical studies. The biographical entries include articles in periodicals and newspapers, essays and addresses, and interviews. The critical entries include books, reviews, and scholarly articles.

Biographical entries suggest that Welty's position in American literature is somewhat paradoxical. Although she is generally recognized as a major writer, she seems to have accepted American society, and it has accepted her. What Katherine Anne Porter observed in her introduction to A Curtain of Green remains true today: Welty is not a "spiritual and intellectual exile . . . groping for native roots." She is a sustaining member of the Junior League, a winner of the First National Bank Award (1964), and an appointee to the National Council on the Arts. Moreover, her talents have not been ignored. She has won at least one prize or award practically every year since 1940, and her books have generally been financial successes. Although her first three books did not reach a wide audience, Delta Wedding brought what Charlotte Capers called "the big money," and her latest books, Losing Battles and The Optimist's Daughter, appeared on the Best Seller List.

Welty's emergence as a major American writer has been steady and almost inevitable. The magazines returned her first work without comment, including the now-famous "Petrified Man," which was rejected so many times that Welty destroyed the original manuscript. But Welty achieved an initial success by publishing "Death of a Traveling Salesman" in Manuscript in 1936 and moved progressively into national and world eminence. Soon, Southern Review was requesting stories (including the rejected "Petrified Man"), and in 1941 Harcourt, Brace & World published her first collection of short stories, A Curtain of Green. It was published with some difficulty in spite of the efforts of Ford Madox Ford, but, when it appeared, Welty's reputation was secure. Perceptive reviewers and critics realized that a major new talent had been discovered; Welty then won O. Henry Memorial Contest Awards in 1942, 1943, and 1969, and published ten more books including The Ponder Heart, which won the William Dean Howells Medal of the Academy of Arts and Letters, and The Optimist's Daughter, which won a Pulitzer Prize.

From a position of eminent respectability, Welty is also one of America's most accessible writers. She grants numerous interviews, lectures at many colleges, and frequently discusses her art in essays. (The interviews are listed in the index under biography.) In the interviews, Welty answers questions about the craft of fiction--to which she is obviously deeply committed--and about her personal life. Welty's numerous critical essays--most of which are listed in this Reference Guide--appear in popular, as well as scholarly, journals and are often used in textbooks to help analyze her

stories. "How I Write," for example, was first published in the
Atlantic Monthly and was later included in Brooks and Warren's Under-
standing Fiction as a commentary on the genesis of "No Place for You,
My Love."

Newspaper accounts reveal Welty's interest in the theatre. As
early as 1949, she expressed a desire to write a musical comedy,
"What Year is This?" to compete with what she considered to be the
mediocre Broadway offerings of the time. She did not make her dramatic debut, however, until 1956 when Chodorov and Fields made a play
from The Ponder Heart, which appeared successfully in New York's Music Box. The play won her the enduring friendship of David Wayne,
who played the part of Uncle Ponder, and created the possibility of a
movie version of the book, a possibility still considered by Wayne.
The glamorous New York production probably made Welty even more famous in Jackson (Mississippi) than her books had done. The Ponder
Heart was performed twice in Jackson by the Little Theatre, once in
the version by Chodorov and Fields, and once in a version revised by
Frank Hains of the Clarion-Ledger Jackson Daily News. The success of
The Ponder Heart was followed by The Shoebird Ballet (based on her
children's book with the same title), A Season of Dreams (in which
she gave a reading), and a musical comedy version of The Robber
Bridegroom in 1974.

The newspapers present Miss Welty as perhaps the most amiable
and inoffensive writer that America has ever produced. According to
clippings from the New York Times and the Clarion-Ledger Jackson
Daily News, she is often helping with charities, submitting recipes
to cookbooks, attending coffees for the Jackson Symphony, and pa-
tiently speaking of her art to school children, college students, and
irascible old critics. For diversions, she accepts honorary degrees
and other awards, gives lectures and readings, and appears on educational television. In fact, Welty seems so amiable and so inoffensive that she belies the subtleties and ironies of her fiction. One
man in Taiwan wrote that he wanted Welty to be a grandmother to his
children. Welty never answered the letter, but, in discussing it
with an interviewer, she revealed another side of her complex personality: "I don't want to be anyone's damn grandmother."

From the seemingly mundane and tranquil world of Jackson,
Welty creates an art that to many readers is unrealistic and hope-
lessly regional. For--like one of her favorite authors, Jane
Austen--Welty depicts the world that she knows best: the world of
home, family, and community. Readers in search of scathing indict-
ments of American society often fail to see in her domestic and local
scenes a universal and enduring art.

In her introduction to A Curtain of Green, Katherine Anne
Porter introduced another aspect of regionalism which has been much
quoted by the critics. When she described "Why I Live at the P.O."
as "a terrifying case of dementia praecox," she inadvertently linked

Welty with those regionalists who had an obsession for Southern deca-
dence. According to the reviewer for Time, most of the characters in
A Curtain of Green were "demented" and "deformed"; only two stories
dealt with "normal" people. Porter also introduced a topic, social
criticism, which has been a persistent concern of the critics. When
Porter said, "Miss Welty escaped social consciousness . . . and she
has not expressed implicitly any attitude at all on the state of politics or the state of society," she set a precedent for critics who
regard the lack of "social consciousness" as a serious flaw. According to Tina Rathborne of the Harvard Crimson (1971.B35), as well as a
considerable number of other reviewers and critics, Welty's entire
literary production is unrealistic because she fails to write about
current social issues. (She did, in fact, write two stories of topi-
cal social interest, "Where is that Voice Coming From," and "The Demonstrators.") So extensive is this criticism of her work that Welty
wrote a rebuttal in "Why Must the Novelist Crusade?"

Porter also predicted what was apparently a persistent concern
for Welty, "The Novel." According to Porter, every publisher expected a novel from gifted writers of short stories. Before Losing Battles, many critics and reviewers were not certain that Welty had
written any novels. To some, The Robber Bridegroom was a long short
story, Delta Wedding was a short story expanded into a novel, and The
Golden Apples was simply a collection of closely related short stories. Even when Losing Battles appeared as an undeniable novel, some
critics insisted that Welty was more gifted as a writer of short
stories.

Porter also first identified one of the most important aspects
of Welty's style, the interplay between the external world and the
imagination, the "mysterious threshold between dream and waking."
(Eunice Glenn, in "Eudora Welty's Use of Fantasy," made the first attempt to analyze this element of Welty's prose). Fantasy is also
closely related to one of the most persistent doubts about Welty's
achievement: her apparent obscurantism. For many reviewers and
critics, this "mysterious threshold" is merely Welty's unsuccessful
effort to make mundane experiences seem profound. For others, however, Welty's prose is often difficult but not obscure, and the difficulties are justifiable since she depicts what she intends to
depict: the mysteries of human relationship and personality.

In addition to Welty's lack of social criticism and her obsession with mystery, five other aspects of her writings have consistently claimed the attention of the critics: her sense of place, her
comic sense, her use of myth and ritual, her use of colloquial speech
patterns, and her manuscripts. Welty's residence in the South and
the essay, "Place in Fiction," have produced considerable interest in
her use of setting. In his review of The Robber Bridegroom, Frederick Brantley noted that Welty used a Southern setting without being
a regionalist (1942.B12). Critics discussed the presence of regionalism in many of her other works, particularly Delta Wedding, The

INTRODUCTION

Golden Apples, and Losing Battles. (For a complete list, See "place" in the index.) For some critics, place is synonymous with regionalism; for others, it is the basis for a universal art.

Appel (1965.A1) and Vande Kieft (1962.A1) devoted chapters of their books to Welty's comic sense, and Seymour Gross contributed an important essay to The Comic Imagination in American Literature (1973.B39), "Eudora Welty's Comic Imagination." All three have helped to define Welty's position in the tradition of American humor. Closely related to the comic sense is Welty's use of colloquial speech. Robert Holland (1963.B10), Louise Blackwell (1965.B2), and Florence Ogden (1971.B32) affirmed the accuracy of Welty's reproduction of the subtleties of Southern speech. Welty's writings have also been the subject of considerable myth criticism. For a complete listing, see "myth" in the index.

W. U. McDonald has done most of the work with Welty's manuscripts. In addition to publishing "Eudora Welty Manuscripts: An Annotated Finding List" (1963.B14, with a Supplement in 1974), he has begun the work of comparing published works with the manuscripts. In two essays about Welty's revisions (1970.B74 and 1970.B75), he comments about Welty's methods of composition and observes that Welty's revisions suggest a concern for social issues. Other bibliographical studies of importance are McKelva Cole's "Book Reviews by Eudora Welty: A Checklist" (1963.B5) and Noel Polk's forthcoming bibliography of works by Eudora Welty, which appears in part in "A Eudora Welty Checklist."

Although numerous essays and reviews have been written, most of the comprehensive studies are yet to be done. Thirty-four years of criticism have produced only four full-length books and two pamphlets. Two of the books, Eudora Welty by Ruth Vande Kieft (1962.A1), and A Season of Dreams by Alfred Appel (1965.A1), are comprehensive introductions to the study of Welty's fiction; two of them attempt to deal extensively with particular aspects of Welty's style: Zelma Howard's The Rhetoric of Welty's Stories (1973.A1), and Marie-Antoinette Manz-Kunz' Eudora Welty: Aspects of Reality in Her Short Fiction (1971.A1). The pamphlets by J. A. Bryant (1968.A1) and Neil Isaacs (1969.A1) are general introductions. The many doctoral dissertations--twenty as of 1975--indicate an interest in analyzing Welty's art, but most of these emphasize the explications of stories rather than Welty's place in a larger critical context. (For the contents of the dissertations abstracted in DAI, see entries from DAI in the Reference Guide.)

In "The Literary Situation in 1953" (1953.B5), Malcolm Cowley explained why comprehensive studies of Welty's fiction are difficult. With their emphasis on symbol and form, Welty's stories are of particular interest to the New Critics. Consequently, they have been treated not so much as part of a literary tradition as they have been treated as separate and self-contained entities. As such, they have received extensive treatment in textbooks (See Landon Burns,

1970.B22 and 1971.B10) and have been analyzed separately in numerous
scholarly journals. In his "Eudora Welty" in A Bibliographical Guide
to the Study of Southern Literature (1969.B2), Alfred Appel notes the
continuing failure of critics to gain a wider perspective on the
achievement of Eudora Welty. By bringing together the diverse explications and reviews of the past thirty-four years, however, this
Reference Guide reveals some definite patterns and helps create a
critical context for Welty's fiction from A Curtain of Green through
The Optimist's Daughter.

　　　　According to Publishers' Weekly (1941.B5), A Curtain of Green
"attracted unusual attention" and sold surprisingly well for a first
book of short stories. But Booklist (1941.B7) made an important
qualification that has characterized the critical reception of Welty's books ever since: the stories are beautifully written, but
their unusual subject matter and style will appeal to only "a few
discriminating readers." Such nondiscriminating readers as the reviewer from Time (1941.B4) could not accept Welty's apparent emphasis
on the "demented" and "deformed," and the reviewer from the Commercial Appeal (Memphis) (1941.B19) noted sardonically that Welty was a
"Jr. Leaguer turned writer." But Marianne Hauser of the New York
Times Book Review (1941.B17) found the stories beautifully poetic,
and Albert Goldstein of the Times-Picayune (1941.B16) found in them a
"superior talent" and a simple, direct style. Since their publication
in 1941, individual stories in A Curtain of Green have received extensive critical commentary, particularly "Petrified Man," "Death of
a Traveling Salesman," "Powerhouse," and "A Worn Path." Also, many
of them have appeared in textbooks for analysis (See Burns, 1970.B22
and 1971.B10). But, except for chapters in Vande Kieft's Eudora
Welty and Appel's A Season of Dreams, no one has attempted to evalu-
ate the significance of the work as a whole.

　　　　The Robber Bridegroom also created sharp distinctions between
"discriminating" and nondiscriminating readers. Booklist (1942.B9)
found that The Robber Bridegroom would "have limited appeal," and
Nathan Rothman of Saturday Review (1942.B24) considered it an experi-
ment that Welty would not repeat. Emily Garnett's comments typified
the reactions of those who liked the book. She considered The Robber
Bridegroom a delightful combination of prose ballad and fairy tale,
with "passages of beautiful writing" (1942.B15). The major critical
response was--and to some extent still is--to Welty's use of folklore
sources. Lionel Trilling (1942.B26) considered her numerous allusions obscure, and John Peale Bishop (1942.B10) thought that she
failed in her effort to blend European fairy tales with American
folk tales. Alfred Kazin, however, considered the book a successful
representation of the American frontier. Because the use of native
folklore was still of critical interest in 1975, Welty spoke on the
topic before the Mississippi Historical Society.

　　　　The Wide Net confounded many of the critics who had admired
A Curtain of Green and The Robber Bridegroom. Although the title

story was generally considered to be a comic masterpiece--good enough to win first prize in the O. Henry Memorial Contest Award in 1942--many reviewers noted a tendency toward obscurantism in the remaining stories. One of the most representative attacks was that of Jean Stafford. In a review appropriately entitled "The Empty Net," she accused Welty of fine writing and deliberate obscurity. Several other reviewers, including Diana Trilling and Isaac Rosenfield, shared Stafford's opinion.

At this point in her literary reputation, Welty received some important support from Robert Penn Warren. In his essay, "The Love and Separateness in Miss Welty," Warren defended Welty against the charge of obscurantism. Although Warren admitted the presence of obscuring elements (for example, metaphors which only "pretend to an underlying logic"), he argued that Welty's style was perfectly suited for her central theme: "separateness."

Unlike Welty's first three books, Delta Wedding reached a large audience. The first edition was sold in three weeks, and the publishing rights were sold in Sweden. Some of the persistent doubts of the reviewers, however, remained. According to Diana Trilling (1946.B51), the book was "self-conscious and dream-like"; Orville Prescott (1946.B45) considered it obscure; and George Dangerfield (1946.B23) considered it a descent into "cloud-cuckoo land." Others noted a lack of plot, a hopeless regionalism, and a presentation of an unreal view of life. Discriminating readers were more sanguine. According to John Crowe Ransom (1946.B47), the novel was not regional in the pejorative sense; it was a beautiful representation of a doomed way of life. And, although admitting a lack of plot or traditional plot structure, Collins (1946.B21) found an impressionistic unity.

The publication of The Golden Apples in 1949 gave critics the first opportunity to find patterns of unity within a collection of Welty's stories. Although the stories had all appeared separately, many writers saw the book as a novel. Others noted the enduring problem of obscurity. According to Lee Cannon (1949.B14), the book suggested a nonexistent philosophic significance, and, according to Theodore O'Leary (1949.B28), Paul Pickrel (1949.B29), and Coleman Rosenberger (1949.B51), the book was unnecessarily obscure. With its title and with its occasional allusions to mythology, The Golden Apples has also provided material for myth criticism. (See "myth" in the index for a complete listing.)

The Ponder Heart created a new side to the critical reception of Welty. According to Carl Little of the Houston Post (1955.B49), Welty had always been a writer for the discriminating few, but, in The Ponder Heart, she wrote a book that could be enjoyed by everyone. Such popularity did not detract from the critical reception of the book. Both Charles Poore of the New York Times Book Review (1954.B40) and Albert Roberts of the Clarion-Ledger (1954.B43)

considered The Ponder Heart her best work. It also won the William
Dean Howells Medal of the Academy of Arts and Letters and was adapted
into a successful Broadway play by Chodorov and Fields. For once, no
one called a work by Welty obscure. Yet, The Ponder Heart was not
universally accepted as a classic. Kingsley Amis found it too sweet
(1954.B17); Kennebeck thought that it lacked human passion
(1954.B35); and Robert Adams (1954.B16) considered it marred by a
self-conscious buffoonery.

After the popular success of The Ponder Heart, Welty redi-
rected her attention to the discriminating few in The Bride of the
Innisfallen. Some critics saw the stories as finely controlled examples of impressionism, but others considered them needlessly obscure. According to Fred Bornhauser (1955.B19) and Louis Rubin
(1955.B63), Welty was in complete control of her material, but the
reviewer for the Times Literary Supplement (1955.B8) found the stories "tediously clever," and Theodore Hoffman thought that Welty made
the experiences of her characters more complicated than they actually
were (1955.B37).

Fifteen years elapsed before Welty at last presented the world
with what Porter had anticipated in 1941, "The Novel." Like A Curtain of Green, Losing Battles was praised by some critics as a major
work and condemned by others as insubstantial. Among the negative
reviews were some predictable patterns. According to Paul Gray
(1970.B45), the world of the novel was too pleasant: Welty did not
seem to be making significant comments about current social problems
in the South. Hugh Holman found the book insubstantial (1970.B54);
William Hamlin considered it forced and labored (1970.B50); and
Carolyn Ruffin lamented that the vulgarity of the Renfros triumphed
over the civilized values of Julia Mortimer (1970.B100). Most critics who disliked the book also considered it tediously long and un-
humorous. Generally, however, Losing Battles was more universally
admired than any of Welty's earlier books: it was her first "best
seller." Among the reviewers, Elmo Howell admired Welty's use of the
comedy of manners (1970.B56), Richard Rupp (1970.B101) and Elizabeth
Janeway (1970.B59) admired the use of folklore and ritual, and Louis
Rubin admired the rich texture of the surface (1970.B99). Losing
Battles has already generated at least one significant scholarly article. In his "Myth and History: The Foes of Losing Battles," Michael Kreyling (1973.B49) discussed Welty's use of myth as structure.

As early as 1936, when she published her first short story in
Manuscript, Welty expressed her desire to sell a collection of her
photographs. She at last succeeded with the photograph collection,
One Time, One Place. Because the collection was the work of a professional writer and an amateur photographer, the critics evidenced
some difficulties in assessing its merits. Madison Jones (1971.B21)
considered the pictures of uneven quality, but Michael Putney
(1971.B34) found Welty's amateurism to be an asset. To him, the pictures seemed natural and unposed. Most admirers of Welty's fiction

INTRODUCTION

also found much to admire in the photographs. However, those critic
who expected Welty to criticize racism in the South were generally
disappointed by a collection which merely recorded honestly and directly a single time and place in American history.

When The Optimist's Daughter appeared in the New Yorker in
1969, Reynolds Price called it Welty's "strongest richest work"
(1969.B17). He preferred the simplicity and clarity of the prose an
the stability of the narrator to the "slow dissolving impressionism"
of The Bride of the Innisfallen. In the context of thirty-four year
of criticism, Price's observation suggests an important aspect of
Welty's critical reputation. Although few reviewers found obscurity
in A Curtain of Green, all of Welty's other work, with the exception
of The Ponder Heart, brought at least some protests of obscurantism.
Moreover, in "How I Write," Welty said that she intended to "sound
mysterious now and then," and she stated as a general principle in
"The Reading and Writing of Short Stories" that "the first thing we
see about a story is its mystery." If Price's observation is sound,
Welty seems to have abandoned the aims and techniques of most of her
fiction. Readers who may have preferred the subtleties of The Bride
of the Innisfallen, however, had serious doubts about the subtlety o
The Optimist's Daughter. To Elizabeth Janeway (1972.B73), Fay was
too simplistic, and to George Trail (1972.B132), Fay should have bee
presented more ironically. Barbara Holliday (1972.B70), however,
justified Fay's one-sidedness as the natural consequence of Laurel's
point of view. The social critics were divided in their estimate.
According to Granville Hicks, Welty questioned social values in the
South, but according to Maxwell Geismar (1972.B56), Welty did not
question the values of the middle class.

This survey of thirty-four years of criticism reveals recur-
rent patterns which I have indexed as "place," "the grotesque,"
"myth," "obscurantism," "social criticism," and "the comic sense."
The total view of Welty criticism that emerges, however, is somewhat
inconclusive. In spite of many excellent shorter writings, most of
the comprehensive work is yet to be done. This Reference Guide gath
ers the work of many critics and hopefully will provide the perspective and the resources for additional full-length critical studies.

I am indebted to the many known and unknown persons who labored
to direct material to the coastal flats of Newport News, Virginia.
I am particularly indebted to Lynn G. Tienken of the Thomas Nelson
Library who diligently and continuously sent out inter-library loans
to Sandy Jirkal of Random House who kindly made available to me reviews of Welty's books, and to Caroline Allen of the Mississippi Department of Archives and History who made me aware of extensive Mississippi material, xeroxed it, and mailed it. I am also indebted to
Richard Guthrie, Kirsten Crain, and Mary Tognozzi who helped with th
translation of articles in German and Italian, to Louise Miller who
graciously talked with me about her former student, Eudora Welty,
and to the hospitable librarians at the College of William and Mary,

the Library of Congress, the New York Public Library, the University
of Cincinnati Library, and the Winthrop College Library who helped
me find material. Finally, I am most indebted to Ronald Gottesman
who conceived the idea of the book but gave me the opportunity to
write it.

Newport News, 1975

List of Periodical Abbreviations

AI	American Imago
AL	American Literature
ArQ	Arizona Quarterly
BB	Bulletin of Bibliography
BSUF	Ball State University Forum
CE	College English
Crit	Critiques and Essays on Modern Fiction
DAI	Dissertation Abstracts International
EJ	English Journal
Expl	Explicator
GaR	Georgia Review
Harper's	Harper's Bazaar
HudR	Hudson Review
JAF	Journal of American Folklore
KR	Kenyon Review
LJ	Library Journal
MarkhamR	Markham Review
MFS	Modern Fiction Studies
MissQ	Mississippi Quarterly
MLN	Modern Language Notes
NConL	Notes on Contemporary Literature
NMW	Notes on Mississippi Writers
NY	New Yorker
PR	Partisan Review
PrS	Prairie Schooner
SAQ	South Atlantic Quarterly
SatR	Saturday Review
SFQ	Southern Folklore Quarterly
SHR	Southern Humanities Review
SLJ	Southern Literary Journal
SoR	Southern Review
SR	Sewanee Review
SSC Rev	Shippensburg State College Review
SSF	Studies in Short Fiction
TCL	Twentieth-Century Literature
TLS	Times Literary Supplement
TQ	Texas Quarterly

LIST OF PERIODICAL ABBREVIATIONS

UR	University of Kansas City Review
VQR	Virginia Quarterly Review
WHR	Western Humanities Review
WVUPP	West Virginia University Philological Papers
YR	Yale Review

Writings About Eudora Welty, 1936 - 1975

1936 A BOOKS - NONE

1936 B SHORTER WRITINGS

1   ANON. "Discovered by Manuscript." Manuscript, 3 (May/June),
        65.
            Tells how Mary Lawhead of Manuscript discovered "Death
        of a Traveling Salesman."

2   ANON. "Notes on Contributors." Manuscript, 3 (September/
        October), 63.
            Welty's first story, "Death of a Traveling Salesman,"
        "was received with loud praise by our readers." The second
        story, "Magic" (included in this volume), is quite differ-
        ent from "Death of a Traveling Salesman," but it demon-
        strates Welty's versatility.

3   WELTY, EUDORA. "The Contributors." Manuscript, 3 (May/June), ?.
            Welty admits that she has suffered less than most
        writers.

1939 A BOOKS - NONE

1939 B SHORTER WRITINGS

1   FORD, FORD MADOX. "Travel Notes." SatR, 20 (June 10), 14.
            Ford includes a letter from a publisher (probably Stanley
        Unwin) which explains why A Curtain of Green will not be
        published. Welty's writing is "'beautiful'" but will ap-
        peal only to "'discriminating readers.'"

2   HANSEN, HARRY. O. Henry Memorial Award Prize Stories of 1939.
        New York: Doubleday, Doran & Co., p. xiii.
            Gives Charles Poore's opinion in "Petrified Man," that
        Welty was able to reveal an entire character in a single
        sentence with "incisive dialogue."

1940

1940 A BOOKS - NONE

1940 B SHORTER WRITINGS

1   ANON. "Local Writer at Bread Loaf Authors' Meet." Jackson
      Daily News (10 August).
          Notes that Welty was one of seven young authors to win a
      fellowship to the Breadloaf Writer's Conference at Middle-
      bury, Vermont.

1941 A BOOKS - NONE

1941 B SHORTER WRITINGS

1   ANON. "Jackson Writers Get Recognition for Recent Work."
      Jackson Daily News (2 May), p. 3.
          Notes the achievements of students and alumnae of Missis-
      sippi State College for Women including Welty's publication
      of her second story--"Why I Live at the P.O."--in the At-
      lantic Monthly. The story is presumably about "one of
      Mississippi's rural communities."

2   ANON. Review of A Curtain of Green. NY, 17 (5 November),
      110.
          The stories are "deceptively simple," but actually "far
      from ordinary." A Curtain of Green is "a distinguished
      book."

3   ANON. "O. Henry Winners Include Jacksonian." Jackson Daily
      News (6 November).
          Announces that Welty won the $200 second place prize
      for "A Worn Path."

4   ANON. "Briefly noted." Review of O. Henry Memorial Award
      Prize Stories of 1941, edited by Herschel Brickell. NY,
      17 (15 November), 110.
          Considers the collection a "much better than average
      lot."

5   ANON. "New Southern Writer Unspoiled by Fads." Review of
      A Curtain of Green. Kansas City Star, (22 November), E,
      p. 14.
          Welty generally avoids the preciousness of style that is
      often found in the "Little Magazines."

6   ANON. "A New Writer." Review of A Curtain of Green. Time,
      38 (24 November), 110-111.

(ANON.)
Welty has "a clear, original prose style," but most of her stories deal with "melodrama" and "the demented, the deformed, the queer, the highly spiced."

7   ANON. Review of A Curtain of Green. Time, 38 (24 November), 110–111.
Welty's prose is clear and original, but she undercuts it with melodramatic elements. Most of her characters are "demented" and "deformed." Of the seventeen stories, only two deal with "normal" people.

8   ANON. Review of A Curtain of Green. Booklist, 38 (15 December), 132.
The stories are well-written and concise, but their unusual style and subject matter will make them appeal to only "a few discriminating readers."

9   ANON. "New Writers." Publishers' Weekly, 140 (6 December), 2099–2100.
Gives a brief biographical sketch and notes that A Curtain of Green "attracted unusual attention" and sold well for a collection of short stories (200 copies per week for three weeks).

10   BARBER, BETTE. "Novel Can Wait, Says Jackson Author." Jackson Daily News, (1 December).
Welty says that she prefers to write short stories in which action is "'secondary'" to "'feeling or emotion.'" Her stories focus not on "world strife" but on "the little people in the world." Welty says that she will continue to write such stories rather than attempt to write a novel.

11   BATES, GLADYS GRAHAM. "Two Southerners." Review of A Curtain of Green. SatR, 24 (22 November), 10.
A Curtain of Green is a promising first collection. Although Welty concentrates on "the odd, grotesque, or sardonic," she shows the effects of incident on character. In a collection of uneven quality, the best is "Lily Daw."

12   BOGAN, LOUISE. "The Gothic South." Review of A Curtain of Green. Nation, 153 (6 December), 572.
Compares Welty's "oblique humor" with that of Gogol's The Inspector General and Dead Souls. Like Gogol, Welty gives minute details to describe character and setting.

3

1941

13   BOYLE, KAY. "Full Length Portrait." Review of A Curtain of
      Green. New Republic, 55 (24 November), 707.
          Enthusiastically praises Welty's talent but notes a se-
      rious flaw: Welty carries objectivity so far, that she
      creates too great a distance between her characters, and
      narrators. As a result of this distance, the characters
      lack human proportions.

14   BRICKELL, HERSCHEL. O. Henry Memorial Award Prize Stories of
      1941. Garden City, New York: Doubleday, Doran & Co.,
      p. xix.
          "Powerhouse" and "Why I Live at the P.O." had been con-
      sidered, and the judges were divided on their opinion of
      the second-prize winner, "A Worn Path." One judge thought
      it "too slight"; another liked "the hidden motive for the
      conflict upon which the story turns."

15   FIELD, ROSE. Review of A Curtain of Green. New York Herald
      Tribune Books, (16 November), pp. 10, 12.
          In a distinctly feminine style, Welty's stories create
      mood but few memorable incidents. Rather than humor, the
      stories are dominated by "bitterness and frustration."
      Also, they reveal "too great a preoccupation with the ab-
      normal and grotesque."

16   GOLDSTEIN, ALBERT. Review of A Curtain of Green. Times-
      Picayune, New Orleans, (23 November), II, p. 10.
          All the stories in the collection "reflect a natural and
      superior talent." Welty's style is simple and direct as
      she recreates people and things of her own experience.

17   HAUSER, MARIANNE. Review of A Curtain of Green. New York
      Times Book Review, (16 November), p. 6.
          Welty does not seem to have learned her techniques from
      anyone or in fact to have patterned her writing after any
      other writers. Her style is spontaneous and poetic rather
      than "intellectual." Her form cannot be analyzed, but it
      is "right."

18   *MULLEN, DALE. "Some Notes on the Stories of Eudora Welty."
      Mississippi Literary Review, 1 (November), 21-24.
          Listed by Noel Polk (1973.B56) in "A Eudora Welty Check-
      list," MissQ, 26 (Fall 1973).

19   PEERY, JAMES ROBERT. "Eudora Welty of Jackson, Mississippi
      Displays Rare Talent in Short Stories." Review of A Cur-
      tain of Green. Commercial Appeal (Memphis), (23 November),
      IV, p. 11.

(PEERY, JAMES ROBERT)
A Curtain of Green demonstrates that Welty has achieved maturity as a writer. In her comprehension of human motivation, she brings "realism to definite focus."

20 PORTER, KATHERINE ANNE. "Introduction," to A Curtain of Green. New York: Harcourt, Brace & World, pp. xi-xxiii.
In introducing Welty as a young writer with great abilities, Porter fears only that critics will attempt to direct Welty's attention away from short stories to novels. Porter discusses Welty's reading, training as a writer, and freedom from social criticism. She also discusses the wide range of Welty's style with particular emphasis on Welty's comic sense and lack of "tolerance or sentimental tenderness toward symptomatic evils. . . ."

21 WEIGLE, EDITH. "Broad Variety of Short Story Fare in These." Review of A Curtain of Green. Chicago Tribune Book World, 19 November, E, p. 2.
Character analysis and emotion are more important than plot. Nevertheless, the style is clear and lyrical.

1942 A BOOKS - NONE

1942 B SHORTER WRITINGS

1 ANON. "Eudora Welty." Wilson Library Bulletin, 16 (February), 410.
Gives a brief history of Welty's rise to literary eminence from a little published protégé of Ford Madox Ford to the writer of A Curtain of Green.

2 ANON. "Mississippi Writer Receives Guggenheim Award." Commercial Appeal (Memphis), (6 April), p. 11.
Notes that Welty is a "Jr. Leaguer turned writer." Her fiction is known for its "characterization and dialogue," and she is interested in photography and painting.

3 ANON. "Guggenheim Fund Gives Eudora Welty Award in Fiction." Jackson Daily News, (7 April).
Notes that Welty was given a cash award so that she could devote her time to writing stories about the Natchez Trace.

4 ANON. "Guggenheim Fellowships Awarded." Publishers Weekly, 141 (11 April), 1408.
Notes that Welty won an award in 1942.

1942

5   ANON. "Guggenheim Fellows." Time, 39 (13 April), 48.
         Notes that Welty was awarded a Guggenheim fellowship "to
     write novels."

6   ANON. "Briefly Noted." Review of The Robber Bridegroom.
     NY, 18 (24 October), 82.
         The Robber Bridegroom is dreamlike and "gorgeous" with
     humor like Candide's. Also Welty's prose is "disciplined"
     and "beautiful."

7   ANON. "Eudora Welty, Jacksonian Wins O. Henry Prize." Jack-
     son Daily News, (14 November).
         Notes that Welty won a first prize for "The Wide Net."

8   ANON. Review of The Robber Bridegroom. Booklist, 39 (15
     November), 103.
         This "long short story" will "have limited appeal."

9   ANON. "Eudora Welty Wins O. Henry Memorial Award." Pub-
     lishers Weekly, 142 (21 November), 2112-2113.
         "The Wide Net" was selected from more than 8,000 possi-
     bilities by a committee which included Herschel Brickell,
     Murial Fuller, and the judges, Joseph Henry Jackson, Amy
     Loveman, and Marjorie Rawlings.

10   BISHOP, JOHN PEALE. "The Violent Country." Review of The
     Robber Bridegroom. New Republic, 107 (16 November),
     646-647.
         The violence of Grimm's "Robber Bridegroom" is well
     suited for Welty's novel. But the combining incidents
     from a European fairy tale with elements of the American
     tall tale produces some confusion. If Welty "meant to es-
     tablish that our tall tale is the equivalent of the Euro-
     pean folk tale she fails to do so."

11   B. R. "Fairy Tale in Modern Manner." Review of The Robber
     Bridegroom. Kansas City Star, (14 November), p. 14.
         Welty includes all the familiar characters of fairy tale,
     but she combines them into a "wonderful" adult book. "It
     is as amoral as an oyster."

12   BRANTLEY, FREDERICK. "A Curtain of Green: Themes and Atti-
     tudes." Review of A Curtain of Green. American Prefaces,
     7 (Spring), 241-251.
         Because she does not stereotype the old decaying South,
     Welty is not a regionalist in the narrow sense of the term.
     But in subtle ways—through a great sense of detail and
     symbolism—she combines the diverse elements of her region

(BRANTLEY, FREDERICK)
into complex statements about the human condition. "The Hitch-Hikers" is a particularly representative example of her method.

13   BRICKELL, HERSCHEL. O. Henry Memorial Award Prize Stories of 1942. Garden City, New York: Doubleday, Doran & Co., pp. viii-ix.
Brickell considered Welty "beyond doubt the most distinguished of the younger short story writers" and "The Wide Net" a well-constructed "original story," but he did not vote to give Welty the first prize.

14   CARR, ARTHUR J. Review of A Curtain of Green. Accent, 2 (Spring), 188-189.
Rather than literal depictions of reality, Welty uses highly compressed images which create "psychological" effects. The characters fail to have a complete comprehension of the actions in which they are involved, but the stories are coherent and unified.

15   GARNETT, EMILY. Review of The Robber Bridegroom. LJ, 67 (15 September), 795.
The book is a delightful and entertaining combination of the prose ballad and the fairy tale. It contains "some passages of beautiful writing."

16   GOLDSTEIN, ALBERT. Review of The Robber Bridegroom. Times-Picayune, New Orleans, (22 November), II, p. 11.
Like Alice in Wonderland, The Robber Bridegroom has no plot; it also has "implications which are not always clear." But the book is "smoothly written" and "is the product of a writer of unusual talent."

17   HAUSER, MARIANNE. "Miss Welty's Fairy Tale." Review of The Robber Bridegroom. New York Times Book Review, (1 November), pp. 6-7.
Although the style is clear and pure, The Robber Bridegroom is filled with "irony," "Humor," "wisdom," and "surrealistic extravaganzas."

18   JACKSON, KATHERINE GAUSS. "In Brief." Review of The Robber Bridegroom. Harper's Magazine, 186 (December), n.p.
The Robber Bridegroom is written in a "highly stylized and delicate prose."

1942

19   KAZIN, ALFRED. "An Enchanted World in America." Review of
      The Robber Bridegroom. New York Herald Tribune Books,
      (25 October), p. 19.
         Welty does what few American writers have been able to
      achieve. She transforms folktales and legends into liter-
      ature. In her reworking of the tales from her own child-
      hood, she recreates the sense of joy and delight of the
      American frontier.

20   KROLL, HARRY HARRISON. "Unusual Story by Eudora Welty Among
      Latest Fiction Publications." Review of The Robber Bride-
      groom. Commercial Appeal (Memphis), 25 October, IV, p. 10.
         The whole book has the quality of a child's dream. It is
      filled with "joyous idiocy" in its blend of fairy tales,
      legends, and the Bible. The dream is one of "exquisite
      beauty" but tires after "the novelty of her method wears
      off."

21   MacF., R. "Natchez Love Woven into Gossamer Tale." Review of
      The Robber Bridegroom. Chicago Tribune Book World, (27 De-
      cember),vi, p. 20.
         Welty's "musical" style heightens the reality of stock
      characters of the Natchez Trace. She makes them more
      "brilliant than those of real life."

22   MARSH, FRED. "Prize Stories." Review of O. Henry Memorial
      Award Prize Stories of 1942. New York Times Book Review,
      (29 November), p. 48.
         Welty's story, "The Wide Net," is "a remarkable tale."
      It is an "odd" and original story.

23   MUNN, L. S. "Eudora Welty's Fantasy Will Delight the Minority
      that Enjoys Airy Madness in Exquisite Prose." Review of
      The Robber Bridegroom. Springfield Union, (22 November),
      E, p. 7.
         Welty creates a world of delightful madness through the
      "magic of metaphor and simile."

24   ROTHMAN, NATHAN. "The Lost Realm." Review of The Robber
      Bridegroom. SatR, 25 (14 November), 16.
         Welty rediscovers the fantasy of childhood in her rework-
      ing of fairy tales and legends. She adds only one element,
      sex. The book is a delightful experiment in which style is
      well suited for expression. However, "It really means
      nothing." It is an experiment, and Welty will probably not
      try it again.

25   SCHIFF, SARAH. "Stories Too Green to Burn." Review of A
      Curtain of Green. Springfield Union, Springfield Republi-
      can, (11 January), E, p. 7.

8

(SCHIFF, SARAH)
Welty writes in the tradition of Wordsworth and Saroyan in that she tries to find significance in the casual passing moments of everyday life. Unfortunately, she never finds significance. She does not give the reader anything to compensate for the lack of significant structure and action.

26 TRILLING, LIONEL. "American Fairy Tale." Review of The Robber Bridegroom. Nation, 155 (19 December), 686-687.
Justifies Welty's use of European fairy tales in an American setting but questions her method. Welty is self-consciously playful and unnecessarily mysterious. She seems to make allusions which have meaning only for herself.

27 VAN GELDER, ROBERT. "An Interview with Eudora Welty." New York Times Book Review, 14 June, II, p. 6.
See 1946.B52.

1943 A BOOKS - NONE

1943 B SHORTER WRITINGS

1 ANON. "Briefly Noted." Review of The Wide Net. NY, 19 (25 September), 68.
The title piece has "wit" and "imagination," as it balances between dream and reality, but the other stories are inferior to Welty's earlier work. They are "labored" and "diffuse."

2 No Entry

3 ANON. "Fine New Stories by Eudora Welty." Review of The Wide Net. Philadelphia Inquirer, (26 September), SO, p. 8.
Welty has "an oddly original touch." The setting is the Natchez Trace, but because of their universality, the stories could have taken place anywhere. This collection "strengthens" Welty's position among "the first rank of American Writers."

4 ANON. "Sense and Sensibility." Review of The Wide Net. Time, 42 (27 September), 100-101.
In contrast to the stories in A Curtain of Green which are rich in comedy and satire, those in The Wide Net are "perplexing and exasperating." The characters do not resemble real people but rather representations of "love,

1943

(ANON.)
enchantment and death." "Asphodel" is more of a case history than literature.

5   ANON. "Books-Authors." New York Times, (19 November), p. 16.
Notes that Welty won first prize in the annual O. Henry awards for the second consecutive year. She is only "outranked" by Stephen Vincent Benet who won three first prizes.

6   ANON. "Books in Brief." Review of The Wide Net. Christian Century, 60 (27 October), 1233.
Welty bases her stories on a realistic setting and attention to details but at the same time evokes "the world of the supernatural."

7   ANON. Review of The Wide Net. Christian Century, 60 (27 October), 1233.
The story is set in the real world, but through the use of great detail, Welty suggests a second world, the supernatural and "an atmosphere suggestive of implicit or impending catastrophe."

8   ANON. "Prize-Winning Story and Lesser Ones." Review of The Wide Net. Chicago Daily News, (17 November), p. 26.
Only the title story is "down-to-earth." The other stories are "90% style and 10% substance." Meanings are lost in fantasy and abstraction.

9   ARMFIELD, EUGENE. "Short Stories by Eudora Welty." Review of The Wide Net. New York Times Book Review, (26 September), p. 3.
In the best stories (e.g., "The Winds"), Welty creates a perfect blend of "fantasy and actuality." But in the less successful stories (e.g., "The Purple Hat"), she loses control of her method and produces mere confusion.

10   B. R. "The Trend in Short Fiction." Review of The Wide Net. Kansas City Star, (2 October), F, n.p.
The collection as a whole is "uneven," and Welty has written better than any of the individual stories. "Asphodel" is "tenuous and unworldly," "First Love" is "oblique," and the title story has Erskine Caldwellian humors."

11   BRICKELL, HERSCHEL. O. Henry Memorial Award Prize Stories of 1943. New York: Doubleday, Doran & Co.
The editors considered "Asphodel" and "The Winds" but

(BRICKELL, HERSCHEL)
gave the first prize for "Livvie," "because of its greater
originality." The story was particularly admired by Esther
Forbes and Carl Van Doren.

12   CLARKE, GEORGE HERBERT. "Women Interpret Women." Review of
The Robber Bridegroom. VQR, 19 (Winter), 140, 142-143.
With imagination, Welty combines the Robin Hood stories,
Hans Christian Anderson, the Grimm Brothers, Peter Pan,
The Wind in the Willows, and the Mississippi of Mark Twain.
The result is a book with precise evocative details which
is "a little classic in its own right."

13   D. H. "Eight Short Tales." Review of The Wide Net. Raleigh
News and Observer, (26 September), X, p. 13.
Particularly in the title story, Welty demonstrates a
gift for "painting word pictures." Other stories in the
collection including "Asphodel" and "Livvie" leave less
to the imagination" and are therefore more conventional.

14   ENGLE, PAUL. "Volumes Stress Vitality of American Short
Story." Review of The Wide Net. Chicago Tribune Book Review, (10 October), p. 17.
Welty's style is distinctly her own. Through attention to
small details, she suggests "extra meanings." This volume shows less effort to reveal personality than does A
Curtain of Green.

15   *FREDERICK, JOHN T. Review of The Wide Net. Bookweek, (26
September), p. 2.
Listed by Seymour Gross in "Eudora Welty: A Bibliography
of Criticism and Comment," 1960. See 1960.B5.

16   JACKSON, JOSEPH HENRY. Review of The Wide Net. San Francisco
Chronicle, (27 September), p. 12.
Welty manages to avoid "the New Yorker style." Within
the limitations of her settings and situations her style
is pictorial and clear; it is also free of uncontrolled
emotionalism.

17   LANE, JOHN. "An Original Newcomer." Review of A Curtain of
Green. TLS, (17 July), p. 341.
Welty's stories are original and interesting but also
somewhat "immature." Imagination sometimes unnecessarily
clouds what would otherwise be the ordinary experience of
life. Welty also seems to have too much of an obsession
for the "bizarre" and the abnormal.

1943

18   LERMAN, LEO. "Daughter of the Mississippi." Review of The
      Wide Net. New York Herald Tribune Book Review, (26 Sep-
      tember), p. 4.
          Welty does not write about the grotesque and the deformed
      to shock. Nor does she "sacrifice" character to style.
      She is primarily interested in human beings. The best
      tales in the collection are "The Wide Net" and "Asphodel"
      (her best tale yet).

19   McCRORY, MARY. "Thre New Collections for Short Story Ad-
      dicts." Review of The Wide Net. Boston Herald, (10 Novem-
      ber), p. 22.
          Welty creates a dream-like atmosphere in most of these
      stories. Some of them are difficult to understand, but in
      general, she "writes beautiful eerie fantasy."

20   MOLLOY, ROBERT. "Elusive Tales from the Pen of a Newcomer."
      Review of The Wide Net. New York Sun, (24 September),
      p. 22.
          The stories have the clear images that Welty learned to
      appreciate as a photographer, but are fanciful to the point
      of preciosity and needlessly obscure. Jesse Stuart could
      have done better with "The Wide Net."

21   PRESCOTT, ORVILLE. "A Handful of Rising Stars." New York
      Times Book Review, (21 March), p. 13.
          In spite of The Robber Bridegroom which "was a disap-
      pointment," Welty is a very promising writer. In A Curtain
      of Green, the "Mississippi marvel" is "firm in her crafts-
      manship."

22   _____. Review of The Wide Net. Cue, 9 October.
      Listed by Seymour Gross, 1960. See 1960.B5.

23   ROBINSON, TED. Review of The Wide Net. Cleveland Plain
      Dealer, (3 October), All Feature Section, p. 3.
          Through tricks of the imagination Welty transforms ordi-
      nary people into subtle works of art.

24   ROSENFIELD, ISAAC. "Consolations of Poetry." Review of The
      Wide Net and Other Stories. New Republic, 109 (18 Octo-
      ber), 525-526.
          In A Curtain of Green, Welty had command of many styles,
      but in The Wide Net, she becomes self-consciously aesthet-
      ic. Consequently, the stories are highly artificial.

25   SHATTUCK, CHARLES. Review of The Robber Bridegroom, Accent,
      3 (Winter), 124.
         Welty synthesizes legends and folktales but tones down
      the "bloodthirstiness" and heightens "the decorative and
      the marvelous." Her style is well-suited to the matter.
      It is filled with clearly defined visual details, particu-
      larly those of Mississippi's forests and landscapes.

26   TRILLING, DIANA. Review of The Wide Net. Nation, 157 (2 Oc-
      tober), 386-387.
         Only the title story and "Livvie" are comprehensible.
      The rest are examples of "fine writing." Technical con-
      siderations are more important than meaning. This tendency
      toward "fine writing" is a departure from Welty's greatest
      strengths as a writer: a "healthy wit" and clear, detailed
      dialogue.

27   WELTY, EUDORA. "Shanty Boat Life." Mississippi: A Guide to
      the Magnolia State, compiled and written by the Federal
      Writer's Project of the Works Progress Administration.
      New York: Viking Press, p. 16.
         Photograph without commentary.

1944 A BOOKS - NONE

1944 B SHORTER WRITINGS

1   ANON. "The Editor's Guest Book." Harper's, 2786 (February),
      73.
         Shows a comic valentine that Welty included with the MS
      of "Some Notes on River Country."

2   *ANON. Review of The Wide Net. Cresset (February).
      Listed by Seymour Gross, 1960. See 1960.B5.

3   ANON. "Eudora Welty." Publishers Weekly, 146 (8 July), 122.
         Gives Welty's publication history and announces that she
      has joined the staff of the New York Times Book Review.

4   *ANON. Review of The Wide Net. Kirkus' (Virginia) Service
      Bulletin, (1 September).
      Listed by Seymour Gross, 1960. See 1960.B5.

5   LANE, JOHN. "Southern Allegory." Review of The Robber Bride-
      groom. TLS, 43 (22 January), 41.
         Welty mixes her genres confusingly and the allegory
      "leaves nothing unsaid." Consequently, The Robber

1944

(LANE, JOHN)
Bridegroom is an "odd and not very successful affair."
Welty has "a bold and individual talent," but in The Robber
Bridegroom, "it seems to overreach itself."

6   READ, MARTHA. "Eudora Welty." PrS, (Spring) 18, 74-76.
Welty's first three books suggest the beginning of a very
unusual writing career. Although she writes about the
South, she is not a regionalist. Although many of her
characters are psychologically abnormal, they do not resemble "the Faulkner-Caldwell school of psychological ab-
normalities." Each of her books and each story within
those books is unique. Unlike O. Henry, Chekhov and Mau-
passant, Welty does not seem to be developing predictable
patterns.

7   STAFFORD, JEAN. "The Empty Net." Review of The Wide Net.
PR, 11 (Winter), 114.
Unlike the stories in A Curtain of Green, those in The
Wide Net are humorless and vague. The Aaron Burr of "First
Love" bears no resemblance to the Burr of history. "The
Winds" has potential, but it is smothered by the density of
thought and language.

8   WARREN, ROBERT PENN. "The Love and Separateness in Miss Welty." KR, 6 (September), 246-259.
Warren's essay is at least in part a response to Diana
Trilling's review of The Wide Net (1943.B26). Warren observes that A Wide Net reveals technical difficulties that
were not very pronounced in A Curtain of Green; and like
Trilling he admits the possibility of insincerity and the
falsely poetic. Warren's essay, as a whole, however, is a
detailed defense of Welty's emerging new style. In specific comments about "The Wide Net," "A Still Moment," and
"First Love," Warren notes excellences that Trilling over-
looked. In "The Wide Net," for example, Welty uses myth
and folklore to support her theme of "separateness." In
such stories as "The Purple Hat," Welty is too self-conscious, but The Wide Net, as a whole, is at least promising.

9   WELTY, EUDORA. "Gathering for a Political Rally." Mississippi: A Guide to the Magnolia State, compiled and written by
the Federal Writer's Project of the Works Progress Adminis-
tration. New York: Viking Press, p. 9.
Photograph without commentary.

10   _____. "José de Creft." Magazine of Art, 37 (February),
42-47.

14

1945

(WELTY, EUDORA)
Welty discusses the life and sculpture of José de Creeft.
She observes that de Creeft's material "directs what he
does with it" and that he "shows real interest in other
people and invites their best ideas."

11   _____. "Literature and the Lens." Vogue, 104 (1 August),
102-103.
Includes three pictures with commentary: Royal Street,
New Orleans, an old ruined house on the Natchez Trace, and
the Church of God in Christ Holiness.

12   _____. "Some Notes on River Country." Harper's, 2786
(February), 86-87, 150-156.
Welty takes the reader on a tour of the Natchez Trace and
surrounding areas. She includes places mentioned in her
fiction such as Rodney's Landing (The Robber Bridegroom),
Windsor Castle ("Asphodel"), and Washington, Mississippi
("First Love").

1945 A BOOKS - NONE

1945 B SHORTER WRITINGS

1 ALLEN, CHARLES. "Regionalism and the Little Magazines." CE,
7 (October), 13.
Welty is among the best of the regionalists but--like her
peers--is "too preoccupied with the region's peculiarity,
its eccentric detail, its uniqueness."

2 LANE, JOHN. "In the Deep South." Review of The Wide Net.
TLS, (5 May), p. 209.
The title story is an excellent example of what Welty can
do at her best. It is imaginative, controlled, and rich in
racy humor. The other stories in the collection, however,
seem to strain toward levels of perception which Welty cannot control. "Asphodel," "First Love," and "A Still Moment" are somewhat "precious" and "lifeless."

3 LEWIS, SINCLAIR. "Obscenity and Obscurity Remarking the Te-
diousness of Two Kinds of Prigs, the Futility of Ivory
Tower Scribes and the Genius of Eudora Welty." Esquire, 24
(July), 140.
Welty has been accepted as "the most distinguished of the
new story-tellers" by Greenwich Village, Taos, and Carmel,
but her prose is neither obscure nor obscene. She has some

1945

      (LEWIS, SINCLAIR)
          interest in symbolism, but her style is as clean and clear
          "as the Gettysburg Address."

4   SPENSER, THEODORE. "Recent Fiction." Review of The Wide Net.
       SR, 53 (Spring), 301.
          The stories are of high quality, particularly those in
       which Welty recreates the Natchez Trace landscape as a
       background for her characters. Many are experimentally in-
       teresting. "First Love" may seem like a mere "tour de
       force," but with its limited point of view, it is an inno-
       vative language experiment.

1946 A BOOKS - NONE

1946 B SHORTER WRITINGS

1   ANDERSON, BARBARA TUNNELL. "A Delta Wedding and a 9-Year
       Old." Review of Delta Wedding. Louisville Courier-Jour-
       nal, (19 May), III, p. 10.
          Although Welty finds great significance in the "common-
       place" and is a sensitive observer of people doing ordinar
       things, the reader would like more "straightforward busi-
       ness" and more action. Welty's first works suggested that
       she would someday write a major work, but that work is not
       Delta Wedding. Welty needs to return to "the frightening
       brand of vulgarity that provokes her to magnificent satire
       ridicule and rage."

2   ANON. Review of Delta Wedding. Booklist, 42 (1 June), 318.
          The novel has no plot, but the shifting point of view
       creates variety.

3   ANON. "Delta Flavor Aptly Caught." Commercial Appeal (Mem-
       phis), (7 April), IV, p. 12.
          In Delta Wedding, Welty depicts the delicate "serenity
       and security" of Southern life in a way which may be only
       fully appreciated by a Southerner. The world she present
       is filled with "smiling, loving life."

4   No Entry

5   No Entry

6   ANON. Review of Delta Wedding. Pictorial Magazine, Cleveland Plain Dealer, (28 April), p. 16.
Delta Wedding transports the reader into "an utterly improbable place," and presents a "self-centered family of loveable lunatics."

7   ANON. "First Edition of Delta Wedding Sold Out." Jackson Daily News, (7 May).
In approximately three weeks, the entire first edition of Delta Wedding, consisting of 10,000 copies, was sold out and a second edition was being prepared. Publishing rights were also sold to the Bonner Publishing Company of Sweden for translation into Swedish.

8   ANON. "A Mississippi Mosaic." Review of Delta Wedding. Minneapolis Tribune, (19 May), G, p. 17.
The reading is difficult, but the reader is rewarded with "long dangling Jamesian sentences," humor, and "human understanding."

9   ANON. "Books Received." Review of Delta Wedding. Christian Century, 63 (22 May), 657-658.
Welty has a delicate touch, but the subject matter of her book is "rather thin."

10   ANON. Review of Delta Wedding. Christian Century, 63 (22 May), 657.
The entire book seems unreal. The plot is frail, and the characters are so delicately drawn that Welty never actually succeeds in penetrating "to their essence."

11   *ANON. Review of Delta Wedding. Wisconsin Library Bulletin, 42 (June).
Listed by Seymour Gross, 1960. See 1960.B5.

12   *ANON. Review of Delta Wedding. Kirkus' (Virginia) Bulletin, 14 (1 April), 152.
Listed by Seymour Gross, 1960. See 1960.B5.

13   *ANON. Review of Delta Wedding. U.S. Quarterly Booklist, 2 (September), 183.
Listed by Seymour Gross, 1960. See 1960.B5.

1946

14 APPEL, DAVID. "Mississippi Delta Nuptials." Review of Delta
    Wedding. Chicago Daily News, (17 April).
        Welty's first full-length novel fulfills the great prom-
    ise of her short stories. Her "sensitive prose" has a
    "lyric beauty" which will be appreciated by discriminating
    readers.

15 BASSO, HAMILTON. "Look Away, Look Away, Look Away." Review
    of Delta Wedding. NY, 22 (11 May), 86.
        Although Delta Wedding is a novel in which "nothing hap-
    pens," it reveals much about character. With humor and
    "Southern speech," Welty gives a portrait of a Southern
    family which is universal and "wonderful."

16 B. C. C. Review of Delta Wedding. Providence Journal, (14
    April), VI, p. 8.
        A book filled with purple passages and mediocre anec-
    dotes, Delta Wedding suffers from "the genealogical falla-
    cy." Certain people and their stories seem "important and
    valuable because they belong to a certain family."

17 BULLOCK, FLORENCE HAXTON. "A Southern Family Sliding Down-
    hill." Review of Delta Wedding. Chicago Sun Book Week,
    4 (14 April), p. 1.
        Delta Wedding "has most of the qualities which distin-
    guish her short stories." Although it may be too "subtle
    and intricate" for some readers, it reflects Welty's abil-
    ity to capture the details of the surface which reveal in-
    ner meanings.

18 *BUTLER, M. Review of Delta Wedding. Best Sellers, 6 (15
    June), 61-62.
        Listed by Seymour Gross, 1960. See 1960.B5.

19 CANFIELD, DOROTHY. Review of Delta Wedding. Book-of-the-
    Month-Club News, (May), p. 7.
        Some readers will be puzzled by Welty's lack of plot and
    by her "shimmering, opalescent, diaphanous" prose. But
    readers who have enjoyed her stories will probably also en-
    joy Welty's first novel.

20 CAPERS, CHARLOTTE. "Eudora Welty Moves into Big Money with
    New Novel, Delta Wedding on Stands April 15." Jackson
    Daily News, (7 April).
        Capers describes Welty's progress from a writer without a
    publisher to the $5,000. advance plus royalties for Delta
    Wedding. She also notes Welty's importance in American
    Literature for her "lucid, timeless prose."

21   COLLINS, L. A.   Review of Delta Wedding.   Commonweal, 44 (21
        June), 242.
            A Curtain of Green and The Robber Bridegroom, though
        giving evidence of extraordinary talent, merely give prom-
        ise of the great achievement of Delta Wedding.   Although
        the novel is essentially plotless, it is held together by
        a unity of impressions which focus on one region and one
        family.   Delta Wedding is an antidote to the harsh realism
        of most contemporary Southern writing.

22   COURNOS, JOHN.   "A Family Gathers to Attend a Wedding."   Re-
        view of Delta Wedding.   New York Sun, (15 April), p. 21.
            Although Welty is "perhaps the best of all our regional
        novelists," and although in her careful depiction of the
        smallest characteristics of people and places, she is un-
        erring, Delta Wedding is not a story.   It has neither plot
        nor structure.

23   DANGERFIELD, GEORGE.   "A Family Rarely in Repose."   Review of
        Delta Wedding.   SatR, 24 (20 April), 12.
            Admirers of Welty's earlier work will be dismayed by
        Delta Wedding.   Unlike the stories in A Curtain of Green,
        Delta Wedding ascends into "cloud cuckoo land."   Its plot
        is buried in disconnected and continuous conversations
        which lead nowhere.

24   _____.   Review of Delta Wedding.   Time, 47 (22 April), 104.
            The novel is seriously weakened by Welty's penchant for
        the eccentric and the abnormal.   The characters do not re-
        semble real people but have a "queer vitality" not of this
        earth.   Such writing is to be expected, however, from one
        who is the daughter of an insurance company executive and a
        member of the Junior League.

25   No Entry

26   *DEXTER, E. H.   Review of Delta Wedding.   Springfield Republi-
        can, (19 May).
            Listed by Seymour Gross, 1960.   See 1960.B5.

27   ENGLE, PAUL.   "Miss Welty's Full Charm in First Novel."   Re-
        view of Delta Wedding.   Chicago Tribune, (14 April),
        pp. 3, 12.
            Welty demonstrates the precision of language of her short
        stories as well as "a slow accumulation of meaning

1946

(ENGLE, PAUL)
impossible for the short stories to achieve." By honestly
presenting the "texture of human experience," she presents
a universal problem: "the struggle of the individual to
attach himself to a group, to acquire the knowledge of be-
longing."

28 GANNETT, LEWIS. "Books and Things." Review of Delta Wedding.
New York Herald Tribune, (15 April), p. 19.
Welty deliberately presents the world of the novel ob-
liquely and suggests "more than she states." Although
Faulkner has similar themes, Welty's "is stiller, deeper
water."

29 GRAY, JAMES. "Family Life is Theme of Eudora Welty Novel."
Review of Delta Wedding. St. Paul Sunday Pioneer Press,
(14 April), Magazine, p. 11.
Delta Wedding is comparable in scope and method to Chekhov's The Cherry Orchard. In a "distinguished" book, Welty
"captures the poignant indecisiveness of the human yearning
for identification one with another."

30 GRUNEWALD, HUDSON. "Eudora Welty Wins High Praise for Superb
Writing." Washington Star, (28 April), C, p. 4.
The prose is "cool' and "clear" and the talent is "extra-
ordinary," but the story is "incomplete."

31 HANSEN, HARRY. "New Novels by Women." New York World Telegram, (27 April), p. 10.
Welty "is an author of delicate sensibility and deep
feeling for the nuances of human relationships," but in
Delta Wedding, she has not done much with plot.

32 HOFFMAN, FREDERICK, CHARLES ALLEN, and CAROLYN F. ULRICH.
The Little Magazine: A History and a Bibliography.
Princeton University Press, pp. 279, 323, 329, 339, 350,
358, 392.
Lists the little magazines in which Welty's stories first
appeared.

33 HOLDER, WILLIAM. "Miss Welty's Enchanted Land." Review of
Delta Wedding. Nashville Tennessean, (21 April).
Delta Wedding is a "regional" novel with a national interest. Although Welty's earlier fiction reached only a
few readers, Delta Wedding should give her "her rightful
place in the literary sun."

34 JACKSON, JOSEPH HENRY. Review of Delta Wedding. San Francis-
    co Chronicle, (22 April), p. 14.
       The novel has all the superb craftsmanship of the sto-
    ries. As in the stories, insight into character is much
    more significant than plot.

35 JACKSON, KATHERINE GAUSS. Review of Delta Wedding. Harper's
    Magazine, 192 (May), front advertising pages.
       Some readers may prefer "a lustier approach to life."
    Delta Wedding is a book in which action is very limited.
    Nevertheless, Welty presents her many characters in minute
    detail.

36 J. S. T. "Rare View of Dixie in Wedding." Review of Delta
    Wedding. Kansas City Star, (11 May), p. 4.
       The action may seem slow to some readers, but Welty's
    first full length novel achieves a "high level." In its
    sensitive portrayal of Laura's impressions, it is "nostal-
    gic" and "delightful."

37 KANE, HARNETT T. "Eudora Welty's Authentic and Vital Talent."
    Review of Delta Wedding. New York Herald Tribune Weekly
    Book Review, (14 April), p. 3.
       Although the book is occasionally obscure and slow paced,
    it is rich in visual details and insight into character.
    It is also poetic, imaginative and virtually free of purple
    passages.

38 K. H. "Su'th'n Family in Full Array." Philadelphia Inquirer,
    (12 May), 50, p. 15.
       Because Delta Wedding is "intricate" and "uninhibited,"
    the "casual reader may expect to be confused."

39 MCGRATH, THOMAS. "Life in Mississippi." Review of Delta Wed-
    ding. Review and Comment, (4 June).
       In her effort to create a world in the manner "of music
    or a symbolist poem," Welty does not always objectify her
    "conflicts." Consequently, the picture that she gives of
    the planter family "lacks the necessary perspective."

40 MEADOR, FRANK. "A Different Group of Southerners." Review of
    Delta Wedding. Boston Daily Globe, (17 April), p. 12.
       Welty's "word pictures are clear," and she depicts "many
    characters with extraordinary skill," but her style is
    sometimes awkward and unnatural.

41 NICHOLS, ELIZABETH P. Review of Delta Wedding. LJ, 71 (15
    April), 587.

1946

(NICHOLS, ELIZABETH P.)
Delta Wedding is Welty's best book so far. It combines
realism and imagination "to a remarkable degree." Also,
the prose is "lucid."

42   NORTH, STERLING. "Delta Alpha, Omega?" Review of Delta Wedding. New York Post, (18 April), p. 30.
See 1946.B43.

43   _____. "Miss Welty Needs to be Untangled." Review of Delta
Wedding. Atlanta Constitution, (21 April), B, p. 10.
The novel is "unbearably slow," and the writing is "need-
lessly obscure and the technique amateurish." Moreover,
Welty is "almost completely humorless."

44   POORE, CHARLES. "A Fine Novel of the Deep South." Review of
Delta Wedding. New York Times Book Review, (14 April),
pp. 1, 41.
As in her short stories, Welty combines the sensibilities
of Virginia Woolf with "an uncommon sense of the American
realistic tradition." Although she has been compared with
many other writers--particularly Mansfield, Porter, and
James--her style and development are distinctly her own.
She presents her world obliquely through detail rather than
through authorial commentary.

45   PRESCOTT, ORVILLE. "Books of the Times." Review of Delta
Wedding. New York Times, (17 April), p. 23.
Although Welty presents a detailed view of the Fairchild's, the book is "distant and unreal." Welty seems to
be making "private experiments with form and cryptic elusive vagaries of style too tenuous for clear communication.

46   _____. "Outstanding Novels." Review of Delta Wedding. YR,
35 (Summer), 765-766.
The book is "fascinating" but also "irritatingly elusive." Welty shifts the point of view from character to
character and thereby "achieves remarkable atmospheric results." But at the same time, she loses control of the
story. The result is a book which is "opaque and even a
little dull."

47   RANSOM, JOHN CROWE. "Delta Fiction." Review of Delta Wedding. KR, 8 (Summer), 503-507.
Ransom admires the book for its intense concentration on
a single family and for its portrayal of a way of life that
is already doomed. Stylistically--with its control of the

(RANSOM, JOHN CROWE)
interior monologue and its intense projection of the characters' feelings--Welty's style closely resembles that of
Virginia Woolf. The Fairchild wedding is "a perfect ana-
logue for Mrs. Dalloway's party." Future critics may dis-
parage the book for the wrong reasons: its lack of con-
demnation of the planter way of life and its failure to
state a political position.

48   ROSENFIELD, ISAAC. "Double Standard." Review of Delta Wed-
      ding. New Republic, 114 (29 April), 633-634.
        Welty preserves folk art in both The Wide Net and Delta
      Wedding, but her methods in The Wide Net are much surer and
      more interesting. Delta Wedding is a dull book because
      Welty does not present a Southern society in actuality but
      merely the "sensations of one."

49   SCRUGGS, PHILIP LIGHTFOOT. "A Southern Miscellany: Crusaders
      and Artists." Review of Delta Wedding. VQR, 22 (Summer),
      448-453.
        Like Tolstoy, a novelist must be both a crusader and art-
      ist, but in Delta Wedding, Welty is neither. The style is
      repetitious and boring; the plot is "hackneyed"; and Welty
      makes no suggestion that society needs to be changed.
      Only Southerners will like the book for its portrayal of a
      plantation family.

50   STEELE, MARY Q. "Little Plot, Enormity of Detail Make Fine
      Book on Delta Folk." Review of Delta Wedding. Chatta-
      nooga Times, (22 May).
        Some readers will find Welty's prose subtle, baffling,
      and "even tedious," but no one can fail to be "delighted
      by the accuracy of her observation" and "by the precision
      and beauty of her prose."

51   TRILLING, DIANA. Review of Delta Wedding. Nation, 162 (11
      May), 578.
        At least in part because Welty's subject is a romantic
      old South, her style is so self-conscious and so dream-
      like, that it is never in touch with the real world.
      Welty's best stories--her early ones--are founded in the
      everyday reality of Southern life. The later stories, as
      well as Delta Wedding, tend to become lost in a dream of
      the "southern past." Although Welty had once seemed to be
      a promising critic of Southern society, she seems in Delta
      Wedding, all too ready to accept all the pride and narrow-
      mindedness of the old South.

1946

52   VAN GELDER, ROBERT. "An Interview with Eudora Welty." Writ-
     ers and Writing. New York: Charles Scribner's Sons, pp.
     287-290.
         Welty gives specific information about her development
     as a writer. Her early stories about Paris (never pub-
     lished) lacked the sense of place that she evokes in her
     later and more successful work. When she turned to the
     Natchez Trace, she discovered the sense of place and found
     enough material there to keep her busy for a lifetime.
     She discusses her art of writing and gives the genesis of
     "Keela the Outcast Indian Maiden."

53   VAN GELDER, ROBERT and DOROTHY VAN GELDER. "Forward." Ameri-
     can Legend: A Treasury of Our Country's Yesterdays. New
     York: D. Appleton-Century Co., p. xii.
         Explains the rationale for making a collection of fiction
     which will "take readers into the living company of people
     of another time, another place." The collection includes
     The Robber Bridegroom.

54   *WILLIAMSON, MARGARET. Review of Delta Wedding. Christian
     Science Monitor, (15 April), p. 16.
         Listed by Seymour Gross, 1960. See 1960.B5.

1947 A BOOKS - NONE

1947 B SHORTER WRITINGS

1   ANON. Review of Delta Wedding. The Tatler and Bystander, (6
     August), p. 183.
         In her short stories, Welty has tended to write in two
     extremes: realistically and poetically. The best are
     those that fall in between, and the worst are those that
     move too much in the direction of the poetic. Delta Wed-
     ding falls beautifully between these two extremes and may
     "come to be recognized as a classic."

2   ANON. "The Editor's Guest Book." Harper's (September), p. 110.
         The Golden Apples is "Welty at her best."

3   *BOWEN, ELIZABETH. Review of Delta Wedding. Tatler and By-
     stander (London), 6 August.
         Listed by Seymour Gross, 1960. See 1960.B5.

4   BRICKELL, HERSCHEL. Prize Stories of 1947, The O. Henry
     Awards. Garden City, New York: Doubleday & Co., pp. xiv-
     xv.

(BRICKELL, HERSCHEL)
"The Whole World Knows" is greatly inferior to Welty's
prize winners, but character and setting are "admirable."

5   LANE, JOHN. Review of Delta Wedding. TLS, 46 (19 July),
     p. 361.
     Delta Wedding is something of a long short story with its
     concentration "on a single scene and group." Its "poeti-
     cal" overtones and intense observation remind one of the
     style of Elizabeth Bowen. And the distance of the world of
     the story creates a strange and dream-like effect. The
     only counterpart for this view of old Southern society is
     in nineteenth century Russia.

6   SNELL, GEORGE. The Shapes of American Fiction 1798-1947.
     New York: E. P. Dutton & Co., p. 301.
     Predicts that Welty--whose work resembles Porter's--may
     "outdistance Miss Porter" in her "unusual refraction of
     her peculiar Southern World."

1948 A BOOKS - NONE

1948 B SHORTER WRITINGS

1   BISHOP, JOHN PEALE. "The Violent Country." Review of The
     Robber Bridegroom. The Collected Essays of John Peale
     Bishop. New York: Charles Scribner's Sons, pp. 257-259.
     Welty uses the Natchez Trace setting along with some of
     its notorious characters to evoke a sense of violence and
     terror, but she fails to make the American tall tale the
     equivalent of the European fairy tale. She does, however,
     develop the important truth that nothing is what it seems
     to be.
     (Reprinted from The New Republic, 16 November, 1942.)

1949 A BOOKS - NONE

1949 B SHORTER WRITINGS

1   ANON. "Literary Awards 1949." Publishers Weekly, 157 (21
     January), 232.
     Welty's name listed as a winner of a John Simon Guggen-
     heim Memorial Fellowship.

2   ANON. "Guggenheim Memorial Foundation." Publishers Weekly,
     155 (23 April), 1740.

25

1949

(ANON.)
 Notes that ten writers including Welty received Guggenheim fellowships.

3   *ANON. Review of The Golden Apples. Kirkus' (Virginia) Serv-
     ice Bulletin, 17 (1 July), 332.
      Listed by Seymour Gross, 1960. See 1960.B5.

4   ANON. "On an Author." New York Herald Tribune Weekly Book
     Review, (21 August), p. 2.
      Gives a brief summary of Welty's publishing history
     through 1949. Welty claims to have had less difficulty be-
     ing appreciated than many other writers.

5   ANON. "Living People Grace Pages of Eudora Welty's New Tale."
     Review of The Golden Apples. Commercial Appeal (Memphis),
     (11 September), IV, p. 12.
      Discusses each story and briefly comments generally about
     the universality of Welty's art. In "June Recital," she
     depicts "a child's viewpoint, unintentionally as cruel as
     nature and as unbiased."

6   ANON. Review of The Golden Apples. Booklist, 46 (15 Septem-
     ber), 35.
      "With artistry," Welty presents indirectly "people as
     they are seen by each other."

7   *ANON. Review of The Golden Apples. Cleveland Open Shelf,
     October, p. 82.
      Listed by Seymour Gross, 1960. See 1960.B5.

8   BAILEY, MARY. Review of The Golden Apples. Book-of-the-
     Month Club News, August, p. 9.
      The stories are loosely linked by time and "marked by
     Miss Welty's flawless sensory perception."

9   BASSO, HAMILTON. "Morgana Mississippi." Review of The Golden
     Apples. NY, 25 (3 September), 63-64.
      Welty uses Faulkner's device of creating a mythical
     Southern setting through an accurate portrayal of Southern
     manners and language. Although the inspiration was prob-
     ably Faulkner's, the style is distinctly her own. She has
     a gift for observing detail, a fine comic sense, and a
     gift for language. The only flaw in a book which is a nov-
     el rather than a series of short stories is "Sir Rabbit."
     The seduction scene is too contrived.

10 BEAUCHAMP, ELISE. "Literature and Less." Picayune (New Or-
     leans), (28 August), II, p. 15.

26

(BEAUCHAMP, ELISE)
Welty is "borgia-like in her malevolence." In her depic-
tion of her "elegant neighbors" in The Golden Apples, she
covers "contempt" with "beautiful writing." her method is
similar to that of Delta Wedding in which she presents "an
idealized portrait of Mississippi, tongue in cheek."

11   BOOKHART, MARY ALICE. "Eudora Welty Writes Another Magic
      Story." Clarion-Ledger (Jackson), (22 August).
      The world of Morgana is both "dreamlike and realistic"
      since Welty combines imagination "with meticulous attention
      to detail." Although each story is complete in itself, the
      stories together make a coherent chronicle of the ficti-
      tious town, Morgana.

12   BREIT, HARVEY. Review of The Golden Apples. New York Times,
      (18 August), p. 19.
      Welty's method is that of pointillism. In her best sto-
      ries--particularly in "Moon Lake"--she creates many seg-
      mented details which all fit together like a Seurat paint-
      ing. "A Shower of Gold" is marred by tiresome dialogue and
      "Sir Rabbit" is "ultimately lost in mystification," but the
      collection as a whole suggests the continuity of a novel
      without "novelistic techniques."

13   BRICKELL, HERSCHEL. "Dragons in Mississippi." Review of The
      Golden Apples. SatR, 32 (27 August), 9.
      Welty is one of the best living short story writers, and
      The Golden Apples is "one of her finest achievements." It
      will be appreciated by "discriminating" readers. Although
      some of the stories appeared separately, the collection re-
      sembles a novel in its complete presentation "of a linked
      group of people."

14   CANNON, LEE E. "Main Street in Dixie." Review of The Golden
      Apples. Christian Century, 66 (7 September), 1039-1040.
      In her accurate descriptions of the lives and manners in
      a Southern town, Welty creates a world "with suppressed de-
      sires and frustrations," but also with a mysterious fluctu-
      ation between the real and the imaginary. With precision
      of phrasing and the stream of consciousness, she reveals
      the inner lives of her characters, but sometimes suggests
      a "philosophic significance which perhaps isn't there."

15   CLARK, ELEANOR. "Old Glamor, New Gloom." PR, 16 (June),
      631-636.
      Welty's treatment of "Death of a Traveling Salesman" is
      subtle and truly tragic, but Miller's Death of a Salesman
      is hackneyed and superficial.

16   *CLARKE, CLORINDA. Review of The Golden Apples. Catholic
      World, 170 (November), 158.
      Listed by Seymour Gross, 1960. See 1960.B5.

1949

17 DEDMON, EMMETT. "Golden Apples of a Writer Are Found to Con-
    tain Worms." Review of The Golden Apples. Chicago Sun,
    (4 September), X, p. 6.
       Welty violates the logic of language in creating the ob-
    scure and maladjusted world of Morgana.

18 FARRELLY, JOHN. "The Long Afternoon." Review of The Golden
    Apples. New Republic, 121 (22 August), 19-20.
       Since characters develop throughout the collection, The
    Golden Apples should be read as a novel rather than as a
    collection of short stories.

19 GUILFOIL, KELSEY. Review of The Golden Apples. Chicago Trib-
    une Book World, (14 August), IV, p. 3.
       Welty presents the details of life, but because she pre-
    sents them from the limited points of view of her charac-
    ters, her stories are often vague and indeterminate. Nev-
    ertheless, they are also "tantalizing and indefinably
    mysterious."

20 HAY, JOHN. Review of The Golden Apples. Commonweal, 50 (30
    September), 609.
       The world of Morgana has both beauty and irritation.
    Welty's style reflects changing stages of sensibility but
    shifts so rapidly from character, that it "sometimes runs
    past its world." It is not always clear which images and
    impressions belong with which characters. Nevertheless,
    Welty's community is unified and captivating.

21 *HORMEL, O. D. Review of The Golden Apples. Christian Sci-
    ence Monitor, (24 August).
       Listed by Seymour Gross, 1960. See 1960.B5.

22 HUTCHENS, JOHN K. "Books and Things." Review of The Golden
    Apples. New York Herald Tribune, (18 August), p. 13.
       Welty's unique style creates "a dream-like world, built
    in exquisite phrases around a core of reality." Much hap-
    pens, but "it is all real, in the sense that a dream is
    real."

23 JACKSON, JOSEPH HENRY. "Miss Welty's Mississippi." Review of
    The Golden Apples. San Francisco Chronicle, (12 Septem-
    ber), p. 14.
       By straining realistic details through her creative imag-
    ination, Welty creates her own Mississippi. (She is no
    imitator of Faulkner.) Her characters have regional traits
    but they are also universal.

24 _____. Review of The Golden Apples. Los Angeles Times,
    13 September, II, p. 5.

(JACKSON, JOSEPH HENRY)
With a style that is more poetry than prose, Welty transforms the details of speech and place into a world of fairy
tale and legend. She is aware of the details of Mississippi, but she moves from local realism to universality.

25 JACKSON, KATHERINE GAUSS. Review of The Golden Apples. Harper's Magazine, 199 (September), 108-109.
Assumes that The Golden Apples is a novel and concludes
that Welty is more successful as a short story writer than
as a novelist. Although each section of the book is beautiful in itself, esoteric allusions to people and places
are somewhat puzzling. "The sound is lovely, but the meaning is obscure." Many people, symbols, and places might
have meaning for Welty, and possibly for other Mississippians, but they are completely baffling for non-Southern-
ers.

26 MARSHALL, MARGARET. "Notes by the Way." Review of The Golden
Apples. Nation, 169 (10 September), 256.
One of Welty's most obvious oversights is her failure to
include Blacks. In an age of racial conflict, such an
omission is evidence of Welty's failure to include the real
world. She has fallen into the nostalgia trap.

27 M. M. "Small Town Dreamers Made Vivid." Review of The Golden
Apples. Los Angeles Times, 28 August, IV, p. 9.
As Elizabeth Bowen noted, "Welty's magic of writing" is
"fully demonstrated in this episodic novel." With its
many scenes and characters, The Golden Apples reads "like
a folk tale."

28 O'LEARY, THEODORE. "Pathos of the Unattained Golden Apples."
Review of The Golden Apples. Kansas City Star, (10 Septem-
ber), p. 14.
The surface details are not nearly as important as the
depths of a human personality which never fulfills itself.
Sometimes Welty probes too deeply for words and instead of
producing the surface, she is "exasperatingly obscure."
Her prose is thus both intense and fragile.

29 PICKREL, PAUL. "Outstanding Novels." Review of The Golden
Apples. YR, 39 (Autumn), 192.
Welty has no theme and no subject in the traditional
sense. Rather, she creates a series of insights into the
lives of characters in a small Mississippi town at various
stages of "their long and troubled lives." The Golden

1949

    (PICKREL, PAUL)
       Apples is not as consistently good as Delta Wedding. It is
       marred by passages which are "perfectly opaque."

30   POORE, CHARLES. Review of Music from Spain. Books of the
       Times, New York Times, (1 January), p. 11.
         The hero is a "milquetoast" like Walter Mitty, and his
       adventures are "as real--as smoke."

31   ROSENBERGER, COLEMAN. "Miss Welty's Trance-like Mississippi."
       Review of The Golden Apples. New York Herald Tribune Week-
       ly Book Review, (21 August), p. 6.
         The book is "skillful" but Welty's tendency to use a pri-
       vate system of symbols makes many of the stories too elu-
       sive. The best are the longest, particularly "June Recit-
       al" which demonstrates Welty's best stylistic technique,
       the accumulation of detail.

32   SHEFFIELD, MARTHA. "Eudora Welty Adds Statue [sic] to Repu-
       tation with Latest Stories, 'Golden Apples.'" Jackson
       Daily News, 18 September, IV, p. 3.
         With a wide range of vocabularies and with a knowledge of
       folklore, Welty creates "a full-blown classic." Its major
       weakness is her unattractive use of the simile.

33   STEEGMULLER, FRANCIS. "Small-Town Life." Review of The Gold-
       en Apples. New York Times Book Review, (21 August), p. 5.
         Although many of the stories have appeared separately,
       they are all strengthened by putting them together in what
       amounts to a "beautiful novel or poem." The sense of unity
       is emphasized by the unity of place in Morgana. The less
       successful stories--"Music from Spain" and "Sir Rabbit"--
       are marred by willful obscurity of language and by overuse
       of myth. The more successful stories are comparable to
       Winesburg Ohio and Huckleberry Finn.

34   TALLEY, RHEA. "Eudora Welty Joins Hegira of Mississippians to
       Europe." Commercial Appeal (Memphis), (17 July), V, p. 4.
         Mentions Welty's forthcoming visit to Paris to write a
       book. Also notes a musical which Welty was to write in
       collaboration with Hildegarde Dolson. As a challenge to
       the poor musical fare in New York, it was to be a series of
       skits entitled "What Year Is This?" No music has yet been
       written, but Welty has listened to songs by "several com-
       posers" including Brown Furlow.

35   No Entry

36   WEEKS, EDWARD. "Eudora Welty of the Delta." Review of The
      Golden Apples. Atlantic, 184 (September), 80.
         Weeks notes that Atlantic first published "A Worn Path,"
      "Why I Live at the P.O.," and "Powerhouse." He considers
      Welty "the best short story teller in the South" and The
      Golden Apples as excellent a portrayal of human nature as
      Winesburg Ohio.

37   WELTY, EUDORA. "The Reading and Writing of Short Stories."
      Atlantic, 183 (February/March), 54-58, 46-49.
         Welty urges both reader and writer to accept the subjec-
      tive response and to be aware of the dangers of overanal-
      ysis. The form of the short story becomes discovered in
      the act of writing it for "the mind in writing a story is
      in the throes of imagination, and it is not in the calcula-
      tions of analysis." Welty illustrates her argument with
      discussions of several writers including Hemingway, Crane,
      Mansfield, Lawrence, and Faulkner.

38   _____. "In Yoknapatawpha." HudR, 1 (Winter), 596-598.
         In a review of Faulkner's Intruder in the Dust, Welty
      discusses Faulkner's humor. "His stories aren't decked out
      in humor, but the humor is born in them, as much as their
      blood and bones. . . ."

39   WEST, RAY B., JR. and ROBERT WOOSTER STALLMAN. The Art of
      Modern Fiction. New York: Rinehart & Co.
         Welty develops "Powerhouse" through theme rather than
      action. The story "is constructed in much the same manner
      as a piece of music." "Powerhouse" is a mythmaker who
      makes art from his "private misfortune."

40   WILSON, DOVER. "Delta Revival." EJ, 38 (March), 121-122.
         Welty is one of the chief figures in the renaissance of
      Mississippi, an area that H. L. Mencken had declared to be
      essentially illiterate. Welty's orientation with this
      area is regional, but she actually lives outside the Delta
      and certainly knows the work of other writers. A chief
      contribution of the revival is the Levee Press which pro-
      duced as its first volume Welty's Music from Spain.

1950 A BOOKS - NONE

1950 B SHORTER WRITINGS

1   ANON. Mississippi Writer Reviewed at Meeting." Commercial
      Dispatch (Columbus, Mississippi), (21 March).

1950

(ANON.)
    Recounts the biographical sketch and review of Delta Wedding given at the Saturday meeting of the Ladies Reading Circle.

2   ANON. Review of The Golden Apples. TLS, 536 (8 September), p. 561.
    Welty's prose is "highly polished" in its appeal to the senses of hearing and seeing. It also displays a "fine control of first-person idiom."

3   ANON. "Awards and Obituaries." Wilson Library Bulletin, 25 (October), 106.
    Announces that Lillian Smith won the Southern Author's Award for Killers of the Dream and that Welty won honorable mention for The Golden Apples.

4   HEAD, BODLEY. "Tales from France." Review of The Golden Apples. TLS, 536 (8 September), p. 561.
    Welty's style is "highly polished" and "appeals to eye and ear." She also controls "first person idiom."

5   HEILMAN, ROBERT B. Modern Short Stories. Westport, Connecticut: Greenwood Press Publishers, pp. 50, 58-59.
    Welty's stories are set in the South but her interests and point of view are universal. She "ranges from a tough comic realism to the poetic and fantastic." Welty creates pathos about a character of low social status without descending into sentimentality.

6   MILLETT, FRED B. Reading Fiction: A Method of Analysis with Selections for Study. New York: Harper & Bros., pp. 159-160.
    Welty's method of narration is impersonal and objective. As a consequence, "Petrified Man" lacks plot but has organic and structural unity.

7   RUBIN, LOUIS D. "Five Southerners." Review of The Golden Apples. Hopkins Review, 3 (Spring), 44-45.
    Praises Welty's use of regional settings to convey universal human feelings. Defends "Sir Rabbit" against Hamilton Basso's contention that the story is contrived. (See 1949.B9 for Basso's comments.) Considers the story a superb example of Welty's subordination of incident to character.

8   *RUNYAN, HARRY. Review of The Golden Apples. Western Humanities Review, 4 (Spring), 171-173.
    Listed by Seymour Gross, 1960. See 1960.B5.

1951

9   SCHMUCKER, WALTER. "A Visit to Eudora Welty in Mississippi."
     Dallas Morning News, 24 December.
          Gives facts about Welty's private life. (Contrary to
     popular belief, she did not sing Methodist hymns with
     Faulkner.) She enjoys seeing her stories translated into
     foreign languages; she dropped a short-story writing class
     at Columbia University after two meetings; Delta Wedding
     began as a rejected short story. Writing is a spontaneous
     product of the mind; it is not entirely conscious.

10   SHORER, MARK. The Story: A Critical Anthology. New York:
     Prentice-Hall, pp. 354-357.
          In "Death of A Traveling Salesman," style and meaning are
     one. Through control of style and language, Welty directs
     the ambiguous interrelationships of the three worlds of the
     story: Bowman's private inner world, the business world
     that shaped Bowman's awareness, and the world of Bowman's
     immediate experience.

11   WELTY, EUDORA. Short Stories. New York: Harcourt, Brace &
     Co.
          See 1949.B37.

12   WYNDHAM, FRANCIS. "New Novels." Review of The Golden Apples.
     Observer, (27 August).
          In a work which may seem obscure to some readers Welty is
     not so much interested in the characters themselves as "in
     the rhythm of their lives. . . ." The entire work has "the
     simple suggestive quality of myth."

1951 A BOOKS - NONE

1951 B SHORTER WRITINGS

1   ANON. "Literary Genius Flourishes and Flowers in Mississippi.
     Faulkner and Allen Illuminate Skies Over Our State Recent-
     ly." Clarion Ledger (Jackson), 8 April, A, p. 13.
          Welty is mentioned briefly as "the first Lady" of Missis-
     sippi.

2   BRICKELL, HERSCHEL. Prize Stories of 1951, the O. Henry
     Awards. Garden City, New York: Doubleday & Co., pp. viii,
     x-xi.

1951

(BRICKELL, HERSCHEL)
Second-prize winner, "The Burning" is "one of the best
things" Welty has written. It is "prose-poetry" filled
with symbolism which becomes "crystal clear" after several
readings. Other judges, however, were less enthusiastic.
Nancy Hale considered the story fascinating but obscure.

3 BROOKS, JOHN. "Twenty-four Storytellers." Review of Prize
Stories of 1951: The O. Henry Awards. New York Times Book
Review, (26 August), p. 4.
The collection as a whole makes "good reading," but the
prize winners "seem disappointing." "The Burning," which
won second prize, "is evocative but miasmal."

4 FELHEIM, MARVIN, FRANKLIN B. NEWMAN, and WILLIAM R. STEINHOFF.
Modern Short Stories. New York: Oxford University Press,
p. 448.
With her "sense of the comic and the grotesque" and a
"highly experimental prose style," Welty is "one of our
most distinguished interpreters of the South." She demonstrates these qualities in "Shower of Gold."

5 HOFFMAN, FREDERICK J. The Modern Novel in America 1900-1950.
Chicago: Henry Regnery Co., pp. 155, 156.
Welty treats the South with "cloying rhetoric." Her best
work is the short story rather than the novel.

6 SHARP, MADORA HALL. "Eudora Welty is Credit to State." Clarion-Ledger (Jackson), (8 April), C, p. 7.
In an interview, Welty shows more enthusiasm for the
landscapes of William Hollingsworth than for her own writing. The interviewer, however, adds her own comments.
Welty and Faulkner "have pulled Mississippi out of the literary doldrums." Welty is a major influence on America's
national literature.

7 SKETTON, B. J. "Double-Take on Mississippi." SatR, 34 (19
May), 20-21.
Although Welty is frequently preoccupied "with the abnormal and demented," she presents her part of Mississippi
"with unusual skill."

8 STRAUMAN, HEINRICH. American Literature in the Twentieth
Century. London, England: Hutchinson's University Li-
brary, pp. 68-69, 119, 125-128.
Welty's subject matter is regional, but through imagina-
tion she transforms this subject into a world of her own.
In this interaction of reality and imagination, she is the

34

(STRAUMAN, HEINRICH)
only modern American who successfully bases her work on
"the absolute autonomy of the imagination." To Welty, the
world of the fabulous is real. Her only difficulty is
structuring her experience. The Robber Bridegroom lacks
discipline and structure.

9   WARFEL, HARRY R. American Novelists of Today. New York:
American Book Co., pp. 447-448.
Warfel states the facts of Welty's educational and work
experiences and comments briefly about Welty's writing
through Delta Wedding.

10   WEST, RAY B. "Three Methods of Modern Fiction: Ernest Hemingway, Thomas Mann, Eudora Welty." CE, 12 (January),
193-203.
Hemingway develops his theme through action, Mann through
psychological theory, and Welty through symbols. Welty's
emphasis on symbolic method in "Powerhouse" is almost the
opposite of Hemingway's emphasis on action in "The Short
Happy Life of Francis Macomber." Whereas what happens in
Hemingway's story is extremely important, what happened--
if anything--is impossible to determine in "Powerhouse."
"Powerhouse" is a symbol of the artist and his insistence
on presenting his own myths "gives form to the doubts and
fears of his race." The words of his myth are as much a
part of his art as the musical improvisations.

1952 A BOOKS - NONE

1952 B SHORTER WRITINGS

1   ANON. "14 Win Admission to Arts Institute." New York Times,
(8 February), p. 18.
Welty was elected to the National Institute of Arts and
Letters as one of those "most likely to win a permanent
place in American culture."

2   ANON. "Long-Heralded Institute of Literature Opens." Jackson
Daily News, (8 February).
Notes that Welty was invited as a guest of the Institute
of Southern Literature at Millsaps College.

3   No Entry

1952

4   ANON. "Writing Good Short Story Rewarding Says Miss Welty."
    Commercial Dispatch (Columbus, Mississippi), (18 April),
    I, p. 1.
        In an address before the Southern Literary Festival
    meeting at Mississippi State College for Women, Welty
    called the short story the "'most individual form of prose
    writing.'" Stories are difficult to write but may "'stim-
    ulate pleasure both for writer and reader.'"

5   ANON. "Author-Alumna Eudora Welty Misses Spiral Fire Tower,
    Finds MSCW Big." Spectator, Mississippi State College for
    Women, 23 April.
        Since she was a "fire chief" of Hastings Hall, Welty is
    disappointed that the spiral fire escape has been removed.
    She also makes some comments about the development of her
    interest in writing and her methods of writing.

6   GLENN, EUNICE. "Fantasy in the Fiction of Eudora Welty."
    Critiques and Essays on Modern Fiction: 1920-1951, edited
    by John W. Aldridge. New York: Ronald Press, pp. 506-517.
        As one of the first scholars to give Welty serious criti-
    cal attention, Glenn makes two contributions: 1. she at-
    tempts to define Welty's place in the tradition of American
    literature and to some extent world literature, and 2. she
    makes a working definition of Welty's use of fantasy. For
    Welty, fantasy is "reality . . . magnified." In most of
    her stories, Welty relates the perceptions of a person with
    "extraordinary acuteness of feeling." From such a point of
    view, the "real world" becomes a place of both horror and
    beauty. The seemingly strange world that her characters
    inhabit is actually the real world magnified. First print-
    ed in A Southern Vanguard, ed. Allen Tate, Prentice-Hall,
    1947.

7   HARDY, JOHN EDWARD. "Delta Wedding as Region and Symbol."
    SR, 60 (Summer), 397-417.
        The novel is structured with the rituals and symbols of
    the pastoral tradition in literature. But the pastoral
    tradition is merely a point of departure. The region is
    distinctly the Mississippi Delta and the Fairchild family
    has its own private system of symbols and rituals (the re-
    peated interest in George's rescue of Maureen, the magic
    lamp, the garnet pin). The most important ritual is prov-
    ing oneself worthy to be a part of the Fairchild clan. To

(HARDY, JOHN EDWARD)
most, worthiness is a right of blood, but the bridegroom
Troy must give evidence of courage and give promise of vi-
rility (a quality implied by his close association with
Negroes who are more oriented with the pastoral world than
the whites).

8   HICKS, GRANVILLE. "Eudora Welty." CE, 14 (November), 69-76.
In brief discussions of several stories from A Curtain
of Green, The Wide Net, The Golden Apples and in brief comments about The Robber Bridegroom and Delta Wedding, Hicks
argues that Welty's writing is not unnecessarily obscure
(as some critics have maintained), nor does it needlessly
emphasize violence, horror and physical deformity. Rather,
through precise control of point of view, and through a de-
piction of her own area of the South, Welty presents a universal view of human personality.

9   MORRIS, HARRY C. "Zeus and the Golden Apples." Perspective,
5 (Autumn), 190-199.
The stories in The Golden Apples are linked by direct
parallels with the legends of Greek mythology. Although
Welty realizes that each age needs to structure its experi-
ence with its own myths, she does seem to consciously im-
pose the structure of Greek myths upon her contemporary
Southern setting. McLain parallels Zeus and dominates the
collection either directly or through his descendants.
Virgie is roughly parallel to Venus and Eugene to Ulysses.
The Golden Apples serve as an ambiguous central symbol.
They can either represent discord or fecundity and rebirth.

10   PORTER, KATHERINE ANNE. "Eudora Welty and A Curtain of
Green." The Days Before. Freeport, New York: Books for
Libraries Press, pp. 101-108.
Reprinted from Introduction of A Curtain of Green. (See
1941.B20.)

11   SCHERMAN, DAVID, and ROSEMARIE REDLICH. Literary America: A
Chronicle of American Culture from 1607-1952. New York:
Dodd Mead & Co., pp. 174-175.
Includes two photographs of the Natchez Trace and brief
commentary. Welty has used the "dream-like Natchez Trace"
in many of her stories and has developed her skills as a
writer apart from any school.

12   WEST, RAY B., JR. The Short Story in America 1900-1950.
Freeport, New York: Books for Libraries Press, pp. 111-
112.

1952

(WEST, RAY B., JR.)
   The quality of Welty's work has steadily declined since
the publication of A Curtain of Green which is "interesting
and competent." (The Wide Net contains two of Welty's best
stories--the title story and "Livvie is Back" but the rest
are inferior to all the stories in A Curtain of Green.)
The Robber Bridegroom failed because of "confused inten-
tions," Delta Wedding is a short story stretched into a
novel, and The Golden Apples reveals a falling off of
quality.

1953 A BOOKS - NONE

1953 B SHORTER WRITINGS

1   ANON. Review of The Ponder Heart. Booklist, 50 (1 November),
       89.
          The Ponder Heart (as it appears in New Yorker) shows the
       brighter side of Faulkner's South.

2   *ANON. Review of The Ponder Heart. Kirkus' (Virginia) Serv-
       ice Bulletin, 21 (1 November), 714.
          Listed by Seymour Gross, 1960. See 1960.B5.

3   BARKER, SHIRLEY. Review of The Ponder Heart, LJ, 78 (15 De-
       cember), 2213.
          "Though marred by an extravagant climax," it is "the
       most amusing piece of humor since Mark Twain."

4   CONNELLY, MARC. "Induction of Newly Elected Members of the
       Institute." Proceedings of American Academy of Arts and
       Letters and National Institute of Arts and Letters. New
       York: Spiral Press, p. 14.
          Gives a brief statement about Welty's qualifications for
       induction. She has produced "subtle portrayal of charac-
       ter" as well as "ironic humor" and vitality.

5   COWLEY, MALCOLM. "The Literary Situation: 1953." Perspec-
       tives USA, 5 (Fall), 12.
          Although Welty is one of the "most considerable" of the
       young novelists, she is too conscious of writing within the
       tradition of the New Criticism. Rather than dealing with
       "social or political subjects," she turns to "inwardness,
       irony, symbolism, and other qualities that the critics
       admire."

6   DANIEL, ROBERT. "The World of Eudora Welty." Southern Ren-
    aissance: Literature of the Modern South, edited by Louis
    Rubin, Jr. and Robert D. Jacobs. Baltimore: Johns Hopkins
    Press, pp. 306-315.
        In a brief discussion of A Curtain of Green, The Wide
    Net, and The Golden Apples, Daniel compares Welty's world
    with the world of Faulkner. Although Welty has never
    claimed to have been influenced by Faulkner, Daniel notes
    some parallels. The white heron in "A Still Moment" has
    its counterpart in Faulkner's "The Bear." Likewise, "Cly-
    tie" is a character who could fit into Faulkner's world of
    fading aristocrats. The major differences are those of
    emphasis. Whereas Faulkner focuses on people within soci-
    ety, Welty is more concerned with the private sensibilities
    and essential loneliness of her characters.

7   HICKS, GRANVILLE. "The Best American Novels Since 1945."
    New Leader, 36 (14 December), 13.
        In its "miracle of sensibility," Delta Wedding is "as
    good as her best short stories. . . ."

8   SIMKINS, FRANCIS BUTLER. A History of the South. New York:
    Alfred Knopf, p. 453.
        Welty's fiction reinforces evidences of strong "sectional
    traditions" that made sociologists call Mississippi "the
    most unprogressive of American States." The Robber Bride-
    groom is a "weird fantasy of the state's frontier," and
    Delta Wedding is a "deft study of an old Southern family in
    decline."

1954 A BOOKS - NONE

1954 B SHORTER WRITINGS

1   ADAMS, ROBERT M. "Formulas and Fictions." Review of The
    Ponder Heart. HudR, 7 (Spring), 145.
        The Ponder Heart is marred by too much "literary serious-
    ness" which gives the characters the "self-conscious buf-
    foonery of television comedians." It does not give much
    evidence of Welty's "genuine talent for language."

2   AMIS, KINGSLEY. Review of The Ponder Heart. Spectator,
    (29 October).
        Amis finds The Ponder Heart too sweet and too quaint.

3   *ANON. Review of The Ponder Heart. Bookmark, 13 (January),
    86.
        Listed by Seymour Gross, 1960. See 1960.B5.

1954

4   ANON. Review of The Ponder Heart. Newsweek, 43 (11 January),
     82–83.
          Unlike Welty's earlier work which "tended to be somber."
     The Ponder Heart is humorous. It is also rich in "small-
     town folklore." The only fault of the novel is its length.
     It should have been shorter.

5   ANON. "It's Funny When You Tell It." Review of The Ponder
     Heart. Chicago Sunday Tribune, (17 January), IV, p. 1.
          Uncle Ponder is "a triumph of comic invention" who paral-
     lels the spending habits of the Federal Government.

6   ANON. "MSCW Library to Observe Eudora Welty Month." Clarion-
     Ledger (Jackson), (17 January), p. 10.
          The publication of The Ponder Heart inspired Mississippi
     State College for Women to have a display of books and rec-
     ords by and about Welty.

7   ANON. "Eudora Welty's Latest Novel is Given Review." Review
     of The Ponder Heart. Jackson Daily News, (21 January).
          Welty takes the difficult theme of the crushing weight of
     the Southern tradition and develops it with "loving humor."

8   *ANON. Review of The Ponder Heart. Durham (North Carolina)
     Morning Herald, (7 February).
          Listed by Seymour Gross, 1960. See 1960.B5.

9   ANON. "The Ponder Heart: Novel of Mississippi." Springfield
     Republican, (14 February), C, p. 5.
          The Review of The Ponder Heart. The humor is quiet rath-
     er than slapstick, but The Ponder Heart is "highly humor-
     ous."

10   *ANON. Review of The Ponder Heart. Wisconsin Library Bulle-
     tin, 50 (March).
          Listed by Seymour Gross, 1960. See 1960.B5.

11   ANON. "Easy to Read and Forget." Review of The Ponder Heart.
     Nation, 178 (6 March), 214.
          The book is delightful, but it is so light that it is
     also very forgettable. It has "Southern charm with none of
     the customary southern gloom."

12   *ANON. Review of The Ponder Heart. America, 91 (10 April),
     52.
          Listed by Seymour Gross, 1960. See 1960.B5.

13   ANON. "The Editor's Guest Book." Harper's, 88 (July), 18.
      Notes that Welty was "a little fearful" of departing from
      the Southern place and character (particularly after get-
      ting lost in Genoa), but she proved in "Going to Naples"
      that she could write well about a foreign place.

14   ANON. Review of The Ponder Heart. Scotsman, 7 (October), 13.
      This "elaborately contrived burlesque" will "either de-
      light or dismay the reader."

15   ANON. "New Novels." Review of The Ponder Heart. Time and
      Tide, (9 October).
      The Ponder Heart is "a superb piece of comic writing."
      Welty presents the town and its people with "sort of con-
      trolled exuberance" that belies her "exceptional skill."

16   BOWEN, ELIZABETH. "Genius of the Deep South." Review of The
      Ponder Heart. Tatler and Bystander, (13 October), p. 108.
      Books from backward parts of the world are often far
      grander than those from more civilized places. The Ponder
      Heart from Mississippi is no exception. "For the joy and
      magic are in Edna Earle's vocabulary."

17   BUTCHER, FANNY. "Cool, Skillful, Amusing Novella." Review of
      The Ponder Heart. Chicago Tribune Book World, (10 Janu-
      ary), IV, p. 5.
      The book is an amusing picture of the old South, but
      much of the meaning runs beneath the surface. It is a
      subtle portrayal of Southern psychology.

18   CAMPBELL, HARRY MODEAN. Journal of Mississippi History, 16,
      291-293.
      Campbell warns readers not to confuse The Ponder Heart
      with Erskine Caldwell's versions of "Southern degeneracy."
      Unlike Caldwell's gentlemen, "Uncle Daniel has a simple
      wisdom of heart that gives him . . . a far greater spirit-
      ual insight than most of his intellectual superiors." The
      Ponder Heart should establish Welty as "one of the three or
      four best living American writers of fiction."

19   CHAPMAN, JOHN. "Witless on the Delta." Review of The Ponder
      Heart. Dallas Morning News, (10 January), VI, p. 15.
      Most of the novel is merely an introduction to the court-
      room scene. Once there, Welty makes comedy out of mental
      deficiency.

1954

20   CHRISS, NICK. "No Pedal Stomper on Dixie Eccentricities, Eu-
        dora Welty Shows Light Side in New Book." Review of The
        Ponder Heart. Tupelo (Mississippi) Daily Journal, (8 May).
        Unlike some Southern writers, Welty does not make a repu-
        tation by tearing down conventions of the old South. But
        in The Ponder Heart, she does show the "lighter side."

21   FRENCH, WARREN. "A Note on Eudora Welty's The Ponder Heart.
        CE, 15 (May), 474.
        Welty borrows the name Edna Earle from the best-selling
        novel St. Elmo by Augusta Evans Wilson. With her self-
        righteous piety and her denial of human sexuality, Welty's
        Edna Earle resembles the Edna Earle of Wilson's novel.

22   GANNETT, LEWIS. Review of The Ponder Heart. New York Herald
        Tribune, (7 January), p. 10.
        One reads The Ponder Heart "for its rhythm" and for "the
        sheer pleasure of hearing Miss Edna Earle talk about her
        beloved Uncle Daniel." One will find little plot.

23   GORLIER, CLAUDIO. "Tre esperienze narrative." Galleria
        (Italy), 4, 349–359.
        "A Still Moment" reveals the dualism of Hawthorne's
        "Ethan Brand": the conflict between love and separateness.
        Even more than Hawthorne, Welty creates in this dualism a
        tragic irony.

24   *GRADY, R. F. Review of The Ponder Heart. Best Sellers, 13
        (15 January), 184–185.
        Listed by Seymour Gross, 1960. See 1960.B5.

25   GRAVES, ALLEN WALLACE. "Difficult Contemporary Short Stories:
        William Faulkner, Katherine Anne Porter, Dylan Thomas,
        Eudora Welty and Virginia Woolf." DAI, 14, 2067–2068.
        (University of Washington, 1954).
        Some modern stories including "Asphodel," "The Burning,"
        "Death of a Traveling Salesman," and "The Wide Net" have
        the "obscurity" of "abstruse modern poetry." They repre-
        sent a radical transformation of the form of the modern
        story.

26   HAMISH, HAMILTON. "The Human Comedy." Review of The Ponder
        Heart. TLS, 53 (29 October), 685.
        The Ponder Heart is one of Welty's "minor works." Her
        ability to sustain Edna Earle's speech patterns "is a
        feat," but it is also tiring for the reader.

27 HICKS, GRANVILLE. "Two Novels about Youth and Age by Jessamyn
    West and Eudora Welty." Review of The Ponder Heart. New
    Leader, (11 January).
        Welty presents "true comedy" without belittling a hero
    with "less than average intelligence." Like Laurence
    Sterne, she is able to write a novel of sentiment without
    being sentimental, and although her work has a Southern
    setting, Welty knows "how to soar above the limitations of
    regionalism."

28 HIERONYMUS, CLARA. "Mississippi Magic." Review of The Ponder
    Heart. Nashville Tennessean, (10 January).
        Welty demonstrates her gifts as a humorist, not with an
    "undertone of melancholy" as in Delta Wedding, but with "a
    gusty sense of the comics." She finds gentle humor in the
    "manners and speech" of her fellow Southerners.

29 HIGHET, GILBERT. Review of The Ponder Heart. Harper's, 208
    (February), 97.
        The Ponder Heart is a highly successful satire of the
    manners of Southern ladies. The only difficulty of the
    book is the narrator whose constant speaking is often so
    nonsensical that she is "a ferocious bore."

30 HUGHES, RILEY. Review of The Ponder Heart. Catholic World,
    179 (May), 152-153.
        After giving a dramatic summary of the plot, Hughes notes
    that "you'll surely want to meet Uncle Daniel."

31 JACKSON, JOSEPH HENRY. "Don't Miss Uncle Daniel Ponder." Re-
    view of The Ponder Heart. San Francisco Chronicle, (19 Jan-
    uary), Bookman's Notebook, p. 15.
        See 1954.B34.

32 _____. Review of The Ponder Heart. Los Angeles Times,
    (19 January), II, p. 5.
        Although the book has serious meanings below the surface,
    it is a comic masterpiece. It demonstrates that in addi-
    tion to being a fine prose stylist, Welty also has a "mag-
    nificent sense of the comic."

33 KENNEBECK, EDWIN. "People of Clay." Review of The Ponder
    Heart. Commonweal, 59 (22 January), 410-411.
        Although the story is "beautifully constructed," it lacks
    human passion and borders on "preciousness." There is hu-
    mor and love, but the humor is "not comic enough," and the
    narrator Edna Earle creates a "general air of sexlessness,
    and a handsome glitter of techniques."

1954

34   *KOGAN, HERMAN. Review of The Ponder Heart. Chicago Sun &
         Times, (10 January).
             Listed by Seymour Gross, 1960. See 1960.B5.

35   LEARY, LEWIS. Articles on American Literature 1900-1950.
         Durham, North Carolina: Duke University Press, p. 301.
         Contains three entries about Welty.

36   O'LEARY, THEODORE M. "Eudora Welty in the Mainstream." Re-
         view of The Ponder Heart. Kansas City Star, (23 January),
         p. 14.
             Welty demonstrates that her humor and art can speak to
         all people.

37   PEDEN, WILLIAM. "A Trial with No Verdict." Review of The
         Ponder Heart. SatR, 37 (16 January), 14.
             The Ponder Heart is Welty's best work since Delta Wed-
         ding. As in Delta Wedding, she controls the subtlety of
         her style. Nothing is completely resolved, but such am-
         biguity is intentional.

38   POORE, CHARLES. Review of The Ponder Heart. New York Times,
         (7 January), p. 29.
             Poore compares Welty's use of the self-effacing author
         with James T. Farrell's. Characters reveal themselves to
         the reader without any sense of an interfering author. She
         "has never written a better story than The Ponder Heart."

39   PRITCHETT, V. S. "Bossy Edna Had a Word for Everything."
         Review of The Ponder Heart. New York Times Book Review,
         (10 January), p. 5.
             Welty presents all the charm of Scotch, Irish or Welsh
         regionalists without lapsing into cliches. Her narrator
         "is a respectable young scold with a long tradition in Eng-
         lish sentimental comedy." She brings "the whole town to
         life" with her gossip.

40   QUEMMEL, PETER. "The Grand Style." Review of The Ponder
         Heart. Daily Mail, (29 October), p. 6.
             Welty is both "an accomplished satirist" and "a literary
         artist." In The Ponder Heart she has written "a brilliant
         extravaganza."

41   ROBERTS, ALBERT. "Ponder Heart is Eudora Welty's Finest
         Achievement." Clarion-Ledger, (3 January), I, p. 3.
             Notes Welty's accurate use of colloquial speech and her
         ability to make characters real without making them either
         biographical or autobiographical.

44

42   ROSENBERGER, COLEMAN. "Eudora Welty Tells a Wise and Comic
      Story of a Mississippi Town." Review of The Ponder Heart.
      New York Herald Tribune Weekly Book Review, (10 January),
      p. 1.
          The Ponder Heart is a "tour de force" of sustained humor
      and story telling. Welty recreates the "symbols" of the
      South "with perfect rhythm of speech."

43   RUBIN, HAROLD. "New Eudora Welty Novel Is a Garrulous Recit-
      al." Times Picayune (New Orleans), (10 January).
          Rubin considers the novel "too garrulous" and "a bit too
      cute and country."

44   SAMPSON, PAUL. "The Ponders of Clay Mississippi: A Richly
      Comic Character Study." Washington Post, (10 January), B,
      p. 6.
          The Ponder Heart is a comic novel "with real literary
      merit." It includes within its range "subtle irony,"
      "broad comedy," and "observation of human foibles."

45   SHRAPNEL, NORMAN. Review of The Ponder Heart. Manchester
      Guardian, (5 October), p. 4.
          The Ponder Heart is a "tenderly funny story." Although
      "loquacious," Welty does not waste words.

46   SMITH, HARRISON. Review of The Ponder Heart. Book Service
      for Newspapers, (9 January).
          The novel has "the material for a sordid and depressing
      novel of the South": Uncle Ponder is weak-minded and Edna
      Earle is a hopeless old maid with a failing boardinghouse.
      But Welty has "filled" the novel "with humor and laughing
      tenderness."

47   SVENDSEN, KESTER. "Uncle Daniel Achieves Immortality," Re-
      view of The Ponder Heart. Daily Oklahoman, (10 January),
      Books, p. 18.
          Welty and Faulkner both write the truth about Mississippi,
      but where Faulkner sees "courage, violence and disorder,"
      Welty sees "a muted struggle, not darkness but light, decay
      but not morbidity." There is also a strong mythic element
      in The Ponder Heart (as in The Robber Bridegroom) which
      suggests Welty's acceptance of life.

48   THESMAR, SARAH. "Mississippi Town Is Locale for Eudora Welty's
      Latest." Commercial Appeal (Memphis), (17 January), U,
      p. 12.
          In The Ponder Heart, Welty combines a heavy theme with a

1954

(THESMAR, SARAH)
    light subject but succeeds in faithfully portraying a proud
    Mississippi family.

49   *____. Review of The Ponder Heart. Commercial Appeal (Mem-
    phis), (17 January).
       Listed by Seymour Gross, 1960. See 1960.B5.

50   WEEKS, EDWARD. Review of The Ponder Heart. Atlantic, 193
    (February), 78.
       Edna Earle tells a moving and beautiful story, particular-
    ly in her portrayal of Uncle Daniel. Her language is
    "rhythmical" and distinctly Southern.

1955 A BOOKS - NONE

1955 B SHORTER WRITINGS

1   A. D. V. "Men and Motives." Review of The Bride of the
    Innisfallen. Hartford Courant Magazine, (8 May), p. 19.
       "Kin" and "Going to Naples" are readable because Welty's
    style is clear. The title story, however, and most of the
    others in the collection are obscured by "a sea of words
    which at times threatens to drown the reader."

2   ABERNATHY, HARRY. "Welty Quality in Tiny Package." Review
    of The Bride of the Innisfallen. Clarksdale Mississippi
    Press Register, (14 May), p. 2.
       The stories tend to lack plot, but the characters are
    often memorable. In fact the collection presents outstand-
    ing examples of Welty's talent for character development.

3   *ANON. Review of The Bride of the Innisfallen. Kirkus' (Vir-
    ginia) Service Bulletin, 73 (1 February), 98.
       Listed by Seymour Gross, 1960. See 1960.B5.

4   *ANON. Review of The Bride of the Innisfallen. Bookmark, 14
    (April), 162.
       Listed by Seymour Gross, 1960. See 1960.B5.

5   ANON. "Collector's Items." Review of The Bride of the Innis-
    fallen. Newsweek, 45 (11 April), 114-115.
       Welty is "a prose mistress at work." With the qualities
    of a French impressionist, she is particularly effective in

1955

(ANON.)
"No Place for You, My Love," the title story and "Going to
Naples."

6 *ANON. Review of The Bride of the Innisfallen. Southern Observer (Nashville), (May).
Listed by Seymour Gross, 1960. See 1960.B5.

7 ANON. Review of The Bride of the Innisfallen. Booklist, 51
(1 May), 368.
Although many of the stories are set outside of the
South, Welty still has a strong sense of place. She is
also "a born poet" who writes in prose.

8 ANON. "Diplomat Extols Rhetoric's Power." New York Times,
(26 May), p. 62.
The National Academy of Arts and Letters and the National
Institute of Arts and Letters presented Welty with an award
"for distinguished achievement."

9 ANON. Review of The Bride of the Innisfallen. VQR, 31 (Summer), lxviii.
Although A Curtain of Green establishes Welty as "one of
our finest short story writers," The Bride of the Innisfallen is not her best work. The stories frequently "lack
point and meaning." The best in the collection are "Kin"
and "Circe."

10 *ANON. Review of The Bride of the Innisfallen. Book-of-the-
Month Club News, (June), 8.
Listed by Seymour Gross, 1960. See 1960.B5.

11 *ANON. Review of The Bride of the Innisfallen. U.S. Quarterly Book Review, 11 (September), 353.
Listed by Seymour Gross, 1960. See 1960.B5.

12 ANON. Review of The Bride of the Innisfallen. TLS, 54
(11 November), 669.
The stories are "archly ingenious, tediously clever."
They lack the strong comic sense that Welty demonstrated in
A Curtain of Green. Welty has fallen into the "quicksand
of whimsy" that has trapped many other women writers.

13 ARP, THOMAS. "Welty's New Book of Short Stories." Review of
The Bride of the Innisfallen. San Francisco Chronicle,
(3 April), This World, p. 16.
All the stories have a single theme: the quest for understanding the mysteries of love, knowledge and happiness

1955

(ARP, THOMAS)
  which forever elude the perceptions of mere human beings.
  Even the god-like Circe cannot find the ultimate answer.
  Unlike earlier collections, The Bride of the Innisfallen
  contains stories that are not set in the South and do not
  deal with Southerners.

14   No Entry

15   BECK, WARREN. "The Realization of Sheer Genius." Review of
       The Bride of the Innisfallen. Chicago Tribune Book World,
       (10 April), IV, p. 3.
         The book is a work of genius, poetic and subtly realis-
       tic. It reveals a wide range of styles and perceptions.

16   BELLAMAN, KATHERINE. "Eudora Welty Praised by Writers and
       Periodicals." Review of The Bride of the Innisfallen.
       Clarion-Ledger, (17 April), IV, p. 6.
         Welty brings her characters to life in tightly controlled
       paragraphs and makes them consistent throughout. Tragedy
       tends to eclipse comic elements.

17   BINDERUP, HORTENSE. "Eudora Welty's Newest Book of Tales
       Called 'Absorbing and Rich in Mood.'" Review of The Bride
       of the Innisfallen. Oregonian (Portland), (23 October),
       III, p. 10.
         Beneath the "surface gaiety" of many of the stories is
       somberness. The world of Welty is strange but "rich in
       mood and atmosphere."

18   BIRD, WILL R. "In the World of Books." Review of The Bride
       of the Innisfallen. Moncton (Canada) Transcript,
       (30 April), p. 16.
         It is "a book of excellent stories" in which "No Place
       for You, My Love" is especially successful.

19   BORNHAUSER, FRED. "Book Reviews." Shenandoah, 7 (Autumn),
       71, 77-81.
         Welty's stories are held together with the themes of
       "separateness" that Warren found unifying The Wide Net.
       She "stabilizes a tragic world, resolves it with vivid im-
       agination; clean control of language, and her comic gift."
       In The Bride of the Innisfallen, she has learned to control
       a difficult and "highly distinguished style."

20   BRESLER, RIVA T. Review of The Bride of the Innisfallen. LJ,
     80 (1 April), 793.
         With a poet's sensibilities, Welty is "one of the finest,
     most original short story writing talents today." The book
     is for "discriminating readers."

21   CARTER, THOMAS H. "Rhetoric and Southern Landscapes." Review
     of The Bride of the Innisfallen. Accent, 15 (Autumn), 293-
     295.
         Welty tends to subordinate subject to style, and the re-
     sult "is disappointing." She evokes a detailed sense of
     place but very little sense of character or action. The
     best stories in the collection are those with a Southern
     setting.

22   COOPERMAN, STANLEY. Review of The Bride of the Innisfallen.
     Nation, 181 (16 July), 62.
         Welty's prose is polished and indirect. She creates su-
     perb "atmosphere" but sometimes sacrifices "substance."

23   DAVENPORT, JOHN. "Micrologophily." Review of The Bride of
     the Innisfallen. Observer (England), (16 October), p. 12.
         The Bride of the Innisfallen is not Welty's best work,
     but it displays an "astonishing eye and ear" and a "fas-
     tidiously disciplined prose." It is also a welcome change
     from her novels which "read like loosely interwoven tales."

24   DAWAIT, GLENDY. Review of The Bride of the Innisfallen.
     Washington, D.C. Post and Times Herald, (17 April), E, p. 6.
         Welty captures the sounds and colors of her world.

25   DOLBIER, MAURICE. "Looking Backward at the Books Which Stood
     Out in 1954." Publishers Weekly, 167 (22 January), 309.
         Notes that The Ponder Heart is "a short novel of pure
     delight."

26   ELDER, WALTER. "That Region." Review of The Bride of the
     Innisfallen. KR, 17 (Autumn), 661-666.
         It is typical of Welty's style but somewhat less of an
     achievement than her first stories which "were her best.
     . . ." As in most of her fiction, all the stories in The
     Bride of the Innisfallen deal with the theme of lost inno-
     cence, a theme which Welty develops through "dimly under-
     stood profundities of emotion." "No Place for You, My
     Love" is the best in the collection.

27   *FRENCH, WARREN. Review of The Bride of the Innisfallen.
     Lexington (Kentucky) Leader, (17 July).

1955

(*FRENCH, WARREN)
Listed by Seymour Gross, 1960. See 1960.B5.

28 FRYE, HARRIET. "Miss Welty's Private World of Whimsey." Review of The Bride of the Innisfallen. Columbus Dispatch, Tab, (17 April), p. 12.
Welty is an important influence on the best modern writing and theater. She is a keen observer and takes the reader into "another world," a world depicting "the comedy of human behavior."

29 *FULLER, RUTH WOLFE. Review of The Bride of the Innisfallen. Boston Herald, (10 April).
Listed by Seymour Gross, 1960. See 1960.B5.

30 GAITHER, FRANCIS. "Of the South and Beyond." Review of The Bride of the Innisfallen. New York Times Book Review, (10 April), p. 4.
The Bride of the Innisfallen is the first book by Welty that is set primarily outside Mississippi, but in these stories Welty's talents have "suffered no adverse sea change." Her talent for recording customs and idiomatic speech is still strong.

31 GANNETT, LEWIS. "Book Review." Review of The Bride of the Innisfallen. New York Herald Tribune, (7 April).
Welty "cares little for plot," but she has a "magic" style which can evoke scene and mood "in a phrase." She also demonstrates in The Bride of the Innisfallen that she can write successfully about places outside Mississippi.

32 *GRADY, R. F. Review of The Bride of the Innisfallen. Best Sellers, 15 (1 May), 28-29.
Listed by Seymour Gross, 1960. See 1960.B5.

33 HAINS, FRANK. "The Bride of the Innisfallen, Published Thursday is Latest Laurel in Eudora Welty's Crowded Crown." Clarion-Ledger (Jackson), (7 April).
Hains takes issue with Orville Prescott of New York Times who called Welty "an ironic, savage observer of the human comedy." Hains accepts the "human comedy" but denies that she is "savage" and "ironic." He also comments about Welty's method of subordinating plot and character to "mood."

34 _____. "Miss Welty Magnificent in Newest Short Pieces." Review of The Bride of the Innisfallen. Clarion-Ledger, (10 April), IV, p. 6.
Each story emphasizes feeling rather than plot, and the

(HAINS, FRANK)
one story that approaches humor, "Circe," is Welty's exper-
iment with a character who has magic but no feelings. Setting is important in each story.

35   HEWITT, DOUGLAS. Review of The Bride of the Innisfallen.
Manchester Guardian, (25 October), p. 6.
Welty's style is "ideosyncratic." She is often successful at presenting passing impressions, but too often her
meaning is unclear.

36   *HOEY, REID A. Review of The Bride of the Innisfallen. Bal-
timore Sun, (10 April).
Listed by Seymour Gross, 1960. See 1960.B5.

37   HOFFMAN, THEODORE. Review of The Bride of the Innisfallen.
PR, 22 (Fall), 561-564.
Welty attempts to make life more complicated than it actually is thus making otherwise transparent things hazy and
dream-like. Welty's detailed descriptions of "clothing and
furniture" which seem to have no interest for the reader
and no place in the design of the stories, are particularly vexing. The most empty stories in a rather empty collection are the title story and "No Place for You, My
Love."

38   HOLZHAUER, JEAN. Review of The Bride of the Innisfallen.
Commonweal, 62 (29 April), 109-110.
Welty's writing is "feminine in both the best and worst
senses." It is perceptive but verbose. The dialogue is
accurate, but it contains too many distracting details.
The result is often "unintentional comedy."

39   HUGHES, RILEY. Review of The Bride of the Innisfallen. Catholic World, 181 (July), 310-311.
Notes that Welty's stories stress the symbolic rather
than the literal.

40   HUTCHENS, JOHN K. "Miss Welty's Somewhat Puzzling Art." Re-
view of The Bride of the Innisfallen. New York Herald
Tribune Book Review, (10 April), p. 2.
The Ponder Heart has the story teller's grace, but The
Bride of the Innisfallen is too carefully contrived.
Rather than using her gifts as a "descriptive artist" Welty
creates needless obscurity by attempting to represent
"states of being."

41   *IVY, FRANCIS. Review of The Bride of the Innisfallen. Commercial Dispatch (Columbus, Mississippi), (27 March).
Listed by Seymour Gross, 1960. See 1960.B5.

1955

42 *JENNINGS, ELIZABETH. Review of The Bride of the Innisfallen.
    Spectator (London), 195 (23 December), 877.
        Listed by Seymour Gross, 1960. See 1960.B5.

43 JESSUP, LEE CHENEY. "Scenes of South in Delightful Stories."
    Review of The Bride of the Innisfallen. Nashville Banner,
    (27 May), p. 32.
        The stories have such divergent themes that there is no
    unity in the volume. But each story stands on its own
    "skill and beauty." The best piece in the collection is
    "Circe" with its "moving and magnetic prose."

44 KALB, BERNARD. "The Author." SatR, 38 (9 April), 18.
        Summarizes Welty's progress from a photographer trying
    to sell her pictures to a winner of prestigious writing
    awards.

45 KELLY, PAT. "Eudora Welty Collection of Stories." Review of
    The Bride of the Innisfallen. Winston-Salem Journal, (24
    April), C, p. 4.
        "'Circe' is a masterpiece," but the other stories in the
    collection are "plotless" and "formless." Welty is more
    a poet than a story-teller.

46 KIRSCHTEN, ERNEST. "Eudora Welty Says Much in Short Stories."
    Review of The Bride of the Innisfallen. St. Louis Post-
    Dispatch, (26 June), C, p. 4.
        Gives a rebuttal to the complaint that Welty's stories
    never lead anywhere and that they are limited in scale.
    Welty is not attempting War and Peace, but within her own
    limitations, a story like "No Place for You, My Love" gives
    a brief but intense insight into human lives.

47 KUNITZ, STANLEY J. "Welty, Eudora." Twentieth Century Au-
    thors First Supplement. New York: H. W. Wilson Co.,
    pp. 1063-1064.
        The chief critical question is whether Welty is a limited
    regionalist or a writer with universal appeal.

48 LEWIS, LAURA L. W. "Eudora Welty in Some Old and New Scenes."
    Review of The Bride of the Innisfallen. Greensboro (North
    Carolina) Daily News, (1 May), Feature Section, p. 3.
        The Bride of the Innisfallen reveals a great diversity of
    methods and subjects and is skillfully written, but as a
    whole, it is inferior to A Curtain of Green.

49 LITTLE, CARL VICTOR. "New Books." Review of The Ponder
    Heart. Houston Press, (8 January).

52

(LITTLE, CARL VICTOR)
   Little is pleasantly confounded that Welty--who had a
reputation as a writer for a small select audience--could
be enjoyed by everyone in The Ponder Heart.

50   *McGRORY, MARY. Review of The Bride of the Innisfallen.
   Washington, D.C. Star, (17 April).
      Listed by Seymour Gross, 1960. See 1960.B5.

51   MALONEY, JIM. "Welty Stories Excel in Character, Mood,
   Style." Beaumont (Texas) Enterprise, (10 April), C, p. 7.
      Like most of Welty's work, The Bride of the Innisfallen
   has an original style, "versatility of setting," uniformity
   of tone, and sharpness in characterization. The major flaw
   is the title story which is obscured by excessive symbolism.

52   MARTIN, TILLMAN L. "Eudora Welty, Master of the American
   Short Story." Southern Observer, 3 (September), 261-266.
      Martin gives comprehensive but superficial appreciation
   of Welty's writings through September of 1955. He intro-
   duces all the stories with one or two sentence plot sum-
   maries, lists some of the criticism, and makes critical
   judgments.

53   *MONROE, HAROLD. Review of The Bride of the Innisfallen.
   Texas Star Telegram (Fort Worth), (15 May).
      Listed by Seymour Gross, 1960. See 1960.B5.

54   MORRIS, HARRY C. "Eudora Welty's Use of Mythology." Shenandoah, 6 (Spring), 34-40.
      Welty uses mythology in three ways: to give order to
   contemporary events, to revive old myths, and to gain
   structural control. Although she writes in the "tradition
   of Poe and Hawthorne," her technique of using "classical
   material in already classical molds," moves the short story
   away from romanticism. This technique is particularly evi-
   dent in The Golden Apples, The Robber Bridegroom and Delta
   Wedding.

55   *NICHOLS, LUTHER. Review of The Bride of the Innisfallen.
   San Francisco Examiner, (10 April).
      Listed by Seymour Gross, 1960. See 1960.B5.

56   NORTH, STERLING. Review of The Bride of the Innisfallen.
   New York World Telegram & Sun, (7 April), p. 22.
      The stories with a Southern setting are the best, but the
   entire collection is excessively obscure.

1955

57   *PATTERSON, MARY KELSEY. Review of The Bride of the Innis-
         fallen. Durham (North Carolina) Herald, (12 May).
         Listed by Seymour Gross, 1960. See 1960.B5.

58   PEDEN, WILLIAM. "The Incomparable Welty." Review of The
         Bride of the Innisfallen and Other Stories. SatR, 38
         (9 April), 18.
            The stories are so allusive and privately symbolic, that
         they seem to be a private game. They are rich in detail,
         but the detail is so excessive that the stories seem to be
         a parody of Welty's earlier work. Only "Ladies in Spring"
         and "Going to Naples" are worthy of Welty at her best.

59   PETTIGREW, RICHARD C. "Her Finest Among These Short Stories."
         Review of The Bride of the Innisfallen. Birmingham News,
         (10 April), E, p. 7.
            Her best stories reveal all the sensuous details of "a
         painter with words."

60   *POWELL, DAWN. Review of The Bride of the Innisfallen. New
         York Post, (10 April).
            Listed by Seymour Gross, 1960. See 1960.B5.

61   PRESCOTT, ORVILLE. "Books of the Times." Review of The Bride
         of the Innisfallen. New York Times, (8 April), p. 19.
            Welty's best books are A Curtain of Green and The Ponder
         Heart. In the others--including The Bride of the Innis-
         fallen--she imitates the faults of Elizabeth Bowen and
         William Faulkner. From Bowen, she derives evasiveness and
         ambiguity; from Faulkner she learns to tell a story from
         the point of view of "a mentally incompetent observer."

62   RICHARDS, ALICE. "7 Spell-Like Tales Brutal and Funny." Re-
         view of The Bride of the Innisfallen. Atlanta Journal,
         (17 April), E, p. 7.
            Most of the stories are "dream-like," but each character
         emerges as a distinct and clearly-drawn personality. Some
         are grim and close to madness, but others, including "Go-
         ing to Naples" are "cruel but nevertheless funny."

63   RUBIN, LOUIS. Review of The Bride of the Innisfallen. SR,
         63 (Autumn), 671-681.
            Even perceptive critics often see only a welter of dis-
         connected details, but Welty structures all the stories in
         the collection with "the search for meaning of time." This
         theme is particularly apparent in "Kin," "No Place for You,
         My Love," "The Burning," and the title story. The primary
         difficulty for the reader is seeing beyond the individual

1955

(RUBIN, LOUIS)
  characters in the stories who often fail to understand the
  significance of their search.

64   SCOTT, ELEANOR. "Perilous Approach." Review of The Bride of
     the Innisfallen. Providence Sunday Journal, (22 May), VI,
     p. 8.
       The travel pieces tend to be unnecessarily vague, ambigu-
     ous, and without form. With the exception of "Circe," the
     stories show style as an end in itself.

65   SHAY, ARTHUR. "Seven Slices of Life Served with Perfection."
     Review of The Bride of the Innisfallen. Chicago Sun-Times
     Book Week, (10 April), III, p. 4.
       Welty's reputation as one of the best living short story
     writers is strengthened by The Bride of the Innisfallen and
     in particular by the best story in the collection, "No
     Place for You, My Love." In a compromise between "the
     slices of life" and the carefully constructed plot, Welty
     depicts the ephemeral nature of human relationships.

66   SHERMAN, JOHN K. "Seemingly Casual Touch Creates Rare In-
     sights." Review of The Bride of the Innisfallen. Minnea-
     polis Sunday Tribune, (22 May), H, p. 12.
       With the touch of a painter, Welty presents impression-
     istic "slices of life." With these impressionistic de-
     tails, she creates some subtle and suggestive characters.
     Sometimes, however, she probes too deeply below the surface
     and makes the reader guess her meaning rather than see it.
     Also, the stories tend to be rather "bloodless."

67   *SINGLETARY, ANNIE LEE. Review of The Bride of the Innis-
     fallen. Winston-Salem Journal, (24 April).
       Listed by Seymour Gross, 1960. See 1960.B5.

68   SPEARMAN, WALTER. "Eudora Welty Describes Own Success." Re-
     view of The Bride of the Innisfallen. Literary Lantern,
     Sunday Star News (Wilmington, North Carolina), (17 April).
       The most successful stories in the collection are those
     with a Southern setting and particularly those with a
     Southern family. When Welty writes about the South, she
     creates a world "hauntingly and nostalgically alive, with
     its sharp edges of reality somewhat smoothed . . . by a
     lyrical and dream-like quality." The stories with foreign
     settings are merely "skillful mood" sketches.

1955

69   *STEGGERT, F. X. Review of The Bride of the Innisfallen.
      Books on Trial, 13 (May), 347.
      Listed by Seymour Gross, 1960. See 1960.B5.

70   STORM, MICHAEL. "Welty's Genius in 7 Stories." Review of The
      Bride of the Innisfallen. Bridgeport Post, (10 April), D,
      p. 4.
          In her earlier works, Welty belonged to "the last strong-
      hold of Southern feudalism" but in The Bride of the Innis-
      fallen, she departs from her native themes and achieves in
      the seven stories, "feats of the imagination."

71   SWADOS, HARVEY. "Some Old Worlds, and Some New Ones Too."
      Review of The Bride of the Innisfallen. HudR, 8 (Summer),
      460.
          At her best--as in "Ladies in Spring"--Welty "writes as
      beautifully as anyone now at work in the U.S." But too
      often in this collection she "is simply not an interesting
      writer." She uses so many techniques to express subtle
      and uncommunicable emotions, that nothing is communicated.

72   *TOWNE, JANE H. Review of The Bride of the Innisfallen.
      Southern Pines (North Carolina) Pilot, (15 April).
      Listed by Seymour Gross, 1960. See 1960.B5.

73   TUNSTALL, CAROLINE. "Eudora Welty's Tales Waver Like Images
      in an Old Mirror." Review of The Bride of the Innisfallen.
      Norfolk Virginian-Pilot Star, (10 April), III, p. 6.
          Welty has two stylistic extremes: "a kind of broad
      farce" (as in "Petrified Man") and a "sensuous, dream crea-
      tion of mood" (as in The Golden Apples). Welty combines
      both styles in The Bride of the Innisfallen (particularly
      in "The Burning").

74   WALFOORT, MARY F. "Eudora Welty Presents Seven Striking Sto-
      ries." Review of The Bride of the Innisfallen. Milwaukee
      Journal, (10 April), V, p. 4.
          Welty tells her stories as though remembering a dream.
      She does not relate events directly but indirectly. Never-
      theless, the stories are rewarding.

75   WASHBURN, BEATRICE. "Editor Slaps at 'Sad Sack' School of
      Southern Writing." Review of The Bride of the Innisfallen.
      Miami Herald, (10 April), F, p. 4.
          Welty is one of Faulkner's "most successful disciples,"
      but like Faulkner's, many of her characters are abnormal.
      In "No Place for You, My Love," however, she shows "her un-
      canny skill in human relations."

76 WEEKS, EDWARD. Review of The Bride of the Innisfallen. Atlantic, 195 (May), 76-78.
Welty has moved away from her preoccupation with Southern
life in the title story and "Going to Naples." By so doing
she shifts from emphasis on place to emphasis on movement.
The prose "is at Miss Welty's best level," filled with
seemingly random details and partially revealed character.

77 WELTY, EUDORA. "How I Write." VQR, 31 (Spring), 240-251.
Each story presents its own problems which are discovered
and solved in the process of writing. Welty explains how
she used this method in the writing of "No Place for You,
My Love."

78 WHITE, ELLINGTON. "Miss Welty is Muted Elegance." Review of
The Bride of the Innisfallen. Richmond Times Dispatch,
(1 May), F, p. 5.
Welty is a master of her craft but because she emphasizes
subtleties beneath the surface rather than the surface itself, her readers will remain few but appreciative.

79 WHITE, MILTON C. "Sensuous Imagery, Vivid Impressions in
Welty's New Collection of Stories." Review of The Bride of
the Innisfallen. State Times (Jackson), (10 April), D, p. 3.
White comments briefly about each story and notes that
as a collection they are "varied and versatile in back-
ground and style."

80 *WILSON, ANGUS. Review of The Bride of the Innisfallen. New
Statesman and Nation, 50 (19 November), 680.
Listed by Seymour Gross, 1960. See 1960.B5.

81 *YOUNG, JAMES D. Review of The Bride of the Innisfallen.
Houston Post, (17 April).
Listed by Seymour Gross, 1960. See 1960.B5.

1956 A BOOKS - NONE

1956 B SHORTER WRITINGS

1 ANON. Advertisement for Music-Box production of The Ponder
Heart, New York Times Magazine, (22 January), p. 44.
Shows three pictures of scenes from the play and comments
briefly about David Wayne, who was to play Uncle Ponder.

2 ANON. "The Trials of Uncle Daniel." Review of the Music-Box
production of The Ponder Heart. Life 40 (5 March), 111-116.

1956

      (ANON.)
          Includes several pictures from the play and some commen-
tary. The reviewer assumes that Uncle Daniel is a disrupt-
ive influence because he is saintly rather than because he
is a half-wit. The play is "scarcely more than a series of
comic portraits suffused with a sunny glow of well-being."

3   ANON. "Wayne's Way." Review of the Music-Box production of
      The Ponder Heart, directed by Robert Douglas and starring
      David Wayne as Uncle Ponder. Newsweek 47 (5 March), 61.
        Wayne makes the character of Uncle Ponder "absolutely
believable."

4   ANON. "Macleish Prods U.S. on Soviet Rivalry," New York
      Times, (4 June), p. 4.
        Notes that Welty received an honorary degree from Smith
College.

5   ANON. "Dr. Wallace to Direct Play from Book by Miss Welty,"
      Clarion-Ledger Jackson Daily News, (5 August), III, p. 1.
        Discusses plans for the Jackson Little Theatre production
of The Ponder Heart.

6   BARBER, BETTE E. "Eudora Welty's The Ponder Heart Gets Rave
      Notices at Broadway Opening." Clarion-Ledger Jackson Daily
      News, (19 February), I, p. 6.
        Describes the atmosphere and critical reception of the
opening of The Ponder Heart at the Music-Box. Includes
comments by Walter Kerr, Brooks Atkinson, and John Chapman.

7   BARON, MARK. Jackson State Times, (17 February).
        Baron comments about the Music-Box production of The Pon-
der Heart and in particular about Welty's reaction to the
successful opening night.

8   BENTLEY, ERIC. "The Ponder Heart, after Eudora Welty by
      Fields and Chodorov." Review of performance of Music-Box
      production of The Ponder Heart. The New Republic, 134
      (12 March), 29.
        One of the major difficulties of the play was caused by
shifting the narrator, Edna Earle, from the center of consciousness that she maintains in the book to the role of a
minor character in the play. The result of this necessary
dislocation is an almost complete confusion of the story.
As a comment on American culture, the play accepts imbecil-
ity as wisdom, "an unconscious confession of spiritual
bankruptcy."

9   BOOKHART, MARY ALICE. "Eudora Welty's Play to Open Wednesday."
      Clarion-Ledger Jackson Daily News,(14 October), Women, p. 25.

(BOOKHART, MARY ALICE)
Describes the opening of the Little Theatre production of
The Ponder Heart in Jackson. Names the local cast and com-
ments about Welty's style.

10 CLERMAN, HAROLD. "Theatre." Review of the Music-Box production of The Ponder Heart by Joseph Fields and Jerome Chodorov. Nation, 182 (10 March), 204-205.
Although the play is "entertaining," Uncle Ponder is a
confused mixture of innocence and simple-mindedness. Consequently, this adaptation of Welty's book is not "completely satisfying."

11 CREEKMORE, HUBERT. "Behind Scenes after The Ponder Heart."
Jackson State Times, (20 February).
Creekmore says the play was "delightful" theatre but not
true to Welty's story. He also describes the reactions of
players and writers--including Welty--after the performance
and after the first successful reviews.

12 FIELDS, JOSEPH, and JEROME CHODOROV. The Ponder Heart: A New
Comedy in Three Acts. New York: Samuel French.
The play begins with a new character, a black maid sweep-
ing the porch. This is followed by a discussion of Uncle
Daniel's impending trial. (Bonnie Dee appears in flash-
back.)

13 GIBBS, WOLCOTT. "Two Views of the South." Review of Music-
Box production of The Ponder Heart. NY, 32 (25 February),
86.
Much of the humor remains, but the play lacks the serious
undercurrents of the book. Welty's compassion and understanding for her characters is sacrificed to the production
of "a bunch of hillbillies in the South" who are equally
"crazy and lovable."

14 HAINS, FRANK. "Ponder Heart Now Out in Dramatic Version."
Clarion-Ledger (Jackson), (27 May), IV, p. 6.
Discusses the difficulties and successes of the dramatic
version of The Ponder Heart. It is a novel of character
rather than of plot and is therefore difficult to transform
into a dramatic medium. In the play, Uncle Ponder "seems
sometimes unhappily near silliness."

15 HALL, JAMES B., and JOSEPH LANGLAND. The Short Story. New
York: Macmillan Co., pp. 329-330.
In "Shower of Gold," the events of King McLain's life
are related by Mrs. Rainey, whose point of view is deter-
mined by local manners and customs. In her telling, King
becomes a mythic figure of Southern folk traditions.

1956

16   HAYES, RICHARD. "A Southern Fiction." Review of the Music-
      Box production of The Ponder Heart. Commonweal, 64
      (6 April), 22, 24.
          The play preserves much of the pathos and humor of the
      novel, but some of the edge has been taken off in the
      fashion of Broadway.

17   HEWES, HENRY. Review of the Music-Box production of The Pon-
      der Heart. SatR, 39 (3 March), 22.
          Lacks the realism of the book but is "as colorful and
      amusing." It is a "benign comedy."

18   HODGINS, AUDREY. "The Narrator as Ironic Device in a Short
      Story by Eudora Welty." TCL, 1 (January), 215-219.
          Welty presents the story, "Asphodel," from the point of
      view of three old maids who only partially understand the
      significance of Sabrina's fanatical effort to suppress the
      life force--the male phallic principle--represented by her
      philandering husband, Don McInnis. Everything about Sab-
      rina suggests suppression of sexuality. Her house is dark
      and tomb-like (even the flowers are "wooden roses"). Her
      husband is the opposite. His house is bright and sunny,
      filled with real roses.

19   KEITH, WILLIAM. "Little Theatre Opens New Season with Eudora
      Welty's 'The Ponder Heart.'" Jackson State Times, (5 Au-
      gust).
          Keith describes preparations for the Little Theatre pro-
      duction of The Ponder Heart in Jackson. He includes com-
      ments by Welty.

20   KREBS, ALBIN. "A Hit or a Miss from Mississippi." Dixie Sun-
      day Magazine of New Orleans Picayune, (5 February).
          Gives some background about the cast of the Fields and
      Chodorov adaptation of The Ponder Heart.

21   PAYNE, WELDON. "'The Ponder Heart' Kicks Off with Smooth
      Mirth, Sadness." Jackson Daily News, (22 October).
          Payne reviews with considerable detail the Little Theatre
      production of The Ponder Heart.

22   SMYTHE, KATHERINE HINES. "Eudora Welty: A Checklist." BB,
      21 (January-April), 207-208.
          Lists all "stories, books, and articles by Eudora Welty
      through the month of July, 1954." The only items not in-
      cluded are book reviews and reprints of short stories in

1957

(SMYTHE, KATHERINE HINES)
anthologies. The list includes not only complete collections, but also individual stories which were later included in complete collections.

23   WELTY, EUDORA. "Place in Fiction." SAQ, 55 (January), 57-72.
Fiction begins with concrete and definable places which
gather "all that has been felt is about to be experienced
in the novel's progress." Fantasy must be grounded in the
concrete facts of place. Place has nothing to do with regionalism, which is a "condescending term." It is the
point from which the artist writes about universal concerns.

24   WYATT, EUPHEMIA VAN RENSSELAER. Review of the Music Box production of The Ponder Heart. Catholic World, 183 (April),
64-65.
Compares Uncle Daniel with "Mr. Pickwick."

1957 A BOOKS - NONE

1957 B SHORTER WRITINGS

1   ANON. American Writing Today: Its Independence and Vigor.
Edited by Allan Angoff. New York: Washington Square New
York University Press, 1957, pp. 183, 188, 189, 219.
Angoff compiles anonymous statements made in the TLS.
He does not give dates and volume numbers.) According to
the statements, Welty's writing is very polished; it is
particularly successful in producing "natural speech
rhythms." The Golden Apples demonstrates that her writing
is becoming "steadily finer" and that she should now be
writing novels.

2   DRAKE, ROBERT Y. "The Reasons of the Heart." GaR, 2 (Winter),
420-426.
Drake compares the novel with Joseph Fields and Jerome
Chodorov's dramatic adaptation and finds that the deficien-
cies of the play help explain the excellences of the novel.
In the play, all the characters are two dimensional. Their
motives are clearly defined and seldom do they act without
reason. The beauty of the novel, however, is the way in
which Welty presents the most beautiful of human paradoxes:
though the mind says one thing, the heart says another, and
the wise will listen to the heart.

1957

3   HARTLEY, LODWICK. "Proserpina and the Old Ladies." MFS, 3,
        350-354.
            Welty subconsciously parallels Marion's visit to an old
        ladies' home with such archetypal descents into the under-
        world as those in The Odyssey, The Iliad, and The Divine
        Comedy. There are parallels for the old man at the en-
        trance (in this case, a masculine lady), the crossing of
        the River Styx (the rippled linoleum), and some "Dantean"
        old ladies.

4   JONES, WILLIAM M. "Welty's Petrified Man." Expl, 15 (Janu-
        ary), Item 21.
            The omission of the article "the" in the title is signi-
        ficant. The story is not about the single man, Mr. Petrie,
        but about all the men. Just as stone men cannot function,
        so all the adult males in the story have been rendered
        useless by the women who so successfully dominate them.
        Only the little boy remains defiant.

5   _____. "Welty's 'A Worn Path.'" Expl, 15 (June), Item 57.
            The name Phoenix is the key symbol of the story. In
        spite of the hostility of landscape, hunter, and city,
        Phoenix--with her simplicity and love--will "return to the
        source of her youth again and again."

6   McBURNEY, WILLIAM H. "Welty's 'The Burning.'" Expl, 16 (No-
        vember), Item 9.
            In "The Burning," Welty uses elements from Tennyson's
        "The Lady of Shallott." The mirror is a central symbol in
        both works. In it, the world is always seen indirectly.
        In both accounts, the knights come through the mirror two
        by two, but in Welty's version not to save, but to destroy.

7   WELTY, EUDORA. "A Sweet Devouring." Mademoiselle, 46 (De-
        cember), 49, 114-116.
            See 1969.A2.

1958 A BOOKS - NONE

1958 B SHORTER WRITINGS

1   ANON. "Eudora Welty Wins Award." New York Times, (11 May),
        p. 56.
            Notes that, because of her "distinction in writing," Welty
        was made Lucy Donnelly Fellow at Bryn Mawr College for
        1958-1959.

1958

2   ANON. "Little Theatre Bill Includes Welty Skit." <u>Clarion-</u>
    <u>Ledger Jackson Daily News</u>, (3 August), C, p. 2.
        Notes that the Little Theatre in Jackson will perform a
    skit written by Welty entitled "Bye, Bye, Brevoort."

3   ANON. "Washington Press Welcomes Miss Eudora Welty on Visit."
    <u>Clarion-Ledger Jackson Daily News</u>, (9 November), D, p. 6.
        Summarizes the following responses to Welty's reading of
    her stories at the Library of Congress: Tom Kelly of the
    <u>Daily News</u>, Paul Simpson of the <u>Post</u>, and John Leyden of
    the <u>Evening Star</u>. Also includes comments by Welty about
    her meetings with Faulkner and about the forthcoming <u>Losing</u>
    <u>Battles</u>.

4   BRADBURY, JOHN M. <u>The Fugitives: A Critical Account</u>. Chapel
    Hill, North Carolina: University of North Carolina Press,
    pp. 105, 248, 258.
        Mentions Welty's early publication in <u>The Southern Review</u>
    and Warren's particular interest in Welty's prose style
    (which he analyzed in "The Love and Separateness of Miss
    Welty").

5   DICKINSON, A. T., JR. <u>American Historical Fiction</u>. New York:
    Scarecrow Press, pp. 128, 204.
        Lists <u>The Robber Bridegroom</u> as an historical novel illus-
    trating "expanding frontiers." The tale is fanciful but
    has an authentic setting. Lists <u>Delta Wedding</u> under his-
    torical novels of the 1930s.

6   DOLLARHIDE, LOUIS. "Welty Wit Sparks Trio Bill at LT." <u>Jack-</u>
    <u>son Daily News</u>, (9 August).
        Dollarhide praises the Little Theatre production of Wel-
    ty's humorous "sketch," "Bye, Bye Brevoort." "Miss Welty
    has a remarkable gift for comedy."

7   HAINS, FRANK. "Miss Welty Reads in Capitol Monday." <u>Clarion</u>
    <u>Ledger Jackson Daily News</u>, (2 November), D, p. 6.
        Notes that on the way to Bryn Mawr as the Lucy Donnelly
    Fellowship Award Winner, Welty will give a reading from her
    works, "probably" from <u>The Golden Apples</u>.

8   _____. "Why Can't Jackson Be More Aware of Its Most Celebrat-
    ed Citizen?" <u>Jackson Daily News</u>, (21 July).
        Welty is "one of the greatest living writers," and yet
    the Jackson Library has difficulty locating her books, and
    few local citizens know who she is.

1958

9   JONES, WILLIAM M.   "Name and Symbol in the Prose of Eudora
       Welty." SFQ, 21 (December), 173-185.
            Welty uses archetypes and mythic characters in a Missis-
       sippi setting. Her technique is fairly obvious in such
       early stories as "A Worn Path," and "Clytie," but in The
       Robber Bridegroom, she is "reaching for a more complex use
       of folk material," and in Delta Wedding, she completely
       submerges her sources in her setting. In The Golden Ap-
       ples, she returns to direct allusions to myths, but in-
       stead of creating new characters in old roles, she creates
       her own legends. Only the symbols which define the old
       legends sometimes remain.

10   WARREN, ROBERT PENN. "Love and Separateness in Eudora Welty."
       Selected Essays Robert Penn Warren. New York: Random
       House, pp. 156-169.
            See 1944.B8.

1959 A BOOKS - NONE

1959 B SHORTER WRITINGS

1   ANON. "Miss Welty at Millsaps Next Sunday." Clarion-Ledger
       Jackson Daily News, (1 March).
            Notes that Welty, "considered by many critics the finest
       living short story writer in the English language," will
       conduct a discussion of the short story at Millsaps.

2   BETTERSWORTH, JOHN K. Mississippi: A History. Austin, Tex-
       as: Steck Co., pp. 504-506.
            Welty rivals Faulkner "as a stylist and as a chronicler
       of Mississippi folk." As "master of the novel and the
       short story," she is "Mississippi's most distinguished
       woman writer." (This point is illustrated by a short ex-
       cerpt from "Kin.")

3   BROOKS, CLEANTH, and ROBERT PENN WARREN. "Interpretation of
       'A Piece of News.'" Understanding Fiction, 2nd ed. New
       York: Appleton-Century-Crofts, pp. 128-132.
            Atmosphere and setting are more important than story in
       defining Ruby's character. Ruby's remoteness and her lack
       of a sophisticated world make exciting dreams possible, but
       these dreams are shattered by reality. Welty develops this
       theme subtly by suggestion rather than by direct statement.

4   GALLI, LORENZA. "La Narrativa di Eudora Welty." S.A. (Studi
       Americani [Roma]), 5, 281-300.

(GALLI, LORENZA)
Galli traces the development of Welty's narrative technique from A Curtain of Green through The Bride of the Innisfallen. She places particular emphasis on the shifting balance between the concrete and the symbolic. She concludes that in Welty's greater focus on the condition of separateness, A Curtain of Green is still her best and most representative work.

5   HARRIS, WENDELL V. "Welty's 'The Key.'" Expl, 17 (June), Item 61.
Like many of the characters in Welty's fiction, Albert and Ellie Morgan are isolated from the normal human world by a physical handicap, deafness. They communicate through symbols, but these symbols frequently fail them. Since all language is made of symbols, Welty suggests a more universal form of human isolation. All symbols are somewhat imprecise and even nonhandicapped people fail to communicate.

6   JONES, WILLIAM M. "Growth of a Symbol: The Sun in Lawrence and Eudora Welty." UR, 26 (October), 68-73.
Following the example of D. H. Lawrence, Welty often uses the sun as a symbol of orientation with the natural world, but Welty's use of the symbol is more subtle than Lawrence's. In "Sun," "The Lovely Lady," and "The Woman Who Rode Away," Lawrence's didactic purpose detracts from the stories. But in "Death of a Traveling Salesman," "Clytie," "A Worn Path," "First Love," and "A Still Moment," Welty succeeds in evoking sun qualities without being didactic.

7   OPITZ, KURT. Neoromantic Als Gestalterin Der Prosa Eudora Welty. Unpublished Doctoral Dissertation der Frein Universitat Berlin.
Opitz traces neoromantic patterns in Welty's fiction. He includes Welty's interest in myth and fable from classical and romantic times, her understanding of Dostoevsky's rationalism and Tolstoy's romanticism, and her interest in the neoromanticism of Virginia Woolf and Yeats. Opitz is particularly interested in the European influence on the American writer.

8   WELTY, EUDORA. "'Cat' Comments by Eudora Welty." Jackson Daily News, (5 February).
Welty discusses the Little Theatre (Jackson) production of "Cat on a Hot Tin Roof." Rather than the performance, she focuses particularly on Williams' awareness of the problems of communications between people.

1959

9   WELTY, EUDORA. "How I Write." <u>Understanding Fiction</u>, 2nd
        ed., edited by Cleanth Brooks and Robert Penn Warren. New
        York: Appleton-Century-Crofts, pp. 545-553.
            <u>See</u> 1955.B76.

1960 A BOOKS - NONE

1960 B SHORTER WRITINGS

1   DRAKE, ROBERT Y., JR. "Comments on Two Eudora Welty Stories."
        <u>MissQ</u>, 13 (Summer), 1123-1131.
            In "Lily Daw and the Three Ladies," Welty develops one of
        her major themes: the difficulty of determining how far to
        help someone without squelching personal growth and self-
        discovery. In "Why I Live at the P.O.," Welty creates a
        "cater-cornered epic," or a mock-heroic story. Epic and
        mock heroic elements are present, but the moral issues are
        more complex than those in a conventional epic or mock
        epic.

2   FIEDLER, LESLIE. <u>Love and Death in the American Novel</u>. New
        York: Criterion Books, pp. 449-451.
            Categorizes Welty as a "distaff Faulknerian" in her ob-
        session with "gothic terror." In Welty's work, the "mascu-
        line vigor" of Faulkner gives way to "nuances of sensi-
        bility."

3   FOLSOM, RAYMOND. "Form and Substance in Eudora Welty." <u>DAI</u>,
        21, 621 (University of Wisconsin, 1960).
            Folsom discusses Welty's fiction in terms of her Southern
        background and in relationship to other contemporary South-
        ern writing. He includes discussions of <u>Delta Wedding</u>,
        regionalism, <u>The Golden Apples</u>, Faulkner and Warren, Kath-
        erine Anne Porter, and Carson McCullers. He concludes that
        Welty's work is more characterized by theme and style than
        by affinities with the South.

4   GRIFFITH, ALBERT JOSEPH, JR. "Eudora Welty's Fiction." <u>DAI</u>,
        20, 2289-2290 (University of Texas, 1959).
            In an analysis of Welty's boldly experimental techniques
        in all her fiction, Griffith discusses place, character,
        style, and theme. Although Welty is not as "broad and
        forceful" as Faulkner, she is "psychologically profound"
        within her own limitations.

5   GROSS, SEYMOUR. "Eudora Welty: A Bibliography of Criticism
        and Comment." <u>Secretary's News Sheet</u>. Bibliographical

(GROSS, SEYMOUR)
Society, University of Virginia, 40 (April), 1-32.
Presents a fairly comprehensive list of critical and bibliographical articles, textbook explications of stories,
and reviews of Welty's fiction through 1955. The list of
reviews is more extensive than any other entries and includes newspaper reviews and reviews in major scholarly
and popular journals.

6 HAINS, FRANK. "Discussion with Miss Welty Recorded in Millsaps 'Stylus.'" Clarion-Ledger Jackson Daily News,
(22 May), C, p. 13.
Contains excerpts from a taped symposium at Millsaps College. Welty answers questions about her favorite book (The
Ponder Heart), the differences between subject and theme,
the function of criticism, and obscurity in modern art.
(The entire transcript was published in Stylus, Spring,
1960.)

7 HOWARD, LEON. Literature and the American Tradition. Garden
City, New York: Doubleday & Co., p. 328.
Includes Welty with "serious writers of fiction" who oc-
casionally publish "'quality'" stories.

8 HÜLLEN, W., W. ROSSI, and W. CHRISTOPEIT. Zeitgenössiche
Amerikanische Dictung Eine Einführung in die Amerikanische
Literaturbetrachtung mit Texten und Interpretationen.
Frankfurt: Hirschgraben-Verlag, pp. 104-109.
Hullen emphasizes the contrast between Bowman's self-
satisfaction in the beginning of "Death of a Traveling
Salesman" and Bowman's sudden recognition that his entire
life has been lived outside the world of natural human de-
sires and satisfactions.

9 JONES, WILLIAM M. "Eudora Welty's Use of Myth in 'Death of a
Traveling Salesman.'" JAF, 73 (January-March), 18-23.
Welty contrasts two ways of life: that of Bowman, who is
a part of the commercial world, and that of Sunny, who is a
part of the natural world. Welty develops this contrast
with probable knowledge of T. S. Eliot's statement in his
review of Ulysses that myth shapes and controls human experience. Bowman's experience is uncontrolled because he
lives without myth, but Sunny's is controlled by his mythic
orientation with the natural world.

10 PEDEN, WILLIAM. Twenty-nine Stories. Boston, Massachusetts:
Houghton Mifflin Co., pp. 336-337.
Like an iceberg, most of the substance of "A Piece of

1960

(PEDEN, WILLIAM)
News" is below the surface. A single incident in Ruby
Fisher's life transforms her entire conception of herself.
Her returning husband--who before was uninteresting to
her--now seems sensuous. He is like a figure from myth-
ology and she a "priestess."

11   RINGE, DONALD A. "Welty's 'Petrified Man'." Expl, 18 (February), Item 32.
In his comments about "Petrified Man" in Expl, 15 (January 1957), William Jones fails to give the complete significance of the name Pike. In New Orleans, a Pike is a nosy
person who "Pikes" (peeks) at his neighbors and knows all
the gossip. Since Welty is well acquainted with New Orleans, and since Mrs. Pike in "Petrified Man" certainly
knows everyone else's business, the name Pike should have
this additional connotation.

12   THORP, WILLARD. American Writing in the 20th Century. Cam-
bridge, Massachusetts: Harvard University Press, p. 257.
Links Welty with Jesse Stuart, Marjorie Rawlings, and
Katherine Anne Porter as a modern local colorist. Like the
other moderns, she confronts "the realities of life," rather than escaping from them in the tradition of the older
local colorists.

13   THURSTON, JARVIS, O. B. EMERSON, CARL HARTMAN, and ELIZABETH
V. WRIGHT. Short Fiction Criticism: A Checklist of In-
terpretation since 1925 of Stories and Novelettes American,
British and Continental, 1800-1958. Denver, Colorado:
Alan Swallow.
Lists criticism of 25 works, from "Asphodel" to "A Worn
Path." For most stories, only one critical work is cited.

1961 A BOOKS - NONE

1961 B SHORTER WRITINGS

1   ANON. "Writers Named to U.S. Posts." New York Times, (14
May), p. 43.
Notes that Welty was appointed an honorary consultant in
American Letters for the Library of Congress.

2   ANON. "Miss Welty Reads Wednesday Noon at St. Andrews."
Jackson Daily News, (7 November).
Announces that Welty will give readings and discussions
of her works at St. Andrews Episcopal Church in Jackson.

1961

3   ANON. "Novelist to Lecture at Smith." New York Times, (3
    December), L, p. 13.
        Notes that Welty had been named William Allen Neilson
    Professor at Smith for the second semester of the 1961-1962
    academic year. She would "meet with students and give a
    series of public lectures."

4   BROOKS, CLEANTH, and ROBERT PENN WARREN. The Scope of Fic-
    tion. New York: Appleton-Century-Crofts, pp. 108-112.
    See 1959.B3.

5   BUSWELL, MARY CATHERINE. "The Love Relationships of Women in
    the Fiction of Eudora Welty." WVUPP, 13 (December),
    94-106.
        Buswell groups Welty's women characters into three types:
    old maids, young unmarried girls, and married women. She
    discusses Welty's thematic treatment of each type in repre-
    sentative stories, and concludes that Welty "accepts the
    traditional attitudes towards the sexes." Welty presents
    no original view of love, but in presenting universal val-
    ues, she is able to "confront the essentials of life."

6   *DANIEL, ROBERT M. "Eudora Welty: The Sense of Place."
    South: Modern Southern Literature in Its Cultural Setting,
    edited by Louis Rubin and Robert D. Jacobs. Garden City,
    New York: Doubleday, pp. 276-286.
        Listed in the PMLA Annual Bibliography for 1962.

7   DUSENBURY, WINIFRED. "Baby Doll and The Ponder Heart." Mod-
    ern Drama, 3 (February), 393-395.
        Williams may have been indebted to Welty for his portray-
    al of the virgin wife in Baby Doll. Both Bonnie Dee Ponder
    and Baby Doll are child brides who flee from the consuma-
    tion of the "trial" marriages. Both are obsessed with the
    possession of furniture. Both have fond and foolish hus-
    bands. And both satirize the "romantic concept of the
    south."

8   GOLD, HERBERT, and DAVID L. STEVENSON, EDITORS. Stories of
    Modern America (alternate edition). New York: St. Mar-
    tin's Press, pp. 145, 165.
        Welty's emphasis on atmosphere and place rather than on
    plot sometimes leads to preciousness and oversensitivity.
    "The Whole World Knows," however, "transcends these dan-
    gers." Because the story is told directly from Ran's point
    of view, the reader is drawn into a "strong emotional re-
    sponse."

1961

9   ROSS, DANFORTH. The American Short Story. Minneapolis,
    Minnesota: University of Minnesota Press, pp. 141-142.
        Discusses "Powerhouse" as an example of Welty's "experi-
    mentation with technique." Welty patterns her story after
    a musical composition. The story of Powerhouse's wife is
    an extension of Powerhouse's music.

10 VANDE KIEFT, RUTH M. "The Mysteries of Eudora Welty." GaR,
    15 (Fall), 343-357.
        Human relationship is mysterious because like the rest of
    the physical world it is constantly changing. Those char-
    acters who are without orientation in place (salesmen) are
    particularly remote from the sense of relationship. But
    all the people in Welty's world have relationships which
    are in imminent danger of falling into chaos. Although
    change is sometimes disastrous, ending in death, it is
    still the essential part of human mystery. In "The Bride
    of the Innisfallen," it renews the relationship between
    husband and wife. On the other hand, Circe cannot perceive
    mystery because her world is fixed and definable. Thus,
    the mysteries of Eudora Welty are her fictitious represen-
    tations of the flux of human relationships.

11 VICKERY, JOHN B. "William Blake and Eudora Welty's 'Death of
    a Salesman [sic] .'" MLN, 76 (November), 625-632.
        Demonstrates many parallels between Blake's Beulah and
    the Beulah in Welty's "Death of a Traveling Salesman."
    The parallels are in symbol, setting, character, and theme.
    For Welty and Blake, Beulah was a descent into the realm
    of self-knowledge and experience.

12 WELTY, EUDORA. "Henry Green: A Novelist of the Imagination."
    TQ, 4 (Autumn), 246-256.
        Welty discusses Green's comic sense and his use of the
    imagination to synthesize the seemingly random experiences
    of daily life.

13 _____. "Miss Welty Urges Books for Hospitals, Institutions."
    The Clarion Ledger (Jackson), (13 April), A, p. 6.
        In her plea to send books to prisons, hospitals, and
    homes for the mentally deficient, Welty discusses the uni-
    versal need for reading. She also makes allowances for the
    relativity of understanding, for "to the scholars, our own
    understanding must seem proportionately childlike."

1962 A BOOKS

1 VANDE KIEFT, RUTH M. Eudora Welty. New York: Twayne Publishers.
      Vande Kieft analyzes all of Welty's fiction through The
   Bride of the Innisfallen with "the kind of patient and loving scrutiny we apply to poems." In addition to careful
   explication of each work, Vande Kieft shows patterns and
   relationships among the stories and ventures to make some
   generalizations about Welty's achievement and her place in
   American fiction. She dedicates chapters to "The Natchez
   Trace," "The Mysteries of Eudora Welty" (Welty's stated
   intention to "mystify"), "The Weather of the Mind" (the impressions of the imagination), "Some Modes of Comedy,"
   "The Season of Dreams" (the flux of dream and reality),
   "The Search for the Golden Apples," and "The Achievement of
   Eudora Welty." In the last chapter, Vande Kieft compares
   Welty's treatment of the South with that of other Southern
   writers and concludes that Welty has less sense of Southern
   history and less concern for the race problem.

1962 B SHORTER WRITINGS

1 ANON. "Eudora Welty Speaks at State." Jackson Daily News,
   (22 October).
      In response to being called "one of the world's best re-
   gionalists," Welty says that the term "regionalist" is
   "'condescending'" and that "'place is secondary to feeling
   and plot.'" She also denies competing with Faulkner.

2 BOWEN, ELIZABETH. "The Golden Apples." Seven Winters and
   Afterthoughts. New York: Alfred A. Knopf, pp. 215-218.
      Unlike "inventive writers" who rely on ready-made forms,
   Welty is "an imaginative writer" who discovers new forms
   and new language in the process of writing. She "would
   seem to have found, for her art, the ideal form." But with
   Welty, "nothing is conclusive."

3 GRIFFITH, A. J. "Welty's 'Death of a Traveling Salesman.'"
   Expl, 20 (January), Item 38.
      Sonny is a Prometheus figure and his wife is an earth
   mother. Sonny offers the archetypal man, Bowman, "primi-
   tive cultural values," but because he rejects these values,
   Bowman (or man in general) is lost.

4 HOLMAN, C. HUGH. "The Novel in the South." A Time of Har-
   vest: American Literature 1910-1960, edited by Robert E.
   Spiller.

1962

    (HOLMAN, C. HUGH)
       New York: Hill and Wang, p. 87.
       Links Welty with Katherine Anne Porter as writers who
    "have used highly refined and almost poetic, brief art
    forms to state their visions of experience."

5   JONES, ALUN R. "Life is the Story." Review of Eudora Welty
       by Ruth M. Vande Kieft. New York Times Book Review,
       (27 May), VII, p. 6.
       Like Mansfield and Woolf, Welty writes prose which "approaches the precision and density of poetry." In her
    analysis of this prose, Vande Kieft is thorough and will
    certainly "further Miss Welty's reputation," but she often
    over-simplifies Welty's prose by explaining it away and is
    often too insistent that Welty has a pessimistic view of
    the world.

6   KLATZO, TONI. "Eudora Welty Tells Students About Writing."
       Clarion-Ledger (Jackson), (19 March), p. 2.
       Welty mentions a new, "longer book" that she is writing.
    She also explains why the South has produced so many outstanding writers, why the artist should not make pronouncements about world affairs, and discusses the importance of
    names in fiction.

7   MIZENER, ARTHUR, ed. Modern Short Stories: The Uses of the
       Imagination. New York: W. W. Norton & Co., p. 465.
       "A Worn Path" exemplifies the distinctly Southern aspects
    of a stable agrarian society, with its fixed and constant
    values. Phoenix's "indomitable love" for her grandson
    keeps her going.

8   O'CONNOR, WILLIAM VAN. The Grotesque: An American Genre and
       Other Essays. Carbondale, Illinois: Southern Illinois
    University Press, p. 13.
       In Welty's stories, "sentiment and sympathy" replace
    righteousness as moral principles. Her world is "eerie"
    and dreamlike.

9   No Entry

10   WELTY, EUDORA. Three Papers on Fiction. Northampton, Massa-
       chusetts: Smith College.
       The three papers are: "Place," "Words Into Fiction,"
    "The Short Story." Place is the starting point for a work
    of fiction. The experience of words comes second and then

(WELTY, EUDORA)
only through "some personal act of vision." The writer
does not solve the mystery of life; he rediscovers it. In
"The Short Story," Welty distinguishes between narrative
and plot (with acknowledgments to E. M. Forster). She discusses Crane's "The Bride Comes to Yellow Sky," Mansfield's
"Miss Brill," Lawrence's "The Fox," and Faulkner's "The
Bear."

1963 A BOOKS - NONE

1963 B SHORTER WRITINGS

1   ANON. "Award of Prize Climaxes Southern Literacy Festival."
    Clarion-Ledger Jackson Daily News, (21 April), F, p. 7.
        Notes that the highlight of the festival was Welty's ad-
    dress, "Words Into Fiction."

2   BEAGLE, BEN. "Writing No Road to Riches, Says Author."
    Roanoke Times, (12 December), p. 17.
        Contains comments gleaned from Welty's remarks during her
    stay at Hollins College as part of the "visiting author
    program." Welty recommends that the "serious writer" have
    a supplemental income. She also comments about the art of
    writing, the "racial situation in Mississippi," and advises
    would-be writers to "'Be aware of what's around you and be
    willing to read.'"

3   BODE, WINSTON. "Eudora Welty Bringing Her Shimmering Prose."
    Houston Chronicle, (13 May).
        Discusses Welty's imminent visit to the University of
    Texas to participate in a "program in criticism."

4   BRADBURY, JOHN M. Renaissance in the South: A Critical His-
    tory of the Literature, 1920-1960. Chapel Hill, North
    Carolina: University of North Carolina Press, pp. 108-110.
        Welty is a "later traditionalist." She is of the second
    generation to be concerned with "the form of symbolic nat-
    uralism," which she learned from Katherine Anne Porter,
    "her chief sponsor." Like Porter, Welty has achieved a
    major place in Southern literature through her short sto-
    ries. Her best stories are in A Curtain of Green; The
    Bride of the Innisfallen reveals a decline of her powers.

5   COLE, McKELVA. "Book Reviews by Eudora Welty: A Checklist."
    BB, 23 (January-April), 240.
        Cole observes that Welty's reviews have appeared in the
    Saturday Review, the New York Post, the Hudson Review, and

1963

(COLE, McKELVA)
"other quarterlies," but he limits his list to all book reviews that Welty wrote for the New York Times between 1943
and 1961.

6   DA PONTE, DURANT. "Books on American Writers." Southern
     Observer, (February).
        Comments about Ruth Vande Kieft's Eudora Welty. Although
     Welty is a "minor" but "genuine" and "skillful" author,
     Vande Kieft's book "is both worthwhile and welcome." In a
     complete analysis of Welty's stories, Vande Kieft helps ac-
     count for Welty's universal reputation, a reputation which
     includes translation into several foreign languages.

7   DOLLARHIDE, LOUIS. "Eudora Welty Receives Annual Bellamann
     Award." Clarion-Ledger Jackson Daily News, (3 February),
     B, 4.
        Dollarhide discusses the extremes of comedy and tragedy
     in Welty's fiction, her acceptance of life (rather than a
     criticism of it), and her "compressed metaphors."

8   EISINGER, CHESTER E. "Eudora Welty and the Triumph of the
     Imagination." Fiction of the Forties. Chicago: Univer-
     sity of Chicago Press, pp. 258-283.
        Welty, more so than any other writer of the 1940s, broke
     with conventions and began "a new school of fiction." Al-
     though her works contain elements of Southern gothicism--
     particularly in the numerous deformed and grotesque char-
     acters--her emphasis is not on the grotesque as a criti-
     cism of Southern society, but on levels of human conscious-
     ness. She emphasizes the synthesizing power of the human
     imagination, a synthesis which combines old myths with
     modern consciousness.

9   HAINS, FRANK. "Eudora Welty Admires Overflow 'Monday Night at
     Library' Session." Jackson Daily News, (2 April), 6.
        Hains describes Welty's reading of "Petrified Man" and
     "Why I Live at the P.O." before a packed assembly room in
     the Jackson Municipal Library. He also summarizes the ad-
     vanced notices given to Welty before she arrived at David-
     son College as "the Book-of-the-Year Visitor."

10   HOLLAND, ROBERT B. "Dialogue as a Reflection of Place in The
     Ponder Heart." AL, 35 (November) 352-358.
        The repetitive mannerisms and stresses of Welty's dia-
     logue reflect the conservative and coherent order of South-
     ern culture, particularly that of the deep South. Communi-
     cation is allusive and elliptical because within the con-
     fines of such a society, the speaker assumes that his audi-
     ence knows the allusions and can readily fill in the gaps.

1963

(HOLLAND, ROBERT B.)
A formal structure which sometimes falls off into the in-
formal creates a bathos but also suggests a society which
is trying to keep up the appearances of order but is slowly
losing the struggle.

11   ISAACS, NEIL D.   "Life for Phoenix."   SR, 71 (Winter), 75-81.
Places the story in the tradition of allegorical "road
literature."   The path is the Christian's road to salvation
and rebirth.   Although the title is pagan, it is also associated with the death and rebirth of Christ.   It suggests
the essentially Christian doctrine that the road to salvation is the road through suffering and death.   Unless man
takes the journey, he cannot pass through sin and death to
redemption and new life.

12   ISAACS, NEIL D., and LOUIS LEITER.   Approaches to the Short
Story.   San Francisco, California: Chandler Publishing
Co., p. 108.
See 1963.B11.

13   JONES, ALUN R.   "The World of Love: The Fiction of Eudora
Welty."   The Creative Present: Notes on Contemporary
American Fiction, edited by Nona Balakian and Charles Simmons.   Garden City, New York: Doubleday & Co., pp. 175-192.
Jones traces Welty's development of the theme of love
from A Curtain of Green through The Bride of the Innisfallen.   He concludes that each story has "a different
challenge" and that "in each she has extended herself in a
new direction."   In The Bride of the Innisfallen, she has
broadened the scope, as well as enriched the texture, of
her writing still further."

14   McDONALD, W. U., JR.   "Eudora Welty Manuscripts: An Annotated
Finding List."   BB, 24 (September-December), 44-45.
McDonald includes the location of Welty's manuscripts for
her published fiction, her unpublished fiction, and her
letters.   The list includes all published fiction to date
(with the exception of The Wide Net), all known unpublished
work (including "Acrobats in a Park," but excluding Welty's
unpublished honors project at the University of Wisconsin,
"All Available Brocade"), and numerous letters.   McDonald
has seen most of the collections and comments briefly about
the condition of the manuscripts and the extent of the revisions.   He observes that there are often substantial differences between the manuscript versions of the stories and
the published versions.   Most manuscripts may be found in

1963

(McDONALD, W. U., JR.)
the Mississippi Department of Archives and History, the
Robert Penn Warren Collection at Yale, and the Millsaps-
Wilson Library in Jackson, Mississippi.

15 _____. "Welty's 'Keela': Irony, Ambiguity, and the Ancient
Mariner." SSF, 1 (Fall), 59-61.
McDonald continues Vande Kieft's discussion of irony in
"Keela, the Outcast Indian Maiden" (See 1962.A1). Vande
Kieft finds the essential irony of the story in the lack
of communication among the three main characters. McDonald
develops this thesis by explaining what "outcast" actually
means to little Lee Roy. Contrary to what Steve believes,
Lee Roy is not outcast until he has been taken out of the
carnival. What seems to Steve to have been a horrible ex-
perience is actually the finest and most exciting part of
Lee Roy's life.

16 PETTY, JANE. "Eudora Welty Headlines Southern Literary Fest."
Clarion-Ledger Jackson Daily News, (14 April), C, p. 4.
Notes that Welty will participate in the Southern Literary Festival at Millsaps College. Quotes from Welty's essay, "Place in Fiction," and announces that Welty will
begin the festival by reading "Words into Fiction."

17 _____. "Eudora Welty Opens Annual Southern Literary Festival
Here." Jackson Daily News, (19 April), p. 3.
Discusses Welty's presentation of her paper "Words into
Fiction." Also notes Welty's comment that "Powerhouse" is
not specifically about Waller; "it is the story of the life
of the artist."

18 ROUSE, SARAH ALLMAN. "Place and People in Eudora Welty's Fiction." DAI, 23, 3901 (Florida State University, 1962).
Rouse demonstrates that Welty's stories and novels reveal
both an accurate view of the South and a universal view of
man. She discusses A Curtain of Green and The Bride of the
Innisfallen in terms of the varied social classes of the
characters, The Golden Apples as a study of the middle
class, and Delta Wedding as a picture of the unchanging
planter class.

19 RUBIN, LOUIS. "The Golden Apples of the Sun." The Faraway
Country. Seattle, Washington: University of Washington
Press, pp. 131-154.
There are two worlds of Mississippi in fiction. One is
Faulkner's, a country of violence, disorder, and tragedy.
The other is a stereotype of Southern tranquility, with

76

1964

(RUBIN, LOUIS)
quiet towns and hospitable, sheltered people. A writer who
depicts the second is likely to be classified a regionalist
with all the negative connotations of the word: provinci-
ality rather than universality, romanticism rather than
realism. All too often, Welty has been classified as this
type of regionalist. However, close readings of Delta
Wedding, "Kin," and The Golden Apples reveal that Welty's
portrayal of her own region is universal and, to some extent, tragic. Although her characters never achieve the
heroic stature of Faulkner's, their seemingly sheltered
world is being undermined by time, which is the universal
enemy of mankind.

20 TRASK, GEORGIANNE, and CHARLES BURKHART, eds. Story Tellers
and Their Art: An Anthology. Garden City, New York:
Anchor Books.
Takes short excerpts from Welty's essay, "Short Stories,"
to help define "Story," "Beauty," "The Writer and the Reader," "Sensibility," and "Form." Also includes the entire
essay, "Place in Fiction," and Porter's "Introduction" to
A Curtain of Green.

21 WELTY, EUDORA. "And They All Lived Happily Ever After." New
York Times Book Review, (10 November), VII-Part 2, p. 3.
The fairy tale is an important element in the modern
short story, since it expresses in "childhood language"
the mysteries of human life. Like life itself, fairy tales
are "wonderfully severe and uncondescending." They are
also rich in irony and present "truths bolder and often
more appalling than we know what to do with . . . ."

22 WEST, RAY B., JR. "The American Short Story at Mid-Century."
Discussions of the Short Story, ed. Hollis Summers. Bos-
ton, Massachusetts: D. C. Heath and Co., p. 39.
Lists Welty with those post-World War II writers whose
works "appear only slightly less important than those of
Hemingway and Faulkner."

1964 A BOOKS - NONE

1964 B SHORTER WRITINGS

1 ANON. "Eudora Welty Named Writer-in-Residence." Major Notes
Millsaps College, (Summer).

1964

(ANON.)
   Quotes the comments of Dr. George Boyd, Chairman of the
Department of English at Millsaps. Dr. Boyd agrees with
critics who consider Welty's work well-structured, humorous, and true to place and language.

2   ANON. "Eudora Welty Will Lecture." Clarion-Ledger (Jackson),
   (7 March), p. 5.
   Announces that Welty will conduct a seminar in American
Literature at the University of Mississippi. She will also
discuss "the technical problems in the writing of short
fiction," with emphasis on the comic mode in The Ponder
Heart and "Why I Live at the P.O."

3   ANON. "Jackson Writer Honored by Journalism Society." Clarion-Ledger (Jackson), (13 March), p. 5.
   Notes that Welty was initiated "into Theta Sigma Phi,
national honorary professional fraternity for women in
journalism."

4   ANON. "Miss Welty Accepts Post at Millsaps." Clarion-Ledger
   Jackson Daily News, (28 June), A, p. 9.
   Briefly discusses Welty's responsibilities at Millsaps
College.

5   ANON. "Miss Welty's Lecture Set for 2 December." Clarion-
   Ledger Jackson Daily News, (29 November), F, p. 7.
   Announces that "America's first Lady of Letters," Welty,
will speak on the subject, "The Southern Writer Today."
Also includes comments by Welty about her creative writing
class at Millsaps.

6   ANON. "Miss Welty to Lecture at Seminar." Clarion-Ledger
   (Jackson), (13 July), p. 5.
   Announces that Welty will address a seminar in American
Studies at Mississippi College in Clinton.

7   ANON. "Pride of Northside." Northside Reporter, (16 July).
   Following a brief biographical sketch, the article notes
that Welty "opened the American Studies Seminar at Missis-
ippi College."

8   ALLEN, WALTER. The Modern Novel in Britain and the United
   States. New York: E. P. Dutton & Co., p. 132.
   Gives Welty only part of one sentence: "Eudora Welty is
much more distinguished as a short-story writer than as a
novelist."

9   BEVINGTON, HELEN. Review of The Shoebird. New York Times
     Book Review, (15 November), p. 50.
          Like Welty, the parrot Arturo loves words. With them, he
     moves from realism to fantasy with great delight. (Recom-
     mended for ages 9-14.)

10   BRADHAM, JO ALLEN. "A Visit of Charity: Menippean Satire."
     SSF, 1 (Fall 1963--Summer 1964), 258-263.
          Bradham defines Menippean satire and then demonstrates
     how all the elements in the definition are present in "A
     Visit of Charity." For example, Menippean satire is "an
     attack on a philosophy;" and in "A Visit of Charity," Welty
     attacks the philosophy of Christian charity.

11   DALY, SAROLYN, R. "'A Worn Path' Retrod." SSF, 1 (Winter),
     133-139.
          Takes exception to the essentially optimistic (and overt-
     ly Christian) interpretations of the story by Neil D.
     Isaacs (1963.B11) and William M. Jones (1957.B5). Phoenix
     encountered not mere difficulty but positive evil. The
     journey is not one of renewal but of repetition. Only the
     existential act makes the journey meaningful. Thus the
     story is more one of existential forebearance than of
     Christian renewal.

12   DOLLARHIDE, LOUIS. "Honors for Miss Welty Recognize State
     'Artist.'" Clarion-Ledger Jackson Daily News, (27 Decem-
     ber), D, p. 9.
          Dollarhide discusses Welty's paradoxical position as an
     artist admired by the bank. (Welty received one of the
     three "First National Bank Awards.")

13   _____. "The One Mississippian Internationally Admired."
     Clarion-Ledger Jackson Daily News, (5 July), E, p. 5.
          Dollarhide discusses Welty's reputation in the world and
     concludes that, with Stark Young and William Faulkner dead,
     "she is probably the one Mississippian admired interna-
     tionally."

14   EMERSON, O. B. "Prophet Next Door." Reality and Myth: Es-
     says in American Literature in Memory of Richard Croom
     Beatty, ed. William E. Walker and Robert L. Welker. Nash-
     ville, Tennessee: Vanderbilt University Press, p. 249.
          Gives Welty credit for helping Faulkner further his repu-
     tation after Sanctuary. (Welty gave the book a favorable
     review.)

1964

15   FELHEIM, MARVIN. "Eudora Welty and Carson McCullers." Con-
      temporary American Novelists, ed. Harry T. Moore. Carbon-
      dale, Illinois: Southern Illinois University Press, pp.
      41-48.
          In a lyrical language, Welty presents the mysteries of
      human relationship and separateness in "A Piece of News,"
      "A Still Moment," and "Moon Lake." With the sensibility of
      a poet and painter, she depicts the linked opposites of
      human experience: "the inevitable sadness of life and the
      surge of redeeming ecstasy."

16   HARDENDORFT, JEANNE B. Review of The Shoebird. LJ, 89 (15
      December), 5012.
          The story is "contrived" and "heavy-handed." It is not
      worthy of "such a talented writer of adult fiction."

17   HARDY, JOHN EDWARD. "Delta Wedding: Region and Symbol." Man
      in the Modern Novel. Seattle, Washington: University of
      Washington Press, pp. 175-193.
          See 1952.B7.

18   _____ . The Modern Talent: An Anthology of Short Stories.
      New York: Holt, Rinehart and Winston, pp. 292-296.
          Establishes two main themes in A Curtain of Green: the
      irrelevance of social conventions of behavior and the
      powerlessness of Mrs. Larkin to control nature.

19   HARRIS, WENDELL V. "The Thematic Unity of Welty's The Golden
      Apples. TSLL, 6 (Spring), 92-95.
          Although the stories in The Golden Apples appeared sepa-
      rately in periodicals, they are united in the collection by
      three interlocking themes. The first is the impact of time
      upon each character. Although characters may seem strong
      and independent, their ultimate fate is "individual fail-
      ure." The second is that of hope. The young see the fu-
      ture as bright, particularly for love, but ultimately, the
      apples are those of discord. The third theme is the ironic
      contrast between ancient myth and the contemporary world.
      The three themes converge in the last story, "The Wander-
      ers," in which Virgie contemplates the Medusa's head and
      concludes that the human fate is "separateness."

20   McKENZIE, BARBARA. "Region and World: The Achievement of
      American Women Writers of Fiction Since 1930." DAI, 24,
      4701 (Florida State University, 1963).
          McKenzie discusses Welty as a regionalist who is also in
      the "spiritual tradition of Western man."

21 MILLER, JAMES E., JR. "Notes for Teaching." The Dimensions
    of the Short Story. New York: Dodd, Mead & Co., p. 30.
        One of the central considerations of "Why I Live at the
    P.O." is the distinction between the narrator's voice and
    Welty's.

22 OPITZ, KURT. "Eudora Welty: The Order of a Captive Soul."
    Crit, 7 (Winter), 79-91.
        All of Welty's characters are trapped by their own isola-
    tion, but have two means to attempt escape: by jumping
    into life (like Jenny in "At the Landing"), or by discover-
    ing the nature of their predicament through introspection
    (like Eugene in "Music from Spain"). As long as Welty sets
    her stories in a specific place, she is able to define this
    existential trap. But in her later work (from The Ponder
    Heart), she relies on stylistic devices which have little
    relationship with real place. Her dominant concern is for
    the idea rather than the people. Welty's obsession with
    ideas and technique has tended to make her drift from real-
    ity in her later fiction.

23 PALMER, MELVIN DELMAR. "Welty's 'A Visit of Charity.'" Expl,
    22 (May), Item 69.
        Shows parallels between incidents in "Little Red Riding
    Hood" and "Through the Looking Glass." Marion is dressed
    like Little Red Riding Hood and confronts old ladies who
    are actually animal-like and who, with their claw-like
    hands, are actually as dangerous as the wolf. "The Wool
    and Water" episodes of "Through the Looking Glass" have
    several parallels in "A Visit of Charity": the sheep lady,
    the shelf which contains something out of reach, the water-
    like linoleum, and the brooch.

24 PEDEN, WILLIAM. The American Short Story: Front Line in the
    National Defense of Literature. Boston, Massachusetts:
    Houghton Mifflin Co., pp. 166-168.
        Notes that Welty has "an individualistic mastery of
    form." Her stories contrast a surface simplicity with
    complex ambiguity of theme and mood.

1965 A BOOKS

1   APPEL, ALFRED, JR. A Season of Dreams: The Fiction of Eudora
    Welty. Baton Rouge, Louisiana: Louisiana State University
    Press.
        Except for Delta Wedding, Appel makes a comprehensive
    study of Welty's fiction through The Bride of Innisfallen.

1965

(APPEL, ALFRED, JR.)
He deals with each story individually and also discusses
elements which are common to groups of stories. In A Curtain of Green, for example, Appel finds a common theme in
"the impact of human separateness on the innocent and de-
fenseless individual." He also groups such stories as
"Lily Daw and the Three Ladies" and The Ponder Heart in a
discussion of Welty's "comic spirit," and devotes chapters
to "The Grotesque and the Gothic," "Form and Technique,"
"Welty's Negro Characters," "The Natchez Trace," "The Gold-
en Apples," and "The Bride of the Innisfallen." Appel concludes that Welty's best stories are "set on home ground"
and evoke "poetry, hope or laughter amidst the circumscrib-
ing absurdity and terror." Each story is a world of its
own and cannot be defined by generalizations.

1965 B SHORTER WRITINGS

1 ANON. "Eudora Welty Lectures December 6." Clarion-Ledger
    Jackson Daily News, (28 November), F, p. 8.
       Announces that Welty will give a lecture at Millsaps en-
    titled "An Appreciation of Katherine Anne Porter." (Later
    published in the Yale Review as "The Eye of Fiction." See
    1965.B21).

2 ANON. "Eudora Welty Plays Scheduled at DSC." Clarion-Ledger
    (Jackson), (12 April), p. 16.
       Discusses student dramatizations of "Why I Live at the
    P.O." and "Asphodel" to be performed at Delaware State
    College.

3 APPEL, ALFRED, JR. "Powerhouse's Blues." SSF, 11 (Spring),
    221-234.
       Notes numerous parallels between Powerhouse's act and
    lines from famous Jazz works and performers (particularly
    those of Billie Holiday). In "Powerhouse," as in Jazz, the
    blues are not an escape from life but a savoring of life's
    agony. Although the blues are generally considered to be
    the voice of oppressed blacks, Welty makes a universal
    statement about the condition of man: his inevitable sepa-
    rateness. Powerhouse is as separate from his fellow blacks
    as from the white audience which does not really understand
    him. His ultimate separateness is playing music that he
    doesn't even like.

4   BLACKWELL, LOUISE. "Eudora Welty and the Rubber Fence Family.
    Kansas Magazine, 30, 73-76.
        Listed by Noel Polk in "A Eudora Welty Checklist," See
    1973.B56.

5   CRAIG, NORMA. "Eudora Welty Gives 'A Part of Me' to Millsaps."
    Clarion-Ledger Jackson Daily News, (23 May), B, p. 5.
        Craig discusses Welty's reading of the "soon to be pub-
    lished [sic]" Losing Battles. "Jack's misadventure is
    typically Southern" and Welty has a "genius" for finding
    "the significant detail which illuminates the character."

6   DOLLARHIDE, LOUIS. "Photographs Show Facet of Her Art."
    Clarion-Ledger Jackson Daily News, (25 April), F, p. 8.
        Dollarhide reviews an exhibition of Welty's photographs
    which appeared at the Old Capital in Jackson. "Each pic-
    ture is composed as carefully as a good painting." (The
    entire collection, including some which did not appear in
    One Time, One Place, is owned by the Mississippi Department
    of Archives and History.)

7   FOSHEE, RUFUS. "On a Quiet Street in Jackson (A Talk with
    Eudora Welty)." Southern Observer, 12 (September), 187-
    188.
        Welty discusses other writers, including Reynolds Price,
    William Styron, and Katherine Anne Porter. She also com-
    ments about her teaching at Millsaps College.

8   GOSSETT, LOUISE Y. "Violence as Revelation: Eudora Welty."
    Violence in Recent Southern Fiction. Durham, North Caro-
    lina: Duke University Press, pp. 98-117.
        Violence in Welty's fiction is a product of "separate-
    ness" and is manifested in the conjunction of the physical
    world and the world of the imagination. As the isolated
    self struggles to achieve relationship, relationship itself
    is sometimes revealed in violence. The violence may be
    physical (as in "At the Landing"), or mental (as in "The
    Whole World Knows"). In either case, it increases self-
    knowledge and establishes momentary relationships.

9   HAINS, FRANK. "Eudora Welty Celebrates 'Blessed Achiever'
    Katherine Anne Porter." Jackson Daily News, (7 December),
    B, p. 8.
        Hains gives a first-hand account of Welty's reading of
    the "Eye of Fiction" in honor of Katherine Anne Porter.
    He notes that many of the comments made about Porter could
    also be made about Welty.

1965

10   HAINS, FRANK. "Welty Delivers Key Tribute to Faulkner."
       Clarion-Ledger Jackson Daily News, (25 April), F, p. 8.
         Quotes from Welty's address to the Southern Literary
       Festival honoring Faulkner. Welty comments about Faulk-
       ner's exactness of detail and the power and scope of his
       imagination.

11   HENLEY, ELTON F. "Confinement-Escape Symbolism in Eudora
       Welty's 'Livvie.'" IEY, 10 (Fall), 60-63.
         Welty skillfully contrasts symbols of confinement--asso-
       ciated with Solomon, his house, and his way of life--with
       symbols of freedom and life--associated with Cash and the
       natural world. Symbols of confinement include not only
       overt images of mouse traps and watches but also images of
       symmetry and order (the opposite of spontaneity and life),
       such as the balanced rose bushes in the front yard. Sym-
       bols of freedom include not only the youth and virility of
       Cash, but also images of spontaneity and disorder. Because
       of her skill with symbols, Welty is justifiably called "one
       of the most important figures of the so-called Southern
       Renaissance."

12   HICKS, GRANVILLE. "Welty's Impact Greater than Quantity of
       Work." Review of Appel's A Season of Dreams. Clarion-
       Ledger Jackson Daily News, (26 December), D, p. 10.
         "Reading Appel is almost as good as re-reading Welty."
       In his explications of texts, he is sometimes "farfetched,"
       but often "suggestive."

13   HUBBELL, JAY B. Who Are the Major American Writers? Durham,
       North Carolina: Duke University Press, 1972. p. 228.
         In a poll taken by Book Week for its 26 September, 1965,
       Book Week, Welty was voted fourteenth of "the Twenty Best
       Writers of Fiction."

14   KENNER, HUGH. Studies in Change: A Book of the Short Story.
       Englewood Cliffs, New Jersey: Prentice Hall, p. 24.
         Welty creates a sense of "dreamlike otherworldliness" in
       "Moon Lake" without directly invoking myth. She does so by
       using a child's point of view and thereby infusing the or-
       dinary with a sense of wonder.

15   LIEF, RUTH ANN. "A Progression of Answers." SSF, 11 (Sum-
       mer), 343-350.
         Ruth Vande Kieft in Eudora Welty goes too far in saying
       that the girl in "A Memory" imposes an order on reality.
       The girl is somewhat innocent, but she is also an adoles-
       cent and poses some questions of sexual desires. The

(LIEF, RUTH ANN)
story is, in part, her discovery of answers to these questions. When she sees the vulgar couple on the beach, she
cannot willfully change them, nor can her presumed innocence shield her from a true knowledge of their sordid
sexuality.

16 MAXWELL, EMILY. "Books: Now and Not-Now." Review of The
Shoebird. NY, 40 (5 December), 221.
     The Shoebird is a "serio-comic fantasy" with elaborate
plays on words. Although it was recommended for ages 8-12,
it exhibits a humor for both children and adults. One
would have to go back to Chaucer's "Parliament of Fowls" to
find anything comparable.

17 PADGE, ROBERT H. "Welty Work Considered in A Season of
Dreams." Review of Appel's A Season of Dreams. Clarion-
Ledger Jackson Daily News, (5 December), E, p. 1.
     Gives a synopsis of Appel's book and notes that it is
naturally more comprehensive than Vande Kieft's.

18 SHATTUCK, HARRY. "No One Can Teach Writing: Welty's Aim 'To
Encourage.'" Jackson Daily News, (3 December).
     Welty comments about her strategies of teaching creative
writing at Millsaps College and mentions the topic of her
forthcoming lecture about Katherine Anne Porter, the eye
of fiction.

19 STEWART, JOHN L. The Burden of Time: The Fugitives and Agrar-
ians. Princeton, New Jersey: Princeton University Press,
pp. 42, 185, 453, 454, 471, 494.
     Links Welty with Porter, Warren, Gordon, and Faulkner
(very briefly). Also notes Warren's comments in his essay,
"Love and Separateness in Miss Welty."

20 VANDE KIEFT, RUTH M. "Introduction" to Thirteen Stories by
Eudora Welty. New York: Harcourt, Brace and World,
pp. 3-14.
     Welty's themes fluctuate between the extremes of comedy
and tragedy, dream and reality, in her quest to portray
"the mystery of the inner life," and in particular the
"changing mystery of human relationships." To show these
dynamic relationships, Welty employs "a variety of fictional points of view." The meaning of her fiction is the
process for both reader and writer; it is not the results.
The reader should let Welty lead and not try to impose his
own concepts of form and structure on the stories.

1965

21   WELTY, EUDORA. "The Eye of the Story." <u>YR</u>, 55 (December),
      265-273.
          With particular emphasis on "Noon Wine," Welty discusses
      Porter's ability to evoke feeling with a limited amount of
      "sensory imagery." Porter is capable of concreteness but
      moves easily between "visibility and invisibility." Welty
      contrasts Porter's method with her own, which she claims is
      almost entirely "visual."

22   _____. "Must the Novelist Crusade?" <u>Atlantic</u>, 216 (October),
      104-108.
          The novelist and the crusader have two different objec-
      tives. The novelist depicts the truths of the human heart
      which are eternal, mysterious, and ambiguous. The crusader
      has a single cause at a single moment in time. If the nov-
      elist were to take up the task of a crusader, his novels
      would oversimplify life and would soon be outdated.

23   _____. "Words into Fiction." <u>Southern Review, N.S.</u>, 1 (Sum-
      mer), 543-553.
          Discusses the subjective nature of words, words as sym-
      bols, and words as changing entities. (<u>See</u> 1962.B10).

<u>1966 A BOOKS - NONE</u>

<u>1966 B SHORTER WRITINGS</u>

1   ANON. "Brandeis Awards 10th Arts Prizes." <u>New York Times</u>,
      (25 April), p. 13.
          Notes that Stanley Kunitz presented Brandeis University's
      10th arts awards medal to Welty.

2   BLACKWELL, LOUISE. "Eudora Welty: Proverbs and Proverbial
      Phrases in <u>The Golden Apples</u>." <u>SFQ</u>, 30 (December),
      332-341.
          Isolates the proverbial sayings and clichés of Edna Earl
      in "Shower of Gold" and finds their origins in fourteen
      dictionaries and reference books. Blackwell concludes that
      Welty had a thorough knowledge of the proverbial language
      of her region and used this knowledge to create the very
      realistic character, Edna Earl.

3   B. O. "An Interview with Eudora Welty." <u>Scholastic Teacher</u>,
      89 (December), 18.
          Tells of Welty's reading of "The Demonstrators" before
      the NCTE annual banquet. Welty does not consider the story
      to be "about civil rights or social protest."

EUDORA WELTY: A REFERENCE GUIDE

1966

4 CAPERS, CHARLOTTE. "Eudora Welty to Date." Tattler, (September), pp. 5, 20.
Capers describes some of the joys and difficulties of being Welty's friend and traveling companion. She includes personal comments about Welty's life patterns and the information that Welty is a "sustaining member of the Junior League of Jackson" who does her own clothes in the launderette.

5 FIRMIN, PIC. "Eudora Shares Experiences in Unusual Christmas Gift." Jackson Daily News, (20 December).
Firman gives an account of Welty's visit to the Great Books discussion group at St. Andrews Episcopal School in Jackson. He notes that the students had been reading Welty's books as part of their study and that Welty answered their questions.

6 GRIFFITH, ALBERT J. "The Numinous Vision: Eudora Welty's 'Clytie.'" SSF, 4 (Fall), 80-82.
Salvation from the oppression of a decaying and oppressive Southern heritage can only be found by discovery of the individual self. Clytie is the only character in the story who makes such an effort. Although her sister, Octavia, believes that sun and rain are destructive forces, Clytie willingly goes off into the sun and rain in search of a face, "a numinous vision."

7 GRIFFITH, BENJAMIN W. "'Powerhouse' as a Showcase of Eudora Welty's Methods and Themes." MissQ, 19 (Spring), 79-84.
Expresses one of Welty's most common themes: the relationship between lover and artist. The artist attempts to communicate two kinds of love, eros and philos, symbolized by the names Little Brother and Valentine. As in many of her stories, "Powerhouse" is also rich in mythic parallels.

8 No Entry

9 TREFMAN, SARA. "Welty's 'A Worn Path.'" Expl, 24 (February), Item 56.
William Jones did not go far enough in identifying Phoenix as simply "the legendary bird of Egyptian folklore (See 1957.B4). Phoenix also has striking parallels with Christ. Her journey is a torturous one over a cold wasteland at Christmas time. She is completely self-sacrificing, and the toy windmill that she bought for her grandchild is a "cross-shaped toy."

87

1966

10   WELTY, EUDORA. "English from the Inside." American Educa-
        tion, 2 (February), 18-19.
          Welty gives her report of her visit to the English Insti-
        tute at Tulane University in New Orleans during the summer
        of 1965. She gives her observations about a class in The
        Sound and the Fury taught by Dr. Marvin Morillo, and re-
        ports on a visit to a composition class.

11   WILD, REBECCA SMITH. "Studies in the Shorter Fiction of
        Elizabeth Bowen and Eudora Welty." DAI, 27, 490-A (Univer-
        sity of Michigan, 1965).
          Welty's work, like Bowen's, resembles the poetry of the
        Seventeenth Century metaphysical tradition. In an analysis
        of six stories by Bowen and Welty, Wild concludes that
        "meaning and form are inextricable."

12   WOESTENDIEK, JO. "Author Eudora Welty Buys Her Own Book."
        Houston Chronicle, (27 November).
          Welty discusses the relationship between reading and
        writing and makes some comments about "The Demonstrators."
        She also mentions the forthcoming novel, Losing Battles.

1967 A BOOKS - NONE

1967 B SHORTER WRITINGS

1   ANON. "Eudora Welty One of Eight Women Honored." Clarion-
        Ledger (Jackson), (22 February), B, p. 8.
          Dr. John A. Logan, President of Hollins College, discus-
        ses Welty's achievements.

2   ANON. "Miss Welty to Lecture at Belhaven." Clarion-Ledger
        Jackson Daily News, (12 March).
          Quotes The New Yorker's comments about the deceptive
        complexity of A Curtain of Green, A, p. 4.

3   ANON. "Welty Heads M.S. Hope Chest Drive in State." Clarion-
        Ledger Jackson Daily News, (7 May), A, p. 4.

1967

(ANON.)
Announces that Welty has been named "honorary chairman"
of the Mississippi "Multiple Sclerosis Hope Chest Cam-
paign."

4   ANON. "Welty, Baroque Music, Stylus Festival Features."
      Clarion-Ledger (Jackson), (8 December), C, p. 17.
      Announces that Welty read "Powerhouse" at the Millsaps
      College autumn fine arts festival.

5   ABERCROMBIE, SHARON. "Housewives Can Write, Too, Says Author
      Eudora Welty." Roanoke Times, (22 February), p. 22.
      Comments about Welty's reception of the Hollins College
      Medal. Notes that Welty is considered "by many literary
      critics the greatest short story writer of the 20th Cen-
      tury." Also records some of Welty's comments about the art
      of writing. The common experiences of the housewife are as
      valuable preparation for writing as more "groveling ones."

6   APPEL, ALFRED. "The Short Stories of Eudora Welty." DAI, 27,
      4241-A (Columbia University, 1963).
      Appel examines Welty's treatment of the inner life as
      compensation for isolation and concludes that her earlier
      work is more successful than The Bride of the Innisfallen,
      which is excessively obscure.

7   BOOTH, WAYNE C. The Rhetoric of Fiction. Chicago: Univer-
      sity of Chicago Press (Phoenix Books), p. 271.
      Places Welty with those writers who use "authorial
      silence."

8   BURNS, ROBERTA. "Short Stories Thrill Audience." Jackson
      Daily News, (17 March).
      Burns gives a first-hand account of Welty's reading of
      "Powerhouse" at Belhaven College. Welty "brought with her
      a love and respect for literature, the South, and mankind."

9   HOFFMAN, FREDERICK J. The Art of Southern Fiction: A Study
      of Some Modern Novelists. Carbondale, Illinois: Southern
      Illinois University Press, pp. 51-65.
      Hoffman demonstrates that Welty is at her best when she
      is writing about her own region. (In this sense, A Curtain
      of Green is her best book.) By observing limited details,
      Welty creates profound insight into character and imagina-
      tion.

10   JONES, WILLIAM M. "The Plot as Search." SSF, 5 (Fall), 37-43.
      The argument is based on a quotation from Welty's article

1967

(JONES, WILLIAM M.)
in the Atlantic Monthly of March 1, 1949: "In any group of
stories we might name as they occur to us, the plot is
search." The method of her fiction, then, is not the arti-
ficial order of plot but the search for order and whole-
ness. Her stories have no consistent order or method; each
is a new kind of search.

11 KEENEY, WILLARD. "'Ripeness is All,' Late, Late Romanticism
and Other Recent Fiction." Review of 13 Stories. Southern
Review, N.S., 3 (Autumn), 1055-1057.
Discusses Welty's ironic humor and the balance between
world and symbol which suggests the symbolic perception of
puritanism. Welty's prose is rich and dense and yet only
occasionally seems obscure.

12 *KUEHL, JOHN. "Commentary." Write and Rewrite, edited by John
Kuehl. New York: Meredith Press, pp. 16-18.
Listed by Noel Polk in "A Eudora Welty Checklist,"
1973.B56.

13 RECHNITZ, ROBERT MAX. "Perception, Identity, and the Grotesque: A Study of Three Southern Writers." DAI, 28 (Oc-
tober-December), 2261-A (University of Colorado, 1967).
In an analysis of works by O'Connor, McCullers, and Welty, Rechnitz derives a definition of the grotesque: "that
which is perceived as a threat to one's identity."

14 RUBIN, LOUIS D., JR. The Curious Death of the Novel. Baton
Rouge, Louisiana: Louisiana State University Press,
p. 135.
Considers Welty among those "in the main stream" of
American literature in the years after World War I.

15 SMITH, JULIAN. "'Livvie'--Eudora Welty's Song of Solomon."
SSF, 5 (Fall), 73-74.
Finds parallels between Welty's "Livvie" and the Song of
Solomon. In both, a rich, powerful man takes a young woman
away from her people. In both, the powerful (but aged) man
tempts unsuccessfully the girl away from her lover. In addition to parallels in plot, character, and theme, there
are also similarities of imagery.

16 THOMPSON, JIMMY. "Eudora Welty Renders 'Worn Path' Reading."
Jackson Daily News, (7 November).
Thompson gives a first-hand account of Welty's reading of
"A Worn Path" before a "packed Parish Hall" at St. Andrews

1968

(THOMPSON, JIMMY)
Church in Jackson. He considers Welty "one of Mississippi's better known products."

17 TINDALL, GEORGE B. The Emergence of the New South 1913-1945.
Baton Rouge, Louisiana: Louisiana State University Press.
Vol. X of A History of the South, edited by Wendell Holmes
Stephenson and E. Merton Coulter. Pp. 682-683.
Welty's writing is not Southern Gothic but pastoral.

1968 A BOOKS

1 BRYANT, J. A., JR. Eudora Welty. Minneapolis, Minnesota:
University of Minnesota Press.
With comments about most of the stories and all the novels, Bryant traces briefly (forty-four pages) the development of Welty's career and style from A Curtain of Green
through the short story, "The Demonstrators." He notes
the movement towards greater complexity of style in The
Bride of the Innisfallen and the corresponding decline in
critical appreciation. He also notes Welty's increasing
ability to control complex metaphors and metaphysical elements of style. He includes a brief discussion of Welty's
criticism.

1968 B SHORTER WRITINGS

1 ANON. "Jackson Ballet Guild to Present World Premiere of
'The Shoebird.'" Clarion-Ledger Jackson Daily News,
(21 January).
Discusses the forthcoming performance of a ballet based
on Welty's The Shoebird, D, 2.

2 ANON. "Eudora Welty Is Member of Millsaps Arts Series."
Clarion-Ledger (Jackson), (18 July), C, p. 9.
A survey taken by the New York Times disclosed that Welty
was among a very few writers to "make significant contributions to American Literature" since World War II.

3 ANON. "Mississippians Mostly Enjoy Eudora's Warm Friendliness." Clarion-Ledger (Jackson), (26 September), E, p. 7.
Comments about Welty's activities in Jackson and about
her discovery of the typewriter in her father's office
(the real beginning of her literary career).

1968

4 ABRAHAMS, WILLIAM. <u>Prize Stories 1968: The O. Henry Awards</u>.
   Garden City, New York: Doubleday & Co., pp. xi, xii–xiii.
   Notes that most of the stories in the collection--includ-
   ing the first-prize winner, "The Demonstrators"--have violent themes.

5 COCHRAN, ROBERT W. "Welty's 'Petrified Man.'" <u>Expl</u>, 27 (December), Item 25.
   Billy Boy's statement at the end of the story--"If you're
   so damn smart why ain't you rich"--suggests the central
   theme of the story: the prostitution of female "gifts."
   Mrs. Pike is not so much a cold fish as cold cash. Her
   cards for three grey-haired gentlemen whom she met at a
   beauticians convention, as well as her late-model Dodge and
   her $500 reward, suggest that men have a place in her life,
   but only on a cash basis.

6 CULBERTSON, JEAN. "Eudora Welty Tells About Jane Austen."
   <u>Clarion-Ledger</u> (Jackson), (6 December), p. 16.
   Summarizes Welty's speech given at the Millsaps Art and
   Lecture Series. Welty discusses Austen's "flawless" style,
   her originality, and her sense of family relationships.

7 CURLEY, DANIEL. "Eudora Welty and the Quordam Obstruction."
   <u>SSF</u>, 5 (Spring), 209–224.
   The vision of Audubon is superior to that of Dow and Merrill. Unlike the other observers of the heron, he is intensely aware of the present moment. He is also the artist
   who is capable of seeing the wisdom of silence. His is a
   vision that Welty has carefully developed in such other
   stories as "Powerhouse," "The Key," "First Love," and "The
   Wide Net."

8 DOLLARHIDE, LOUIS. "Eudora Welty's Words: Air of Recovered
   Speech." <u>Clarion-Ledger Jackson Daily News</u>, (9 June), F,
   p. 10.
   Review of the New Stage production of "A Season of
   Dreams," a series of dramatic readings from Welty's work
   selected by Ellen Walker and Jane Petty. Dollarhide ob-
   serves musical parallels and the extremely oral quality of
   Welty's prose.

9 HAINS, FRANK. "Great Privilege to Have Worked on Welty Script
   at New Stage." <u>Clarion-Ledger Jackson Daily News</u>, (26 May),
   E, p. 5.
   Discusses the standing ovation for Welty after the Jackson performance of "A Season of Dreams" and Welty's reputation for affability in her home town.

1968

10   HARDY, JOHN EDWARD. "The Achievement of Eudora Welty." SHR,
     2 (Summer), 269-278.
        With feminine perception and "no sentimentality," Welty
     comes to terms with some of the fundamental problems of the
     modern age. She faces "the reality of the absurd" in
     "Flowers for Marjorie," and "The Hitch-hikers." She con-
     fronts "the racial problem" in "The Demonstrators" and
     "Powerhouse," and she shows a "courageous, creative intel-
     ligence" that is "not in spite of her femininity but in a
     sense because of being a woman."

11   HUCK, WILBER, and WILLIAM SHANAHAN. The Modern Short Story.
     American Book Co., pp. 26-28.
        Huck breaks "Petrified Man" into the three-part struc-
     ture, beginning (exposition), middle, and end.

12   INGE, THOMAS M. "Eudora Welty as Poet." SHR, 2 (Summer),
     10-11.
        No critical commentaries mention Welty's poetry. How-
     ever, Welty wrote and published poetry at age fifteen,
     before she published fiction. One poem, "There," was pub-
     lished a few months after her first story, "Death of a
     Traveling Salesman," in 1936. (Inge includes the poem.)

13   JONES, BETH GRIFFIN. "Welty's Short Stories in World Premiere
     Here." Clarion-Ledger Jackson Daily News, (12 May), F,
     p. 5.
        Jones describes the scope and method of the New Stage
     Theatre performance of "A Season of Dreams," a dramatiza-
     tion of parts of Welty's work.

14   TATE, ALLEN. "A Southern Mode of the Imagination." Allen
     Tate: Essays of Four Decades. Chicago: Swallow Press,
     pp. 557, 578.
        Tate considers Welty "quite as gifted as Mr. Faulkner, if
     somewhat below him in magnitude and power ...." He also
     considers her to be one of those several writers who would
     make the backward South a "formidable" force in writing
     even without Faulkner.

15   WAGNER, WILLIS. American Literature: A World View. New
     York: New York University Press, p. 265.
        Mentions Welty briefly as an "outstanding" author whose
     books deal with some aspect of love and "present a sympa-
     thetic picture" of Southerners.

1969

1969 A BOOKS

1 ISAACS, NEIL. Eudora Welty. Austin, Texas: Steck-Vaughn Co.
   Southern Writers Series.
      Introduces the reader to Welty's life and works and to
   some of the critical approaches to her fiction. Summarizes
   the plots of numerous stories and novels and makes some
   critical comments about them, particularly about place and
   myth.

2 WELTY, EUDORA. A Sweet Devouring. New York: Albondocanti
   Press.
      Welty tells which books she read as a child and explains
   how important reading was in her life. "The pleasures of
   reading itself--who doesn't remember? were those of a
   Christmas cake, a sweet devouring." Welty's early reading
   was indiscriminate but extensive and enthusiastic, but she
   soon developed taste. She switched from The Camp Fire
   Girls to Mark Twain. (See also, Mademoiselle, 1957.B7.)

1969 B SHORTER WRITINGS

1 ANON. "Five Tributes." Shenandoah, 20 (Spring) 36-39.
      Cites brief statements of praise by Malcolm Cowley, Mar-
   tha Graham, Walker Percy, Robert Penn Warren, and Allen
   Tate. Cowley admires her kindness but also her strength;
   Graham admires her individual style; Percy admires her
   ability to live in harmony with place; Warren admires her
   richly connotative style; and Tate admires her craftsmanship.

2 APPEL, ALFRED, JR. "Eudora Welty." A Bibliographical Guide
   to the Study of Southern Literature, edited by Louis D.
   Rubin, Jr. Baton Rouge, Louisiana: Louisiana State University Press, pp. 320-322.
      Makes a list of forty-two entries and notes that Welty's
   work has been subjected to close textual analysis but has
   seldom been placed in "some context" or evaluated critical-
   ly. However, the best criticism--notably that of Robert
   Penn Warren, Ruth Vande Kieft, and Granville Hicks--"has
   also been able to take a longer view."

3 BROWN, ASHLEY. "Eudora Welty and the Mythos of Summer."
   Shenandoah, 20 (Spring), 29-35.
      Applies Frye's definition of romance in Anatomy of Criti-
   cism to The Robber Bridegroom. Concludes that because of
   Welty's use of the supernatural and the triumph of youth

(BROWN, ASHLEY)
and love over the forces of evil, the novel is a romance.
But Welty adds a new dimension. Whereas the usual hero of
romance is merely virtuous, Welty presents all things doubly. Jamie is both bridegroom and seducer, merchant and
thief.

4   BURGER, NASH K. "Eudora Welty's Jackson." Shenandoah, 20
    (Spring), 8-15.
        As a lifelong friend of Welty, Burger gives numerous en-
    tertaining and useful facts about Welty's childhood and her
    gradual emergence to fame.

5   GRAHAM, KENNETH. "La Double Vision D'Eudora Welty." La
    Nouvelle Revue Francaise, 34 (November), 744-753.
        Like Blake, who saw the duality of good and evil, Welty
    presents a universe which can be taken doubly. Energy is
    usually a life force--as in the case of Virgie Rainy--
    though it can also be disruptive of social order. The dou-
    ble vision for Welty includes the comic and the tragic.
    Many of Welty's tragic stories, including "A Curtain of
    Green," contain the triumphant elements of comedy.

6   GRESSET, MICHEL. "Eudora Welty." La Nouvelle Revue Francaise,
    34 (November), 656.
        In a brief biographical sketch, Gresset notes that, like
    Faulkner, Welty is a Southern regionalist. She is a master
    of reproducing the dialect of the oral tradition of the
    American South. Her regionalism, however, does not explain
    why her work is so reknowned. The biographical sketch is
    followed by a French translation of "A Memory" ("Un Sou-
    venir") translated by Georgette Garrigues.

7   *GRIFFIN, ROBERT J. "Eudora Welty's A Curtain of Green." The
    Forties: Fiction, Poetry, Drama, edited by Warren French.
    Deland, Florida: Everett/Edwards, pp. 101-110.
        Listed by Noel Polk in "A Eudora Welty Checklist"; See
    1973.B56.

8   HAINS, FRANK. "Distinguished Writers Pay Tribute to Eudora
    Welty." Clarion-Ledger Jackson Daily News, (3 August), H,
    p. 1.
        Summarizes comments made in Shenandoah (Spring 1969) by
    Martha Graham, Robert Penn Warren, Allen Tate, Malcolm Cow-
    ley, Diarmuid Russell, Robert B. Heilman, Alun R. Jones,
    Joyce Carol Oates, Reynolds Price, and Nash K. Burger.

1969

9   HEILMAN, ROBERT B.   "Salesmen's Deaths: Documentary and
        Myth." Shenandoah, 20 (Spring), 20-28.
            Notes the popular tendency to compare Welty's "Death of
        a Traveling Salesman" with Miller's Death of a Salesman,
        but considers the comparison to be only partially justifi-
        able. Both deal with the theme of salesmen who are lonely,
        but Welty's version shows greater depth of vision. Mil-
        ler's is about Salesmen, but Welty's is about the condition
        of man.

10 HOWELL, ELMO. "Eudora Welty's Civil War Story." NMW, 2
        (Spring), 3-12.
            Although Welty's story is true to the facts of the civil
        war, it is not primarily historical fiction, nor, in spite
        of Delilah's survival, a story about the durability of the
        Negro race. It is "a victory of untrammeled human nature
        over the civility of an ordered world." Delilah's limited
        perception of what happens intensifies the tragedy of the
        loss of something fine, since the Negroes, as well as the
        soldiers, do not understand what had been lost.

11 ISAACS, NEIL. "Four Notes on Eudora Welty." NMW, 2 (Fall),
        42-54.
            In Delta Wedding, Pinchy is part of the "theme of renew-
        al." Her appearances parallel the central ritual of the
        novel, the marriage of Dabney to Troy.
            The name Edna Earl in The Ponder Heart also appeared in
        The Wide Net. Consequently, Welty had been considering
        the connotative powers of the name as early as 1942.
        (Isaacs notes French's observation that the source is Jane
        Evan's novel, St. Elmo.)
            In "Kin," the main theme of the story is the impossibili-
        ty of knowing why Uncle Felix conjured the name Daisy--
        only a Cockney would confuse it with Dicy--and why Dicy
        cannot account for her own "misdirected" message.
            In The Golden Apples, many of McLain's illegitimate chil-
        dren may be identified on the basis of their golden hair
        and their sensuality.

12 JONES, ALLUN R. "A Frail Traveling Coincidence: Three Later
        Stories by Eudora Welty." Shenandoah, 20 (Spring), 40-53.
            Discusses three stories which are not set on the Natchez
        Trace: "The Bride of the Innisfallen," "No Place for you
        My Love," and "Going to Naples." In each story, Welty
        comes to terms with the rapidly changing landscape of the
        twentieth century. Each is a story of traveling and sug-
        gests the plight of people suspended in time and space.

(JONES, ALLUN R.)
Each is about a temporary relationship that interrupts the
essential rootlessness of traveling.

13 JONES, WILLIAM M. Fiction: Form and Experience: 30 Stories
with Essays. Lexington, Massachusetts: D. C. Heath and
Co., p. 387.
Includes Jones' essay, "Name and Symbol in the Prose of
Eudora Welty." See 1958.B9.

14 KIRKPATRICK, SMITH. "The Anointed Powerhouse." SR, 77 (Winter), 94-108.
Powerhouse is the voice of the artist, and his message,
like Welty's, is a prophetic one. In his music, he imposes
a temporary order on the strange and terrifying forces of
life. The form of that order is love, which transfigures
the hearts of all people and saves them momentarily from
separateness. In the depths of his separateness and in
his quest for unity and love, Powerhouse is in a sense all
men, and Alligator Mississippi is the world.

15 MAY, CHARLES E. "The Difficulty of Loving in 'A Visit of
Charity.'" SSF, 6 (Spring), 338-341.
In "A Visit of Charity" (as in Fromm's Art of Loving and
the Bible), man's chief unhappiness is caused by his failure to love. When Adam ate the apple, he became aware of
differences rather than similarities; consequently, he
became separate from his fellow man and lonely to the point
of despair. When Marion visits the old ladies' home, she
and the ladies are only aware of their differences. They
never reach the common ground that they are all human, and,
therefore, all lonesome.

16 OATES, JOYCE CAROL. "The Art of Eudora Welty." Shenandoah,
20 (Spring), 54-57.
Oates admires the delicate way Welty blends the serene,
ordinary events of everyday life and the horrors which un-
derlie and often intrude upon that serenity. The result is
"indeed frightening." Oates discusses how Welty achieves
this effect in Delta Wedding and "The Demonstrators."

17 PRICE, REYNOLDS. "The Onlooker Smiling: An Early Reading of
The Optimist's Daughter." Shenandoah, 20 (Spring), 58-73.
The Optimist's Daughter is Welty's "strongest, richest
work." Unlike the narrators in some of Welty's earlier
work (particularly those in The Bride of the Innisfallen),
Laurel has a controlled and lucid point of view. Her language is efficient and essentially free of simile,

1969

(PRICE, REYNOLDS)
    metaphor, and "slow dissolving impressionism" (faults that marred some of her earlier work).

18   RUSSELL, DIARMUID. "First Work." Shenandoah, 20 (Spring), 16-19.
    Notes the influence of Ford Madox Ford and Katherine Anne Porter on Welty's early writing; also discusses the difficulties Welty had publishing her stories and the even greater difficulty she had publishing her first collection, A Curtain of Green. In spite of small sales, however, the work endures.

19   VANDE KIEFT, RUTH M. "Demonstrators in a Stricken Land." The Process of Fiction, ed. Barbara McKenzie. New York: Harcourt, Brace & World, pp. 342-349.
    Listed by Noel Polk in "A Eudora Welty Checklist." See 1973.B56.

20   WELTY, EUDORA. "From Where I Live." Delta Review (November-December), p. 69.
    Welty discusses the advantages a writer has by living in the South. He or she has the sense of a place that has changed relatively little. Consequently, he can focus on a human nature which has remained constant. (Man's "aspirations are the same," and his motives for good and evil do not change.) Also, in the South, he writes about a people who are "born to love a good tale." Welty briefly mentions the importance of the agrarian movement in formulating these Southern values.

21   _____. "A Note on Jane Austen." Shenandoah, 20 (Spring), 3-7.
    Discusses the importance of the mundane affairs of life in Austen's humor and in her comic vision.

1970 A BOOKS - NONE

1970 B SHORTER WRITINGS

1   ALDRIDGE, JOHN W. "Eudora Welty: Metamorphosis of a Southern Lady Writer." Review of Losing Battles. SatR, 53 (11 April), 21-22, 35-36.
    In Losing Battles, Welty demonstrates for the first time her ability to present on a large scale all that she has been doing on a small scale. She "accumulates the materials of moral evaluation and with it depth." She begins by

1970

(ALDRIDGE, JOHN W.)
   showing the family in superficial joy, celebrating themselves and their own egos. But through the point of view
   of Julia Mortimer, Welty eventually undercuts their pre-
   tentions and values and gives "a civilized and profound
   criticism of life."

2 ANON. Review of Losing Battles. Time, 95 (4 May), 100.
      Welty's theme of togetherness becomes tiresome and repe-
   titious. The people of Banner are backward and ignorant;
   they refuse to accept the ways of the modern world. And
   yet Welty seems to accept this old way in her praise of
   Jack, who places his family above the progressive values of
   his wife, Gloria.

3 No Entry

4 ANON. "Books in Brief." Honolulu Star-Bulletin (Hawaii),
      (10 May), Aloha, p. 31.
      Welty's "artistry" has never been better. Losing Battles
   is a book with dialogue and action which are "funny" but
   often have "serious and somber tones."

5 ANON. "Military Justice is to Justice as Military Music is to
      Music." Review of Losing Battles. Portland Oregonian
      (Oregon), (10 May), F, p. 6.
      Welty has a "rich" cast of characters and a sense of the
   "comedy and tragedy" of Mississippi.

6 ANON. "The Family Resembles a Breughel Painting." Review of
      Losing Battles. Des Moines Register, (17 May), T, p. 9.
      Losing Battles "may well be her masterpiece," but it does
   not deal with "issues that dominate Southern writing."

7 ANON. Review of Losing Battles. VQR, 46 (Summer), lxxxviii.
      With folk humor and a rich sense of detail, Welty recre-
   ates a "bucolic peace out of times past." The book seems
   simple but is actually rich and sometimes bewildering.

8 ANON. Review of Losing Battles. Hollywood Reporter (Selma,
      Alabama), (3 July).
      Losing Battles is "a masterwork by one of America's few
   major writers." Unlike many of the anti-novels which are

99

1970

(ANON.)
being written, Losing Battles is carefully structured, and
every word, every fragment of conversation, is carefully
fitted to the whole.

9   ANON. "The Book Nook." Review of Losing Battles. Sacramento
Union (California), (5 July), Magazine, B, p. 10.
Losing Battles will "be recognized as a classic." In
spite of their great numbers, Welty's characters "come vi-
brantly and individually to life."

10   ANON. Review of Losing Battles. Tulsa World (Oklahoma),
(5 July), p. 6.
Losing Battles is "wildly funny at times, deeply poignant
at others."

11   ANON. Review of Losing Battles. Booklist, 66 (15 July),
1383.
As in Delta Wedding, Losing Battles portrays a large
planter family of Mississippi. In this case, however, the
poor land and the lack of initiative are "wearing down the
family."

12   ANON. Review of Losing Battles. Washington Star, (29 November), Washington, p. 42.
Notes that, with Losing Battles, Welty "is coming into
her own as a novelist."

13   ANON. "Welty Hailed as Enduring." Mississippi State College
for Women Alumnae News Bulletin, (Winter), p. 9.
Makes comments about the success of Losing Battles (including criticism) and gives some biographical material
which extends from Welty's college days to the present.

14   ANON. "The Critics are Saying." New York Post, (12 April).
Summarizes some of the reviews of Losing Battles in Newsweek, Life, New York Times Book Review, New York Times
(daily), Book World, and Saturday Review.

15   BITKER, MARJORIE M. "Reunion in Mississippi: A Matriarch
Turns 90." Review of Losing Battles. Milwaukee Journal
(Wisconsin), (26 April), V, p. 4.
Losing Battles is more than a family reunion; "it is a
searching into the meaning of life." With "fine" descriptions and "oft-told tales" in dialogue, Welty has presented
a comedy "enriched by its underlying wisdom."

16   BOARDMAN, ANNE CAWLEY. "Eudora Welty's New Novel of South
     Worth the Wait." Minneapolis Star (Minnesota), (29 April),
     B, p. 4.
          Welty had already proved that she was master of the short
     story. In Losing Battles, she proves that she is also "at
     ease within the novel's larger dimensions." She presents
     a "sheer and wonderful comedy."

17   BOATNER, MAXINE TULL. "Mississippi Experience." Review of
     Losing Battles. Hartford Courant (Connecticut), (17 May),
     Magazine, p. 29.
          Through her attention to details and her insight into
     the character of her fellow Mississippians, Welty has cre-
     ated an authentic version of people and places. She pre-
     sents them in a comedy with "both pathos and sadness."

18   BOATWRIGHT, JAMES. "Review of Losing Battles." New York
     Times Book Review, (12 April), pp. 7-1, 32-34.
          Unlike The Bride of the Innisfallen and The Golden Ap-
     ples, which have the complexities of a poem, Losing Battles
     has a "surface of mock simplicity." In its sure comic
     sense and in its presentation of the complexities of human
     relationships, Losing Battles is "a major work of the
     imagination...."

19   BRADLEY, VAN ALLEN. "The Year's Twelve Best in Fiction and
     Nonfiction." Chicago Daily News (12 December), Panorama,
     p. 8.
          Losing Battles is "easily the year's most distinguished
     work of fiction by an American."

20   BRADY, CHARLES A. "Novel to End All Novels of the South."
     Review of Losing Battles. Buffalo News (New York),
     (9 May), B, p. 8.
          Welty takes the "anecdotal" Southern novel to its "reduc-
     tio ad absurdum." It is a "meandering stream of speech"
     of "inordinate length."

21   BRODLEY, VAN ALLEN. "Eudora Welty's New Novel a Triumph."
     Chicago Daily News (11 April), Panorama, p. 8.
          With "the subtlety, the lyricism and the beauty of its
     style," Losing Battles is worth fifteen years of effort.
     Welty captures the speech of Mississippi hill people and
     demonstrates that they are in a sense "triumphant in spir-
     it" even though they lose their battles.

22   BURNS, LANDON C., JR. "A Cross-Referenced Index of Short
     Fiction and Author-Title Listing." SSF, 7 (Winter), 214.
          Lists Welty's stories with the textbooks and collections
     in which they appeared through 1969. Indicates which

1970

(BURNS, LANDON C., JR.)
  collections contain comments and which instructors' manuals
  contain comments. See 1971.B7.

23 CALDWELL, DAVID S. "Sad Old Clan Loses All with a Shiny Ex-
      ception." Review of Losing Battles. Pittsburgh Press
      (Pennsylvania), (12 April), VI, p. 6.
        It is a novel of people talking, not Faulknerian people
      who often "reveal abject degradation," but ordinary people
      who lose all the unimportant battles of "status, power,
      recognition by others" and win the battle of life itself
      through "love."

24 CHENEY, WINIFRED GREEN. "Famous Lady Fixes Figs." Christian
      Science Monitor, (27 August), p. 5.
        Gives Welty's recipe for figs. Also comments that Wel-
      ty's word choice is as discriminating as her cooking.

25 CLAYTON, ROBERT. Review of Losing Battles. LJ, 95 (15 March),
      1050.
        Welty evokes the sense of place and the sense of charac-
      ter, but the book has some serious shortcomings. The pace
      is "lumbering and awkward" and "the comic elements really
      lack the very substance of mirth." Unlike much of her
      earlier work, the style is labored rather than lyrical.

26 CLEMONS, WALTER. "Meeting Miss Welty." New York Times Book
      Review, (12 April), 2-VII, p. 46.
        In a long, desultory interview, Welty discusses the writ-
      ing of Losing Battles, the stage production of The Ponder
      Heart, her work with the WPA, her early writing, her meet-
      ing with E. M. Forster, and her distinguished career as a
      war correspondent under the pseudonymn Michael Ravenna.

27 CULBERTSON, JEAN. "Local Talent Makes Local ETV 'First.'"
      Clarion-Ledger Jackson Daily News, (8 November), A, p. 10.
        Discusses preparations for the production of "A Season
      of Dreams" by Mississippi Educational TV.

28 _____. "Ponder Heart at NS Makes You Feel Better." Clarion-
      Ledger (Jackson) (22 May), C, p. 9.
        Culbertson reviews the New Stage performance of The Pon-
      der Heart in Jackson. She observes that Welty created the
      characters "right out of life."

29 DAVENPORT, GUY. "Mozartean Music in Mississippi." Review of
      Losing Battles. Life, 68 (17 April), 10.

1970

(DAVENPORT, GUY)
   In a style which makes music of the speech of common
people, Welty tells "one of the best stories the world has
ever heard." The concerns of the novel are "timeless,"
and its characters suffer defeats which are universal.

30   DAVIS, CHARLES EDWARD. "Eudora Welty's Art of Naming, DAI,
     30, 4446-A (Emory University, 1969).
         Davis shows how Welty's art of naming describes character
     and reveals theme in her depiction of "The Twentieth Cen-
     tury South." Sometimes the names are humorous, but in
     subtle ways, they often suggest "the disintegration of the
     old South."

31   DAVIS, LEILA M. "Eudora Welty." Hollins Critic, 7 (June), 7.
         Unlike artists who escape from the world with their art,
     Welty considers her social life directly related to her
     writing. She writes of "a world peopled with those who are
     true and human."

32   DOLLARHIDE, LOUIS. "Eudora Welty's Losing Battles is Magnifi-
     cent Feast." Mississippi Library News, (June), pp. 96-98.
         Losing Battles is "a major work by a major writer." Dol-
     larhide discusses Welty's ability to make her characters
     distinctly individual and life-like. He also discusses her
     comedy with its mixture of pathos and her mastery of the
     English sentence.

33   DONNELLY, TOM. "Delicious Things to be Enjoyed by All." Re-
     view of Losing Battles. Washington News, (17 April), p. 26.
         Welty's style is poetic and humorous. Throughout the
     book, "there is something lively, or something funny...."

34   DRAKE, ROBERT. "Miss Welty's Wide World." Review of Losing
     Battles. Christian Century, 87 (17 June), 766-767.
         Welty is redoing her one theme: the conflict between the
     quest for individualism and the pressures of the group or
     family to suppress that individualism. The major flaw of
     the novel is "an extremely dense texture." Too many char-
     acters and too many themes are developing simultaneously.
     She is also too conscious of being artistic.

35   DUHAMEL, P. ALBERT. Review of Losing Battles. Boston Herald
     Traveler (Massachusetts), (13 April).
         Welty's hill people are comparable to Faulkner's in their
     "uneducable innocence." Like Faulkner's books, Losing Bat-
     tles is also "highly complicated" and "a technical tour de
     force."

1970

36   ELDER, PAUL. "Birth of a Classic Novel." Review of Losing
      Battles. San Francisco Examiner (California), (8 May),
      p. 37.
         Losing Battles is "a classic-to-be." Although "nothing
      much happens," the people tell several generations worth
      of happenings. Welty tells these tales in a style with
      "rich, beautiful imagery and metaphor."

37   FOSTER, JANE. Review of Losing Battles. LJ, 95 (15 Novem-
      ber), 1050.
         In spite of a leisurely pace, the book is enriched by
      many "nuances that make it sparkle."

38   FRANKLIN, PHYLLIS. Review of Losing Battles. Cabellian,
      (Autumn), 42-45.
         Using storytelling "as a kind of incantation," Welty
      creates a wide perspective by showing her people and their
      values from three different points of view: the tall tale
      perspective, the human perspective, and the ironic per-
      spective. The tall tale places incidents "at a safe emo-
      tional distance," but the human perspective makes the read-
      er see the characters as "energetic, loving, and kind."
      Finally, the ironic perspective reveals the pathos of lim-
      ited people fighting cosmic battles. All three points of
      view present the central theme, "that of forgiveness."

39   GAINES, ERVIN J. "16 Years Later...Eudora Welty is Still a
      Master." Minneapolis Tribune (Minnesota), (26 April), E,
      p. 9.
         Welty is "an impeccable craftsman" in her sense of detail
      and in her use of dramatic narrative. But even more impor-
      tant "is her abiding humanity."

40   GERSTENBERGER, DONNA, and GEORGE HENDRICK. The American Nov-
      el: A Checklist of 20th Century Criticism on Novels Writ-
      ten since 1789. Chicago: Swallow Press, pp. 359-360.
         Gives a very brief listing of works about Delta Wedding
      and The Ponder Heart; also lists eight general works.

41   GIBSON, DAVID. "Books." Review of Losing Battles. Catholic
      Accent, Greenburg, Pennsylvania, (4 June).
         In her exploration of the nature of love, cruelty and the
      mystery of the human heart, Welty creates "a humorous and
      sensitive novel."

42   GILREATH, EMILY. "Miss Welty Loses the Battle of Words." Re-
      view of Losing Battles. Cleveland Press (Ohio), (17 April),
      Showtime, p. 23.
         The serious story of poverty and ignorance suggests that
      all is not well on Banner Top, but Welty uses too much

(GILREATH, EMILY)
   description and too much meaningless talk and action to
   make this "serious message" interesting.

43   GORDON, JAMES. "A Season of Dreams: The Vision of Eudora
     Welty." Jackson Daily News, (20 November).
       Gordon discusses the various roles in this production of
     Welty's work by the Mississippi Center for Educational
     Television. The roles included Welty, who opened the pro-
     gram with a reading from "A Memory," William Wallace (from
     "The Wide Net"), Ruby and Clyde Fisher (from "A Piece of
     News"), Rosamond (from The Robber Bridegroom), Leota (from
     "Petrified Man"), and Edna Earle (from The Ponder Heart).

44   GOSSETT, LOUISE. "Welty's New Novel: The Comedy of Loss."
     SLJ, 3 (Fall), 122-137.
       Losing Battles is less cryptic and mysterious than most
     of Welty's early work, but it still captures the infinite
     possibilities of every moment in life--possibilities of
     emotions, perceptions, and wisdom. Although Welty does not
     impose an intellectual order on this world, she does pre-
     sent two points of view which threaten to fixate meaning.
     Julia Mortimer threatens the family's happiness by insis-
     ting on books and education. And Gloria threatens to take
     Jack outside the family structure. Both of these restric-
     tive points of view, however, are doomed to defeat. Fam-
     ily pride and ignorance will prevail.

45   GRAY, PAUL EDWARD. Review of Losing Battles. YR, 60 (Au-
     tumn), 103-104.
       Losing Battles is a novel "bursting with talk." The talk
     is usually excellent, but the central theme of love for
     everyone becomes somewhat tiresome. Welty should have add-
     ed some occasional malice to contrast with the pervasive
     good humor.

46   GRIFFIN, ROBERT J. "The Ballad of Banner, Mississippi." Re-
     view of Losing Battles. Nation, 210 (1 June), 662-664.
       Losing Battles begins with a series of metaphors which
     seem to be mere "'poetic embroidery.'" The book, however,
     is rich in humor and in its rustic story is a "bucolic bal-
     lad." It is "Miss Welty's The Reivers, a mellow comic
     tale."

47   HAINS, FRANK. "Eudora Welty Talks about Her New Book, Losing
     Battles." Clarion-Ledger (Jackson), (5 April), F, p. 6.
       Welty comments about Losing Battles before it is re-
     leased. She "anticipates some unfavorable reviews because

1970

(HAINS, FRANK)
   the book is not manifestly about contemporary problems."
   She also notes that the family is based on several families
   that she met while working for the WPA and comments briefly
   about symbolism. Hains observes that Welty is preparing a
   book of essays.

48 _____. "'Transcendentally Beautiful' Novel Wins Accolades for
   Miss Welty." Clarion-Ledger Jackson Daily News,
   (19 April), C, p. 9.
   Gives excerpts from several reviews of Losing Battles:
   Life (Guy Davenport), Virginia Kirkus, Newsweek (Jack
   Kroll), New York Times (James Boatwright), Atlantic Monthly
   (Joyce Carol Oates), and Chicago Sun-Times (Elizabeth Jane-
   way). Notes that the reviews have been generally favorable
   in spite of some "mild detractors here and there."

49 HALL, WADE. "Welty Novel a Dazzling Linguistic Tour de
   Force." Review of Losing Battles. Courier-Journal & Times
   (Louisville), World of Books, (10 May), F, p. 4.
   Hall considers Losing Battles a "major achievement."
   Through accurate use of folk language, Welty presents her
   major theme: human personality is ultimately unknowable,
   but it can be better perceived through the actions and
   speeches of a family at a reunion than through the statis-
   tics at the courthouse. (In a letter, Welty thanked Mr.
   Hall for his clear insight into the novel.)

50 HAMLIN, WILLIAM C. "The Multitudes Arrive and the Talk Goes
   On." Kansas City Star, (10 May), H, p. 10.
   Losing Battles lacks the sense of artlessness of Welty's
   earlier work. It is labored, and the result is forced
   humor, sentimental love, and endless and uninteresting conversation.

51 HART, NANCY. "A Southern Drawl from Eudora Welty's Pen."
   Memphis Press-Scimtar, (15 May).
   Welty recreates the home-spun folk qualities of her native Mississippi. The pace of the novel is slow, but the
   slowness is part of the total effect of a world which
   changes little in its preoccupation with the small concerns
   of life.

52 HARTLEY, LODWICK. "Intricate Folk Comedy." Review of Losing
   Battles. News and Observer (Raleigh, North Carolina),
   (10 May), IV, p. 6.
   Welty's mastery of concrete detail and folklore is every-
   where apparent. She presents an entire narrative through

(HARTLEY, LODWICK)
    the dialogues of rustics. The only shortcoming of her
    method is the danger that characters--like people--who are
    always talking will seem tedious.

53 HOBBY, DIANA. "Get Behind a Barefoot Boy and Push." Review
    of Losing Battles. Houston Post, (10 May), Spotlight, p. 14.
        "The glory" of Losing Battles "is its life." But Welty
    fills it with so much conversation, "so much talent, wis-
    dom, wit, and beauty," that she reaches excess.

54 HOLMAN, HUGH C. "Mississippi Fantasy." Review of Losing Bat-
    tles. Progressive, (August), pp. 42-43.
        Welty's "reproduction" of conversation is "effective,"
    but the novel lacks plot and is surprisingly indifferent to
    economic and social realities. (In fact, she does not in-
    clude a single black.) Thus, in spite of "great skill,"
    the novel "has the insubstantiality of fantasy."

55 HOWARD, ROBERTA. "Novelist Says Eudora Welty Influenced His
    Career." Jackson Daily News, (12 February), A, p. 2.
        In a speech at Bellhaven College, Reynolds Price told
    the audience that Welty's encouragement helped him decide
    to become an author.

56 HOWELL, ELMO. "Eudora Welty's Comedy of Manners." SAQ, 69
    (Autumn), 469-479.
        Welty depicts the Southern aristocracy with all its
    pride and narrow-mindedness, but also with its great sense
    of tradition and its belief in the sacredness of the land.
    In her concern for blood ties, Welty resembles Faulkner
    and is probably indebted to him, but the scope of Faulk-
    ner's fiction is greater than Welty's. Faulkner, like
    Scott, is concerned with the great themes of mankind; Wel-
    ty, like Austen, is more concerned with the manners of a
    particular Southern family.

57 HOWELL, ELMO. "Eudora Welty's Negroes: A Note on 'A Worn
    Path.'" XUS, 9 (Spring), 28-32.
        Howell challenges the views of Appel in A Season of
    Dreams (1965.A1), who sees the story as a criticism of the
    white society's treatment of the Negro. The focus of the
    story is not on social criticism, but on the person of
    Phoenix, whose position in the story and in her relation-
    ship to white society is true to the world and time that
    Welty is describing. Welty does not "defend a caste soci-
    ety," but she does not attack it either.

1970

58   IDEMA, JAMES. "Backwoods America Comes Alive in Losing Bat-
      tles." Denver Post, Roundup, (19 April), p. 16.
         With "dazzling poetry of descriptive narrative," and
      "metaphysical style," Welty has written "an American mas-
      terpiece." In a harsh world which threatens human surviv-
      al, she harmonizes many voices in a hymn to family unity.

59   JANEWAY, ELIZABETH. "Comic Novel with Epic Characters and
      Unpredictable Action." Review of Losing Battles. Chicago
      Sun-Times, Book Week, (12 April), pp. 2-3.
         Welty's characters seem to emerge from the "tradition and
      legend" of "pre-literate society." With their folktales
      and their ritualistic closeness to the earth, they are
      comic and unpredictable but ultimately heroic.

60   JEANS, PEGGY. "'Ponder Heart' Holds Over." Jackson Daily
      News, (1 June), p. 27.
         Jeans notes that Jackson loved the Little Theatre pro-
      duction of The Ponder Heart so much that it would be held
      over two days. According to Jeans, the play reveals Wel-
      ty's ability to make people aware of the people around
      them.

61   JEANES, WILLIAM. "Being Smart Takes A Lot Out of Them."
      Jackson Daily News, (19 May), p. 17.
         Charlotte Capers and Jane Petty--both of whom played the
      part of Edna Earle--compare the New York Music Box produc-
      tion of The Ponder Heart with the forthcoming second Jack-
      son production. Both agree that the new Jackson produc-
      tion, with its greater emphasis on Edna Earle's point of
      view, is closer to Welty's intentions in the story. Ac-
      cording to Jane Petty, "we've gone back to the book to tell
      the story as Eudora did, completely from Edna Earle's point
      of view."

62   _____. "Uncle Daniel Pace Change for Suave Tom Spengler."
      Jackson Daily News, (18 May).
         Tom Spengler, who was to play the role of Uncle Ponder in
      the New Stage production of The Ponder Heart in Jackson,
      discusses the play. He notes in particular the loving
      qualities of Uncle Ponder.

63   KENNEDY, MONSIGNOR JOHN S. "Hill Country, Ill Country." Re-
      view of Losing Battles. Catholic Transcript (Hartford,
      Connecticut), (22 May).
         Losing Battles is a delightful book that may be read many
      times. The reader eavesdrops "on a real community" and the
      words that he hears suggest unity and devotion to place.

64 _____. "Hill Country, Ill Country." Our Sunday Visitor
    (Western edition.) Springfield, Illinois, (24 May).
    See 1970.B63.

65 KISSEL, HOWARD. "Book Making." Review of Losing Battles.
    Women's Wear Daily, (15 April), p. 14.
        Losing Battles is "a cosmic masterpiece." Welty chooses
    extremely limited characters and settings, but through
    careful attention to details, she raises the seemingly
    "mundane" to "the timeless and the mysterious." Through
    humor which is often "sharp," Welty keeps the story from
    becoming "a sentimental period piece."

66 KOVACH, BILL. "Eudora Welty Receives MacDowell Medal."
    Clarion-Ledger Jackson Daily News, (30 August), D, p. 22.
    See 1970.B67.

67 _____. "Eudora Welty Receives the MacDowell Medal." New York
    Times, (24 August), p. 36.
        The award was presented by Russell Lynes, president of
    the MacDowell Colony, who found in Welty "'a force of
    life'" and "'one of the most remarkable novelists of our
    time.'" Welty comments about the South, about young peo-
    ple, and about the craft of fiction.

68 KROLL, JACK. "The Lesson of the Master." Review of Losing
    Battles. Newsweek, 75 (13 April), 90-91.
        Welty's intense language elevates the common affairs of
    a single family to almost epic proportions. This energetic
    literary style celebrates through brilliant bursts of meta-
    phor one of the primal forces of the human experience:
    love of family.

69 KUEHL, LINDA. "Back to Backwoods Mississippi for Granny's
    90th Birthday." Review of Losing Battles. Commonweal, 42
    (18 September), 465-466.
        Losing Battles cannot be restated in intellectual terms,
    because it is a lyrical rendering of "life's mysteries."
    It is in one sense an expression of the joy of life, but
    the joy never degenerates into sentimentality.

70 LEARY, LEWIS. Articles on American Literature 1950-1967.
    Durham, North Carolina: Duke University Press.
        Contains fifty-five entries about Welty.

71 LEHMANN-HAUPT, CHRISTOPHER. "Too Slow and Not Terrific
    Enough." Review of Losing Battles. New York Times,
    (10 April), p. 37.

1970

(LEHMANN-HAUPT, CHRISTOPHER)
The characters in Losing Battles are in perpetual motion,
but the reader has the sense of time standing still. For
all the talk and frantic action, nothing ever changes.
Most action accomplishes nothing, and most of the talk is
merely talk. By imitating the ordinary, Welty often creates "banality" and "sentimentality."

72 MAXWELL, ALLEN. "Strong Fiction for Spring." Review of Losing Battles. Dallas News (Texas), (5 April), F, p. 10.
Considers the novel for which Welty's readers waited fifteen years a "blockbuster."

73 McDONALD, W. U., JR. "Eudora Welty's Revisions of 'A Piece of
News.'" SSF, 7 (Spring), 232-247.
Much may be learned of Welty's craftsmanship and the
workings of her imagination by comparing the first published versions of her stories with the collected versions.
The version of "A Piece of News" which appeared in Southern
Review (3 [Summer, 1937], 80-84) is substantially different from the version that was collected in A Curtain of
Green. In doubling the length of the story for A Curtain
of Green, Welty reveals some qualities of her mature art.
She adds details to enrich character. (Ruby is more of a
dreamer and more sensuous and animal-like. Clyde is even
more kind.) She also enriches setting. In the revision,
she adds details to make fuller use of the symbolic possi-
bilities of the storm.

74 _____. "Welty's Social Consciousness: Revisions of 'The
Whistle.'" MFS, 16 (Summer), 193-198.
Although Welty is primarily concerned with the inner
life, she is much more aware of social injustice than many
of her critics have indicated. She depicts the Mortons as
the victims of an oppressive economic system which is represented by the landlord, Mr. Perkins. In her revision of
her story for A Curtain of Green--the story first appeared
in The Prairie Schooner, 12 (Fall, 1938)--she changes details to place greater emphasis on social injustice.

75 MOODY, MINNIE HITE. "Mississippi Kinfolk Posed for a Portrait." Columbus Dispatch (Ohio), (3 May).
Not "a masterpiece," Losing Battles is an example of "regional realism" filled with talk and the varieties of local
human experience. It has comedy but lacks depth.

76   MOSS, HOWARD. "The Lonesomeness and Hilarity of Survival."
     Review of Losing Battles. NY, 46 (4 July), 73-75.
          The scope is universal, including birth, love and death
     represented by three rituals: "a birthday, a wedding, and
     a funeral." It is a novel of talk and humor that reaches
     into the archetypal past and carries it into the present.
     There are no tragedies, only the human comedy of endless
     wasted effort.

77   MURRAY, DANNY. "Welty Collection is Most Valuable." Jackson
     Daily News, (25 June), p. 4.
          The Mississippi Department of Archives and History (in
     Jackson) has the best collection of Welty manuscripts "in
     the world." It includes everything extant except the manu-
     scripts for one short story (unnamed), which is at the Uni-
     versity of Texas.

78   MURRAY, MICHELE. "Talk Is Art in Miss Welty's Losing Bat-
     tles." Review of Losing Battles. National Observer, 9
     (27 April), 19.
          Like Gogol, Welty superbly balances between comedy and
     the sense of loss. She does so through the dialogue of the
     Southern oral tradition which, even more than setting,
     characterizes the old South.

79   OATES, JOYCE CAROL. "Eudora's Web." Atlantic, 225 (April),
     118-122.
          The world of Losing Battles is already an "extinct" one,
     and so Welty has a difficult task making it seem real to
     the modern reader. But through her use of commonplace de-
     tails--a possible debt to Jane Austen--she makes the Ren-
     fros believable. However, it is not as successful as
     Delta Wedding and The Ponder Heart, since "its serious so-
     cial and psychological concerns are muted."

80   OVERMYER, JANET. "Many Battles Lost." Cincinnati Enquirer
     (Ohio), (9 July), p. 49.
          Welty has "surpassed even her own high excellence." The
     book is filled with accurate dialogue and "subtleties of
     characterization."

81   PETROSKI, CATHERINE. "A Mississippi Family Holds Its Annual
     Reunion." Austin American Statesman (Texas), (31 May), T,
     p. 34.
          Although the density of Welty's prose may confuse the
     reader, Losing Battles is "awesome and beautiful." In a
     complex story about the "collision" of the old and new
     ways, Welty makes every piece fit into a complex whole
     which "stirs the emotions as well as the intellect."

1970

82 PRENSHAW, PEGGY. "Cultural Patterns in Eudora Welty's Delta
    Wedding and "The Demonstrators." NMW, 3 (Fall), 51-70.
       In Delta Wedding, ritual and tradition provide continui-
    ty and, to some extent, help define self, but they also
    tend to eclipse the needs of the individual. In "The Dem-
    onstrators," Welty depicts a world in which the old tradi-
    tions have been lost and the individual is too much alien
    and too much alone. Such a conflict between the needs of
    the individual and those of society are not confined to
    the South. Welty's theme is a universal one.

83 PRENSHAW, PEGGY JOYCE WHITMAN. "A Study of Setting in the
    Fiction of Eudora Welty." DAI, 31, 1810-A (University of
    Texas at Austin, 1970).
       Through close readings of "representative works," Pren-
    shaw demonstrates how Welty uses the details of setting
    both mimetically and symbolically.

84 PRICE, REYNOLDS. "Frightening Gift." Review of Losing Bat-
    tles. Washington Post-Times-Herald (Washington, D.C.),
    (17 April), C, pp. 1, 4.
       Losing Battles is comparable "for depth and breadth"
    with The Tempest, The Winter's Tale, and War and Peace.
    It is also "the funniest novel since Huckleberry Finn."
    Welty's language is almost entirely based on human speech;
    and in the rich, figurative words of a world which is con-
    stantly shifting into metaphor, Welty demonstrates that
    "everything is and is not what it seems...but slides as we
    watch and listen into some other things...."

85 PRYCE-JONES, ALAN. "Almost a Winner." Review of Losing Bat-
    tles. Newsday (Garden City, New York), (2 June).
       Losing Battles is "less a story than a fresco." Although
    the opening pages are a delight, "the life of Banner be-
    comes tiring." It is too intense and too long.

86 RHODES, RICHARD. "The Family Way." Review of Losing Battles.
    Washington Post Book World, 4 (12 April), 3.
       Losing Battles is a deliberate masterpiece which is per-
    haps too carefully constructed. It has none of the excess
    genius of Moby Dick or Leaves of Grass or Emerson's es-
    says. Nevertheless, the book "is immensely entertaining
    and brilliantly written."

87   . "The Family Way." Review of Losing Battles. Chicago
     Tribune Book World, (12 April).
     See 1970.B88.

88   RICKS, CHRISTOPHER. "Female and Other Impersonators." Review
     of Losing Battles. New York Review of Books, 15 (23 July),
     10.
        The book is "meticulous" but somewhat insubstantial. The
     country people are simply too idyllic. Not even their own
     pervasive ignorance upsets the harmony of their world. The
     metaphors never achieve a "proper density." Too often
     they have "nowhere to go."

89   ROBBINS, J. ALBERT. "Voices of a Mighty Family." Review of
     Losing Battles. St. Louis Post-Dispatch, (19 April), B,
     p. 4.
        Losing Battles is a "comic novel," but it also is a seri-
     ous study of human nature. In spite of considerable diver-
     sity, the family is held together by bonds of love, and in
     spite of the fact that many battles are lost, "the human
     spirit is resilient."

90   ROGERS, W. G. "The Bridge Collapses and...." Review of
     Losing Battles. Grand Rapids Press (Michigan), (19 April),
     E, p. 2.
        The plot is held together by three central "links": the
     bridge, the safe, and the ring. Although Welty is not con-
     cerned with social problems in the South, her writing is
     subtle and precise and, in places, is "pure delight."

91   . "Eudora Welty." Book of the Week Service for News-
     papers (edited especially for newspapers every week by the
     Saturday Review), (11 April), pp. 1-3.
     See 1970.B92.

92   . "The Literary Scene." New York Post, (13 April).
     See 1970.B92, p. 50.

93   . "Mid-'30s Mississippi and its People." Review of
     Losing Battles. Chicago Today, 12 April, NOW, p. 12.
     See 1970.B92.

94   ROSE, JEANNE. "Land of Laughter But with a Catch." Review of
     Losing Battles. Baltimore Evening Sun (Maryland),
     (26 April), D, p. 5.
        Losing Battles "is not a novel; it is an experience."
     Reading it is exhausting but elating. Beneath the gusto
     and the humor is "profound wisdom."

1970

95   ROSENFELD, RUTH. "Flawless Ear for Speech Adds Flavor to Wel-
      ty Book." Dayton News (Ohio), (7 June).
            Unlike Faulkner's characters, the tragedy of Welty's is
      not so much greed as "overpowering backwardness."

96   RUBIN, LOUIS D., JR. "Books: Delight Ending in Wisdom in
      Welty Novel." Washington Star (Washington, D.C.),
      (26 April), D, p. 10.
            Losing Battles is a book of the surface, but it is a
      "thick-textured" surface worthy of careful reading. Al-
      though many people are present and many people are talking,
      each character is very much alone and "helpless against
      time and change." Losing Battles will endure as "a master-
      piece by one of the greatest and deepest of all American
      literary artists."

97   _____. "Everything Brought Out in the Open: Eudora Welty's
      Losing Battles." Hollins Critic, 7 (June), 1-12.
            Welty is "one of the three or four most important writers
      to come out of twentieth-century America." Losing Battles
      presents difficulties for the reader which may prevent it
      from being a popular success, but the difficulties are very
      much a part of Welty's craft of fiction. There is nothing
      beneath the surface, but the surface is so rich and complex
      that the reader is expected to see the complex relation-
      ships of multitudes of details, details carefully selected
      to distinguish the trivial from the important. The reader
      who takes the time to read carefully will find "delight
      ending in wisdom."

98   RUFFIN, CAROLYN F. "Sensitivity Runs a Poor Second." Review
      of Losing Battles. Christian Science Monitor, (11 June),
      p. 13.
            The novel shows the triumph of ignorance and vulgarity
      over sensitivity. The cruelty of the conquerers is done
      "with the best of intentions."

99   RUPP, RICHARD. Celebration in Postwar American Fiction 1945-
      1967. Coral Gables, Florida: University of Miami Press,
      pp. 59-75.
            Welty uses myth and folklore to celebrate the ritualized
      elements of life: birth, death, and love. The Robber
      Bridegroom is a juvenile version of this celebration, in
      which fantasy "transcends the violence." Delta Wedding is
      a more mature and complex celebration of love and marriage.
      Her best works of celebration are "The Wide Net," "A Still
      Moment," and "Powerhouse," which use ritual elements.

100 SHAFFNER, CLAIRE. "For Those Who Like Downright Good Story-
     Telling..." Review of Losing Battles. Charlotte Observer
     (North Carolina), (12 April), F, p. 5.
        Welty is a master of telling stories as they are told in
     the South, rather than as they are related by literary
     schools. Because she does not belong to a particular
     school of writers, Welty is able to capture her experiences
     first hand. These experiences have a "humanness" obtain-
     able by few other writers.

101 SHAW, FRED. "Gifted Authors Keep Literature Alive in South."
     Review of Losing Battles. Miami Herald (Florida),
     (24 May), K, p. 7.
        Compares Welty briefly with Katherine Anne Porter.

102 SIMMONS, MABEL C. "Long Wait Is Rewarded--New Welty Novel Is
     Here." Review of Losing Battles. New Orleans Times-Picay-
     une, (26 April), II, p. 2.
        In Losing Battles--as well as in The Ponder Heart--the
     tales within tales of the family reunion are ritualistic
     in their annual reoccurences, and the new incident of
     Jack's imprisonment and revenge on Judge Moody will be a
     part of the following year's ritual.

103 SIMPSON, LEWIS P. "The Chosen People." SoR, 6 (Summer),
     xxii-xxiii.
        Deals with three accounts of the Great Depression, in-
     cluding Losing Battles. In her account, Welty depicts the
     struggle between the agrarian and the industrial societies
     "obliquely" but in "a completely significant way." She
     matches the family (and tribal solidarity) of the Vaughans
     and Beechams against the bourgeoisie commercialism which
     Julia Mortimer tries to instill in her pupils. The end of
     the struggle--like that of life itself--is survival.

104 SPACKS, PATRICIA MEYER. "Losing Battles--A View of Life in
     Mississippi." Review of Losing Battles. Boston Globe
     (Massachusetts), (2 May), p. 12.
        Emphasizes human significance rather than social signif-
     icance and elevates the everyday struggles of human beings
     to "mythic dignity." As human experience, the novel is
     rich in pathos and comedy. However, Welty seems to find
     more profundity in the trivial than is warranted by the
     facts.

1970

105   SPARROW, BONITA. "New Welty Novel Written to Endure." Review
       of Losing Battles. Commercial Appeal (Memphis, Tennessee),
       (12 April), VI, p. 6.
            In the richness of its imagery and in its recreation of
       the tales and speech patterns of rural Mississippi and,
       above all, in its inspiration, Losing Battles "was written
       to endure." It may be Welty's "finest." The manner of
       tale telling is comparable to Chaucer's Canterbury Tales.

106   THOMAS, WILLIAM. Interview with Welty. Akron Beacon Journal,
       (22 November).
            See 1970.B109.

107   _____. "Miss Eudora at Home." Houston Chronicle (Texas),
       (15 November), Zest, p. 9.
            Thomas records an interview which deals primarily with
       Welty's early development as a writer, but also includes
       some comments about Losing Battles and Welty's attitudes
       toward social injustice. Although she has never been a
       "crusader," Welty claims that her work has always presented
       the harder aspects of life. She is opposed to the modern
       tendency to replace ideas with obscenity but believes in
       writing that is "honest."

108   THOMPSON, FRANCIS J. "Belief is the Loser." Tampa Tribune
       (Florida), (24 May), C, p. 5.
            Although Welty is "one of America's 10 best novelists,"
       she fails to achieve "'a willing suspension of disbelief'"
       in Losing Battles. The characters and scenes are "more
       like an animated cartoon" than a real picture of life.

109   THORNTON, EUGENIA. "The Vital Eudora Welty." Review of
       Losing Battles. Cleveland Plain Dealer (Ohio), (19 April),
       H, p. 7.
            In a clearly defined setting, Welty brings together an
       "enormous" group of people and yet presents each one as a
       distinct individual. Although they have lost many battles,
       they have won with gusto and vitality the only important
       one: family unity and love.

110   TORGERSON, MARGARET. "Major Literary Event." Review of
       Losing Battles. Worcester Telegram (Massachusetts),
       (26 April).
            Losing Battles is "an enjoyable book" which gives "the
       celebration for which Harvey Cox pleads." In her rendition
       of human speech, Welty is not "a tape recorder," but "a
       marvelous artist and craftsman."

116

111   VANDE KIEFT, RUTH. "Granny's Big Re-union." Review of Losing
      Battles. Boston Herald-Traveler (Massachusetts),
      (26 April), p. 3-4.
         As the work of "one of our best American fiction writ-
      ers," Welty's depiction of a hill country reunion is well
      worth serious attention. With its mixture of the comic
      and the serious, Losing Battles is a celebration of life.

112   V. P. H. "Tobacco Road Types, Talk, and Din Abound in Eudora
      Welty's New Book." Review of Losing Battles. Omaha Morn-
      ing World-Herald (Nebraska), (26 April), Entertainment,
      p. 39.
         Losing Battles is a "superior piece of writing," parti-
      cularly the figurative language, but the prevalence of ig-
      norant characters talking makes an essentially boring book.
      There is nothing "very amusing in ignorance."

113   WALSH, ANNE C. "Roots and Relationships--The Supporting
      Mesh." Review of Losing Battles. Phoenix Gazette (Ari-
      zona), (18 April), p. 22.
         Welty's Mississippians are comparable to Faulkner's, but
      they are more optimistic. They are supported through
      life's struggles by enduring relationships.

114   WARD, JOY. "Praise and Criticism for Losing Battles." Bir-
      mingham News (Alabama), (17 May), E, p. 7.
         Welty shows great "humanness," but is also somewhat long
      and tedious. Losing Battles has too many scenes which do
      not seem like the work of a professional. Nevertheless,
      Welty preserves the tradition of a humane society which
      may not be known again.

115   WARREN, CLIFTON. "Comic Southern Tale Applauded." Review of
      Losing Battles. Oklahoma City Oklahoman, (12 July),
      Showcase, p. 9.
         As in her short stories, Welty demonstrates in Losing
      Battles that--in the words of Jessamyn West--she is "'the
      most skilful craftsman writing in America today.'"

116   WELLEJUS, ED. "The Book Shelf." Erie Times (Pennsylvania),
      (7 June), E, p. 14.
         In the Southern tradition, Losing Battles is "a book of
      talk." It is funny, but "sometimes a little overdone"
      and "underneath are serious, even somber tones."

1970

117   *WELTY, EUDORA.   Comment about "A Worn Path," This is My Best,
        ed. Whit Burnett.   Garden City, New York: Doubleday, p. 532.
        Listed by Noel Polk in "A Eudora Welty Checklist," See
        1973.B56.

118   WERRY, RICHARD.   "Familial Love in Mississippi."   Review of
        Losing Battles.   Detroit News (Michigan), (10 May), E, p. 5.
          Losing Battles is a compressed novel of "good humor" and
        "familial love" written by a "patient craftswoman" with the
        perceptions of "a great artist."

119   WHITE, EDWARD M.   "'Battles' Lifts Novelist to Major Rank.'"
        Review of Losing Battles.   Los Angeles Times Calendar, (10
        May), p. 39.
          Before Losing Battles, Welty wrote some excellent short
        stories and a few good novels, but with Losing Battles,
        she becomes an "important modern American novelist."   With
        "originality" and "toughness of mind," she maintains for a
        whole novel the artistic control of her best short stories.

120   WILLIAMS, ERMA.   "Novelist Loses One in Her Latest Book."
        Buffalo Courier Express (New York), (14 June).
          Welty loses her "delicate touch" and thereby loses a
        "battle with words."   The patterns of similes and metaphors
        are cumbersome, and plot and character are lost "in a
        morass of words."

121   WILLIAMS, SHIRLEY.   "Bookends."   Louisville Courier-Journal
        (Kentucky), (8 February), D, p. 5.
          Announces the forthcoming publication of Losing Battles,
        "a four-generation comedy about a mammoth family reunion."

122   WILSON, EMERSON, W.   "Family Reunion in Mississippi."   Review
        of Losing Battles.   Wilmington News (Delaware), (29 April).
          As the work of "one of our finest Southern writers,"
        Losing Battles is a "real literary event."   For it, Welty
        should receive the National Book Award.

123   WINFREY, LEE.   "'Losing Battles' an Author's Triumph."   Review
        of Losing Battles.   Detroit Free Press (Michigan), (19
        April), B, p. 5.
          Losing Battles is a "long, deep novel" which sympatheti-
        cally portrays ignorant people trapped by life.   It is a
        masterpiece that few people will read.

124   WOESTENDIEK, JO.   "Eudora Welty Emerges as 'Very Important'
        American Writer."   Houston Chronicle (Texas), (12 April),
        Zest, p. 12.
          Welty proves in Losing Battles that the written word is
        still a viable medium of expression.   No film could capture

(WOESTENDIEK, JO)
her way of seeing the world. This "serio-comedy" is a major achievement and should make Welty a candidate for book
awards.

125   YARDLEY, JONATHAN. "The Last Good One?" Review of Losing
Battles. New Republic, 162 (9 May), 33-36.
Losing Battles may not prove to be Welty's best work because it is too long and somewhat uncontrolled, but it has
the subtle humor and deft portrayal of character that is a
part of Welty's best work. It develops the paradox that
even in losing, the people in the book have attained a kind
of triumph: against impossible odds, they have gone on
trying. Because most of the younger writers are too far
removed in time, Welty may have produced the last good book
about the old South.

126   _____. "Losing Battles: Farewell to the 'Southern Novel.'"
Greensboro News (North Carolina), (12 April), E, p. 3.
Welty is neither regional nor sentimental. Losing Battles is "a description of a ritual, a celebration of the
idea and fact of family." And the family is a "symbolic
microcosm of the world.

127   ZINGMAN, BARBARA. "Welty Novel Is Rich in Humor." Review of
Losing Battles. Louisville Times (Kentucky), (20 May), A,
p. 13.
Losing Battles "reads like a play" and is filled with
myth and humor. It is "a notable contribution" to the
"regional novel in America."

1971 A BOOKS

1   MANZ-KUNZ, MARIE-ANTOINETTE. Eudora Welty: Aspects of Reality in Her Short Fiction. Bern, Switzerland: Francke
Verlag.
The chapters are entitled, "The Writer and Her Work,"
"Reality as an Experience of Rhythm," "The Secrets in the
World," "Lone Wanderers of Experience," "Hegira into Fantasy," and "The Aspects of Reality." Manz-Kunz finds the
source of some confusion about Welty's work in the separa-
tion of her characters from the world and in their attempt
to find a "new integration." Like James and Joyce, Welty
records the inner experiences of her characters. The result is a view of reality which changes with the dynamics
of individual perception.

2 WELTY, EUDORA. <u>Short Stories</u>. New York: Harcourt, Brace &
Co. (Folcraft Library Edition limited to 1500 copies).
  Was originally delivered at the University of Washington
in August 1947 with the title, "Some Views on the Reading
and Writing of Short Stories," and was published in a much
shorter form in <u>Atlantic</u> (183). Welty notes that the power
of the imagination and the power of analysis are opposite
states of mind. The first belongs to the creative artist;
the second belongs to the critic. The critic cannot replay
the creation of a story like a film in reverse, but Welty
plays the critic--at least in part--and discusses the following works: Hemingway's "Indian Camp," Crane's "The
Bride Comes to Yellow Sky," Mansfield's "Miss Brill,"
Chekhov's "The Darling," James' "The Jolly Corner," Faulkner's <u>The Bear</u>, Woolf's <u>The Searchlight</u>, Lawrence's <u>The
Fox</u>, and James' "The Real Thing." Welty prefers those
writers for whom "form is evolved." Poe's form is too perfect. Unlike Lawrence, he does not write of human relationships "in terms of eternity."

1971 B SHORTER WRITINGS

1 ANON. "Miss Welty Receives Award from Commission." <u>Clarion-
Ledger</u> (Jackson), (26 February), B, p. 4.
  Notes that Welty received the "First Annual Award of Ex-
cellence" from the Mississippi Arts Commission.

2 ANON. "Eudora to Get Honorary Degree." <u>Clarion-Ledger</u> (Jack-
son), (17 April), p. 5.
  Announces that Welty will receive an honorary Doctor of
Letters degree from the University of the South.

3 ANON. "Eudora Welty Honored by Denison University." <u>Clarion-
Ledger</u> (Jackson), (30 April), B, p. 6.
  Notes that Welty was the first Beck lecturer in residence
at Denison and that she will receive an honorary doctorate
of literature degree.

4 ANON. Advertisement for <u>One Time, One Place</u>. <u>San Francisco
Sunday Examiner and Chronicle</u> (California), <u>This World</u>,
(21 November), p. 42.
  Includes two pictures from the book--"Carrying the Ice"
and "Saturday Off, Jackson"--and a brief descriptive
commentary.

5   ANON. "Notes on People." New York Times, (9 December), p. 3.
        Notes that Welty was elected to the American Academy of
        Arts and Letters.

6   AVANT, JOHN ALFRED. Review of One Time, One Place, LJ, 96
        (15 December), 4086.
            The beauty of Welty's photographs is captured rather than
        planned. The pictures "suggest the potentially mythic
        resonances of ordinary lives...."

7   BOYLAN, MILDRED. "10 Candidates for 'National Book Award.'"
        Rochester Times Union (New York), (6 February).
            As "one of our great authors," Welty has written a mas-
        terpiece. However, her interpretation of the South is
        different from Faulkner's. Faulkner concentrates on "tra-
        dition, history and politics," while Welty focuses on "in-
        dividuals and their surroundings."

8   BRADFORD, M. E. "Looking Down from a High Place: The Sereni-
        ty of Miss Welty's Losing Battles." Recherches Anglaises
        et Americaines, 4, 92-97.
            Because Julia Mortimer tries to enlighten the family and
        thereby change it, she is a threat to survival. Welty's
        art--like that of most new Southern literature--does not
        attempt to change life, but to record it and to accept the
        cosmic and unchanging values of "honor, courage, charity,
        honesty, loyalty, and memory." Anyone who threatens these
        values is a threat to life itself.

9   BROOKS, CLEANTH. "American Literature: Mirror, Lens or
        Prism?" A Shaping Joy: Studies in the Writer's Craft.
        New York: Harcourt Brace Jovanovich, pp. 168-172.
            Discusses "A Piece of News." In her depiction of a poor
        illiterate girl whose imagination has been stirred by the
        printed word, Welty mirrors the truth of the human heart.
        But she also shows some of the qualities of a prism in
        breaking up "the common light of day" and showing the hid-
        den depth of apparent simplicity.

10 BURNS, LANGDON C., JR. "Supplement to a Cross-Referenced Index
        of Short Fiction and Author-Title Listing." SSF, 8
        (Spring), 407.
            Makes corrections of 1970 list and adds several new en-
        tries. See 1970.B22.

11 No Entry

1971

12   CHENEY, FRANCIS NEEL. "Sharp, Shrewd Eye, True as a Tuning
     Fork." Review of One Time, One Place. Nashville Banner
     (Tennessee), (19 November), p. 56.
        The book contains the direct, honest picture of a writer
     with a "sharp, shrewd eye," rather than those of a social
     worker in search of social commentary.

13   CLEMONS, WALTER. "Meeting Miss Welty, Author of 'Ponder
     Heart.'" Jackson Daily News, (20 May), p. 24.
        See 1970.B26.

14   COCKSHUTT, ROD. "Of Welty, Wine, and a Welshman." Review of
     One Time, One Place. News and Observer (Raleigh, North
     Carolina), Book World, (21 November), IV, p. 6.
        Welty could say much more with words than with pictures.
     Nevertheless, the book reveals Welty's interest in the
     people and folklore of her own Mississippi. In these pic-
     tures, the reader senses the unmistakable presence of
     Welty, the story-teller.

15   FINLEY, ELEANOR. "Miss Welty Caught Depression on Film."
     Atlanta Journal (Georgia), (7 November), C, p. 11.
        The photographs are remarkable in that Welty took them
     with a simple camera. They demonstrate the "superb visual
     perception" of "a fine writer."

16   FOFF, ARTHUR, and DANIEL KNAPP, eds. Story: An Introduction
     to Prose Fiction, 2nd edition, Belmont, California: Wads-
     worth Publishing Co., pp. 10-11.
        The action of "The Wide Net" is Wallace's effort to un-
     derstand his wife. The conflict is, therefore, symbolic
     as well as physical.

17   GILL, BRENDAN. "The Inconstant Past." Review of One Time,
     One Place. NY, 47 (25 December), 66-68.
        Welty knew the art of photography and was able to capture
     her subjects in "a nearly perfect book." It is a book of
     "gestures and feelings," into which the viewer looks for
     small but significant details.

18   GOVIAN, CHRISTINE. "True Understanding." Review of One Time,
     One Place. Chattanooga Times (Tennessee), (5 December), B,
     p. 4.
        Welty's pictures reflect her interest in people; and
     whether she intends to do so or not, she does make a social

(GOVIAN, CHRISTINE)
commentary. She shows man's ability to survive and demonstrates "that whites do have compassion."

19   HAINS, FRANK. "One Time, One Place: Photographs of Her
     Mississippi by Eudora Welty." Clarion-Ledger (Jackson),
     (31 October), C, p. 8.
       Welty's photographs reveal a quality present in her writ-
     ings: her ability to focus on "the single gesture," to
     capture "the essence of the moment."

20   HOWARD, ZELMA TURNER. "Meaning through Rhetoric in Eudora
     Welty's A Curtain of Green, The Wide Net, and The Golden
     Apples. DAI, 31, 6552-A--6553-A (University of Northern
     Colorado, 1970).
       Howard shows Welty's use of the "'silent'" author. In a
     discussion of rhetoric and point of view, she demonstrates
     why Welty's earliest work delighted scholars but dismayed
     critics.

21   JONES, MADISON. Review of One Time, One Place: Mississippi
     in the Depression. New York Times Book Review, (21 Novem-
     ber), VII, pp. 60, 62, 64.
       Although the photographs are of uneven quality--some are
     over-exposed, or under-exposed--they are true to Welty's
     intentions: they show the humanity of her subjects. The
     pictures do not criticize a social system which leaves
     some people poor; they merely show people as they are,
     filled with "a trust now almost entirely vanished."

22   KIHSS, PETER. "2nd Off Broadway Play Wins Pulitzer." New
     York Times, (4 May), p. 1.
       Notes that the fiction judges for the Pulitzer Prize re-
     jected Losing Battles, along with two other candidates.

23   KOON, WARREN. "Welty Mirrors Depression Years." Review of
     One Time, One Place. Natchez Democrat (Mississippi), (17
     November), B, p. 5.
       The photographs are sometimes "magnificent." Welty's
     perception of "the comic, the pathos of the times was ex-
     cellent."

24   KRAUS, KEITH W. "Welty's Petrified Man." Expl, 29 (April),
     Item 63.
       Earlier critics interpreted the name Fletcher as a maker
     of bows and arrows. But there is another possible connota-
     tion. Fletcherism was a health fad of the early twentieth
     century. To be a healthy person, one could eat anything

1971

(KRAUS, KEITH W.)
   but had to chew it carefully. Mrs. Fletcher hears how the
   petrified man chews his food but finds the results to be
   somewhat ironic. Instead of improving his health, the
   process turns him into stone.

25   LANDESS, THOMAS H. "More Trouble in Mississippi: Family vs.
   Antifamily in Miss Welty's Losing Battles." SR, 79 (Autumn), 626-637.
      Although Losing Battles has been criticized for what is
   supposedly an idyllic representation of life, it is actually a book filled with discord. The family is at a reunion,
   but the sense of unity does not run deeply. The novel is
   a major work, but has some serious flaws. No major incidents bring the main conflicts of the novel into sharp focus. Also, the style is less controlled than in some of
   Welty's earlier works. It is burdened by so many surplus
   metaphors that narrative progress is much impeded.

26   McFARLAND, RONALD E. "Vision and Perception in the Works of
   Eudora Welty." MarkhamR, 2 (February), 94-99.
      To have vision is to perceive in flashes of insight the
   significance of details. Vision is painful and sometimes
   self-destructive, but it is necessary for obtaining self-
   knowledge. In many of her stories (including "First Love,"
   "Death of a Traveling Salesman," and "Keela the Outcast
   Indian Maiden"), Welty depicts characters who obtain vision. Only those characters who accept vision "achieve
   meaningful lives."

27   MASSERAND, ANNE M. "Eudora Welty's Travelers: The Journey
   Theme in Her Short Stories." SLJ, 3 (Spring), 39-48.
      Welty's fiction often contains two central symbols: the
   home as the place of worth and security (but also of ignorance), and the journey as the unidentifiable place of dan-
   ger (but also of initiation into the mysteries of life).
   The traveler in many of Welty's stories is a magnificent
   stranger who, with his knowledge gleaned from the journey
   of life, brings insight to the nontravelers. The insight,
   however, is often blurred with ambiguity.

28   M. H. M. "Photo Album, Deep South, In the '30's." Review of
   One Time, One Place. Columbus Dispatch (Ohio), (19 December), Tab, p. 17.
      The collection is more than a money-maker for the pub-
   lisher. It is an honest record of "happy faces, both black
   and white."

29   MIZNER, ARTHUR. Instructor's Manual for Modern Short Stories:
     The Uses of the Imagination. New York: W. W. Norton &
     Co., pp. 178-180.
        In telling a story of "unconscious heroism," Welty moves
     skillfully between objective narration and first-person
     narration. By so doing, she "takes us into old Phoenix's
     mind with great delicacy."

30   *MOSS, GRANT, JR. "'A Worn Path' Retrod." College Language
     Association Journal (Morgan State College), 15 (December),
     144-152.
        Listed by Noel Polk in "A Eudora Welty Checklist," See
     1973.B56.

31   O'CONNOR, WILLIAM VAN. "The Novel and the 'Truth' about
     America." Studies in American Culture: Dominant Ideas
     and Images, edited by Joseph J. Kwiat and Mary C. Turpie.
     Minneapolis, Minnesota: University of Minnesota Press,
     p. 81.
        O'Connor links Welty with writers who depict "grotesques,
     the comedy and pathos of the misfit."

32   OGDEN, FLORENCE SILLERS. "Tribute to Eudora Welty for Dialect
     So Direct." Clarion-Ledger Jackson Daily News, (16 May),
     F, p. 4.
        Discusses Welty's use of Southern speech in Losing
     Battles.

33   PAWLOWSKI, ROBERT S. "The Process of Observation: Winesburg,
     Ohio, and The Golden Apples." UR, 37 (Summer), 292-298.
        Both writers achieve a total vision of life, a vision
     filled with the illogic and chaos of human experience.
     Both set their stories in a small town, which becomes a
     microcosm of the universe. Both are richly symbolic. Both
     use the "spatial concept" of the cubists. Both present
     characters dramatically rather than through authorial
     commentary.

34   PUTNEY, MICHAEL. "Gift Books: Land, Sea, and the Faces of
     Man." Review of One Time, One Place. National Observer,
     10 (4 December), 22.
        Welty makes an amateur's family album, but her very lack
     of professionalism enables her to capture the candid moods
     of her fellow Mississippians.

35   RATHBORNE, TINA. "Review of One Time, One Place." Harvard
     Crimson, (1 December).
        The photographs are admittedly amateurish and sometimes

1971

(RATHBONE, TINA)
poor in quality, but Welty reveals her ability to come to
terms with social realities. If she were to turn this
perception to her writings, her work would be much more
powerful. As it is, Losing Battles reads "like a Walt
Disney script" rather than a novel, because Welty does not
deal with the realities of "politics and money and newspapers and race...." She is too insecure as a woman "deal-
ing with a man's world."

36 RICHMOND, LEE J. "Symbol and Theme in Eudora Welty's 'Petrified Man.'" EJ, 60 (December), 1201-1203.
The theme is the "corruption of love," and the key symbols are the beauty parlor, the mirror and the petrified
man. The parlor and the mirror suggest a world in which
appearance is more important than love. Petrified man includes the petrified women, Leota and Mrs. Fletcher,
whose hearts have turned to stone and whose spiritual values have become petrified.

37 SPEARMAN, WALTER. "A Mississippi Scrapbook of Depression
Years." Review of One Time, One Place. Chapel Hill Weekly
(North Carolina), (21 November), p. 4.
Welty presents "impressive and revealing photographs"
which show her to be a "perceptive, compassionate, caring
person...." She does not attempt to make a social com-
mentary, but merely records unposed moments in the lives of
Mississippi's poor. Welty "should have won the Pulitzer
Prize or the National Book Award--or both" for Losing Bat-
tles.

38 VINSON, CLYDE MARSHALL. "Imagery in the Short Stories of Eudora Welty." DAI, 31, 5431-A--5432-A (Northwestern University, 1970).
Using Philip Wheelwright's Metaphor and Reality as a
guide, Vinson studies the "function of the imagery in Eudora Welty's thirty-nine collected short stories." He emphasizes patterns within stories rather than relationships
among the stories.

39 WASSON, BEN. "Welty Hits Again." Review of One Time, One
Place. Delta Democrat-Times (Greenville, Mississippi),
(31 October).
Welty sees the Mississippi of the Depression "with the
clarity of a poet." She presents a series of pictures
which reveal her "native wisdom" and her "marvelous and
elusive humor."

40 WELTY, EUDORA. "Jane Austen." Atlantic Brief Lives, edited
    by Louis Kronenberger. Boston, Massachusetts: Little,
    Brown and Co., pp. 23-25.
       The family, with its conflicts and seemingly trivial con-
    cerns, is Austen's main subject. Although it is a limited
    subject in terms of settings and interest, it is also
    universal.

41 WEST, CONN. Review of Losing Battles. GaR, 25 (Fall), 375-
    376.
       Welty has a thorough knowledge of the people and customs
    of Mississippi in the depression years, and she elevates
    this factual knowledge to "pure art." In relating the
    humor and sadness of existence, she fits every metaphor
    and adjective "in building the complete tight-knit story."

1972 A BOOKS - NONE

1972 B SHORTER WRITINGS

1   ALDRIDGE, JOHN W. The Devil in the Fire: Retrospective Es-
    says on American Literature and Culture 1951-1971. New
    York: Harper's Magazine Press, in association with Harper
    and Row, pp. 249-256.
       Welty's work before Losing Battles showed promise but
    considerable limitations of scope and technique. In Losing
    Battles, however, she has greatly expanded her scope and
    gained new authority and new complexity. She presents what
    might have become Southern stereotypes in a complex and
    often ironic framework.

2   ALEXANDER, HOLMES. "The Dimension of Character." Tampa Trib-
    une (Florida), (21 May).
       Shows thematic parallels between Laurel Hand and Deck,
    the central character in Larry McMurtry's novel, All My
    Friends are Going to be Strangers.

3   ALLEN, BRUCE. Review of The Optimist's Daughter. LJ, 97 (1
    June), 2119-2120.
       Welty develops a theme and character type from her earli-
    er works: a sensitive person seeking to impose order on a
    harsh, chaotic world. To an extent, Laurel succeeds in
    creating her own order.

4   ALVERSON, TOM. "He's Pessimistic Over Optimist's Daughter."
    Cleveland Press (Ohio), (26 May), G, p. 8.
       The book "fails" because Welty's effort "to explode the

1972

(ALVERSON, TOM)
   validity of optimism" has been done in "more interesting"
   ways by other writers. The real optimist may be Fay, and
   Laurel "may be an expression of modern existential fatal-
   ism," but Welty does not make such distinctions clear.

5   ANON. Review of One Time, One Place." Booklist, 68 (15
        January), 413.
           As in Losing Battles, Welty shows great "sensitivity" to
        people. In an "artless way," she does not intend "social
        documentary," but she does give "an honest revelation of
        social conditions."

6   ANON. "Notes on People." "Honors in the Arts." New York
        Times, (26 January), p. 27
           The National Institute of Arts and Letters named Welty
        and Henry Steele Commager as winners of gold medal awards.

7   ANON. "Welty is Medalist of NIAL." Clarion-Ledger (Jackson),
        (27 January), A, p. 10.
           Notes that Welty won the Gold Medal of the National Acad-
        emy of Arts and Letters, "the highest award that any Ameri-
        can writer can receive."

8   ANON. "A Gold Medal for Eudora Welty Latest Honor for Gracious
        Lady." Clarion-Ledger (Jackson), (3 February), A, p. 14.
           In addition to summarizing Welty's achievements, the
        article comments about Welty's local reputation. She is
        "esteemed and beloved by fellow Mississippians."

9   ANON. Review of One Time, One Place. New Republic, 166 (12
        February), 30-31.
           Because the book does not focus on social injustice, it
        gives a far more comprehensive view of poor people in Mis-
        sissippi than works by writers and photographers who in-
        sist in seeing Mississippi as the epitomy of indifference
        to the Bill of Rights. The photographs fall short of the
        work of professionals, but they are competent and express
        rural scenes and rural people with great sensitivity.

10   ANON. "Miss Welty Gets Another Writing Prize." Clarion-
        Ledger (Jackson), (30 March), F, p. 4.
           Announces that Welty was presented "a special award" by
        Theta Sigma Phi (society for professional women in journal-
        ism and communications). Notes that Welty "is one of the
        outstanding authors of the day" and that she has this dis-
        tinction without catering to the vulgarity of popular
        taste.

11   ANON. "Notes on Current Books." Review of One Time, One
     Place. VQR, 48 (Spring), lxxiv.
        The pictures show sensitivity, amusement, and "a warmth
     and affection seldom seen in the work of the professional
     photographer."

12   ANON. "Miss Welty Will Receive Degree." Clarion-Ledger
     (Jackson), (28 May), A, p. 8.
        Announces that Welty will receive an honorary degree from
     Washington and Lee University.

13   ANON. "Of Life and Living." Review of The Optimist's Daugh-
     ter. Sacramento Bee (California), (18 June).
        Welty writes with "economy and wit" but the novel is
     somewhat "mysterious" and the character of Laurel is diffi-
     cult to understand.

14   ANON. Review of The Optimist's Daughter. Booklist, 68 (15
     July), 975.
        In a "Southern setting," Welty presents "again a simple
     but sensitive exploration of human relations."

15   ANON. "Best Sellers." Publishers Weekly, (7 August).
        Lists The Optimist's Daughter as Number Ten on the best
     seller list.

16   ANON. "Named by Nixon to Council on Arts." New York Times,
     (19 August), p. 30.
        Nixon appointed "the novelist" Welty to serve a six-year
     term on the National Council on the Arts. She was to give
     advice on the spending of federal funds for "cultural en-
     deavors in the United States."

17   ANON. "Notes on Current Books." Review of The Optimist's
     Daughter. VQR, 48 (Autumn), cxx.
        It is "almost perfect in its concept and execution." It
     has a surface simplicity but portrays "a complex pattern of
     human behavior...."

18   ANON. Review of The Optimist's Daughter. Choice, 9 (Septem-
     ber), 819.
        Lacks many of the virtues of Welty's earlier master-
     pieces: comic realism, myth and "stylistic charm." Never-
     theless, the book "probes many human mysteries left unex-
     plored" by her contemporaries.

19   ANON. "Notable Nominations." Review of The Optimist's Daugh-
     ter. American Libraries, 3 (October), 1015.

1972

(ANON.)
It is an "extraordinary short novel" with a central conflict between two "contrasting value systems" represented
by the two women.

20   ANON. "Welty, Percy to be 'Firing Line Guests.'" Clarion-
Ledger Jackson Daily News, 24 December, F, p. 4.
Summarizes Welty's comments on "Firing Line." See
1973.B23.

21   ARP, TOM. "From Eudora Welty, Patient Love." Dallas Morning
News (Texas), Books, (28 May), E, p. 8.
Welty has become a literary figure, "our contemporary
Henry James or Jane Austen." Although The Optimist's
Daughter reiterates earlier themes--particularly the theme
of discovering a past which is already on the point of be-
ing lost forever--it demonstrates that Welty's powers as
a writer continue to develop.

22   BANNON, BARBARA. Review of The Optimist's Daughter. Publisher's Weekly, 201 (20 March), 61.
Welty's poetic qualities are at their best. The book is
"moving without being sentimental." It is comparable to
Agee's A Death in the Family.

23   BEAM, ALVIN. "The Welty Sense of Life." Review of The Optimist's Daughter. Cleveland Plain Dealer (Ohio), Books,
(4 June), H, p. 7.
The Optimist's Daughter occasionally is flawed and is
sometimes "too pat" in its comments on life and death, but
on the whole, it is the beautiful work of a mature and
able writer with a sure ear for the "spoken word."

24   BOATNER, MAXINE TULL. "The Character of Memory." Review of
The Optimist's Daughter. Hartford Courant (Connecticut),
(28 May), F, p. 11.
With the "seemingly simple dilemma" of Judge McKelva's
second marriage, Welty "weaves a touching and at times a
chilling story."

25   BOATWRIGHT, JAMES. "The Continuity of Love." Review of The
Optimist's Daughter. New Republic, 166 (10 June), 24-25.
The central theme of the novel is the continuity of love.
Unlike her parents' marriage, Laurel's is short, full of
ease, and perfect. It has not lasted long enough to fail.
But it also lacks continuity. With all her parents' blind-
ness--literal as well as figurative--they continued their

1972

(BOATWRIGHT, JAMES)
   relationship until the wife's death. Laurel does not recognize the value of this continuity until Fay demonstrates
   the horror of a life without love.

26   BOOZER, WILLIAM. "Optimist's Daughter is Vintage Welty."
     Commercial Appeal (Memphis, Tennessee), (11 June), p. 1.
        Like Faulkner, Welty writes of the "old verities and
     truths of the heart." The book is "beautiful," artistic,
     and "sad." It also has a humor which "is subtle and
     believable."

27   BRAVERMAN, MILLICENT. "KABC's Book of the Day." Radio review
     of The Optimist's Daughter. KABC Radio, Los Angeles,
     California, (1 May).
        With a rich sense of the comic and the mythological and
     an "uncanny ear for colloquial speech," Welty has written
     "a beautifully realized novel" which ranks with A Death in
     the Family.

28   BROYARD, ANATOLE. "Elegy with a Southern Accent." New York
     Times, (18 May), p. 45.
        Welty contrasts Mississippi traditionalism with Texas
     progressivism, but the extremes are too great. The old or-
     der of Mississippi is overly mystical, refined and obscure.
     The new order of Texas is overly comic, "like something
     drawn out of L'l Abner." The Optimist's Daughter would have
     been a better book if Welty had found some "middle ground."

29   BUNTING, CHARLES T. "The Interior World: An Interview with
     Eudora Welty." SoR, 8 (Autumn), 711-735.
        Welty discusses her early writing career, her methods of
     composition, the value of literary criticism, and the
     teaching of fiction. She also discusses at some length her
     use of the objective point of view in Losing Battles. In
     spite of the symbolism which many critics have found in her
     work, Welty insists that her primary interest was to use
     names and places that were true to particular regions.
     Even the much discussed name Phoenix is to Welty not pri-
     marily symbolic. She also insists that The Golden Apples
     is not a novel.

30   BUSWELL, MARY CATHERINE. "The Mountain Figure in the Fiction
     of Eudora Welty." WVUPP, 19 (July), 50-63.
        Drawing upon her own observations of forty years of vaca-
     tioning in the mountains of West Virginia and using descrip-
     tions of mountain people given by Horace Kephart in Our
     Southern Highlanders (New York: Macmillan, 1913), Buswell
     concludes that Welty's depiction of the mountain figure is
     accurate in both essential types and language. She bases
     this conclusion on discussions of three main types in Wel-
     ty's fiction: "The primitive who lives in isolation," "the

1972

(BUSWELL, MARY CATHERINE)
mountain man who has some family traditions," and "the more affluent mountain family." Welty's fiction deals primarily with the second type (for example, Troy Flavin in Delta Wedding).

31 C. A. B. "Welty Captures Bit of America in 'Optimist.'" Review of The Optimist's Daughter. Buffalo Evening News (New York), (12 August), B, p. 16.
Losing Battles is a "valorous failure," but The Optimist's Daughter is a success because Welty returns to her most successful subject, "the human heart."

32 CALLAWAY, JOHN. "Review of The Optimist's Daughter." CBS Radio, (15 July).
In its simplicity and perfection, The Optimist's Daughter is "one of the finest short novels in the history of American Literature." The funeral scene in particular "is a classic...."

33 CHENEY, FRANCIS NEEL. "Profound Novel of Love, Death, Old Age." Review of The Optimist's Daughter. Nashville Banner (Tennessee), (19 May), p. 58.
The novel "is beautifully structured and beautifully written." In this "profound" story of "early death, love and old age," Fay is "one of the most unlovable of Miss Welty's characters...."

34 CLARK, BETTY GAIL. "The Search for Fulfillment in the Fiction of Eudora Welty." Master's thesis, Lamar University, 1972 (Abstract, 14-v).
A major theme in Welty's fiction "is women's search for fulfillment." Such fulfillment is never complete, but those women are the most happy who "follow their own drives," particularly sexual drives, and "subordinate some of their drives to those of men." The others, through "false pride," do not allow themselves to form relationships, and thus "become frustrated, even suicidal."

35 CLEMANS, WALTER. "Chorale of Blunderers." Review of The Optimist's Daughter. Newsweek, 79 (22 May), 101.
The Optimist's Daughter is "one of the best things she has ever done." Like Losing Battles, it is a "choral work." Many characters speak their own tales in many different voices. The primary sound, however, is the chorus of people "'blundering.'"

36 CONKLIN, RICHARD W. "Novel that Relives Memories." South Bend Tribune (Indiana), (2 July), p. 9.

(CONKLIN, RICHARD W.)
Welty expresses the theme of the indelibility of "the
touch of love" better than any other writer. She makes
language serve nuance."

37 COPPEL, ALFRED. "The Keenly Reasoned Welty Prose." Review of
Losing Battles. San Francisco Examiner and Chronicle (California), This World, (25 June), p. 30.
There is not much plot and not much action, but in a distinctly feminine manner, Welty captures the essence of her
characters in concise, exact statements. In the control of
the English language, Losing Battles is "an absolutely
first rate novel."

38 CORRY, JOHN. "Intellectuals in Bloom at Spring Gathering."
New York Times, (18 May), p. 49.
Welty attended the annual ceremonies of the American
Academy of Arts and Letters and the National Institute of
Arts and Letters, where Katherine Anne Porter called her
"'one of my dearest friends'" and commented, "'I love her
and everything she ever wrote....'"

39 CURLEY, DANIEL. "A Time Exposure." Review of One Time, One
Place. NMW, 5 (Spring), 11-14.
The book is significant in two ways: it shows scenes
which appear in her fiction; and the introduction is a
brilliant commentary on her own work. A revealing aspect
of the pictures is the inclusion of many scenes and people
from Jackson.

40 CUSHMAN, SUSAN. "Eudora Welty Novel Unknowns of Life, Death,
Probed." Review of The Optimist's Daughter. Minneapolis
Star (Minnesota), (19 August), A, p. 16.
Welty's "resignation" is a "strength" rather than a lim-
itation. As in Losing Battles, she recreates "authentic
tongues" of the South. The novel is "sparing, yet powerful...."

41 DAVENPORT, GUY. "Primal Visions." Review of The Optimist's
Daughter. National Review, 24 (23 June), 697.
As in much of her earlier fiction, particularly in her
"masterpiece," Losing Battles, Welty builds upon the cyclical patterns of existence in the natural world and on the
myths that portray those patterns. Laurel is like Psyche,
and her husband Phil, Philos. Fay is "Psyche's nasty,
hateful sister." There is also a suggestion of Persephone
(as in Losing Battles), and the myth of "regenerative
virginity." In her portrayal of Fay, Welty returns to

1972

(DAVENPORT, GUY)
"Petrified Man," in which she depicts "conduct without morals or values." Laurel's is the vision of rebirth and redemption.

42   DAVIS, CHARLES E. "Welty's Old Mr. Marblehall." Expl, 30 (January), Item 40.
The source for the name "Marblehall" is probably the first line of "I Dreamt I Dwelt in Marble Halls," a romantic "escape" poem by Alfred Bunn. The allusion is very appropriate, since Mr. Marblehall "is an habitual dreamer." Mr. Marblehall's second name, Bird, is also significant with its associations of soaring above the realities of the earth.

43   DAVIS, ROBERT GORHAM. "A Worn Path." Instructor's Manual, Ten Masters: An Anthology of the Short Story, 3rd edition, New York: Harcourt Brace Jovanovich, pp. 58-59.
Notes significant patterns of development: the "purposeful journey," the movement between "the real world and the dream world," the representation of the old relationship between master and slave, and the mixture of literate and illiterate diction and grammar in Aunt Phoenix's speech.

44   _____. "Eudora Welty." Instructor's Manual, Ten Masters: An Anthology of the Short Story, 3rd edition. New York: Harcourt Brace Jovanovich, p. 58.
Comments briefly about Welty's development as a writer and specifically about several representative stories.

45   _____. "The Demonstrators." Instructor's Manual, Ten Masters: An Anthology of the Short Story, 3rd edition. New York: Harcourt Brace Jovanovich, pp. 60-62.
Welty explores the question, "is art a weapon in social struggles?" She describes the social reality of defensive whites suppressing blacks, but does not insist upon an easy answer to the social problem. The fact that she concentrates on the conservative doctor rather than upon a militant black or a liberal white suggests that the whole town—with its "sick" values—"is doomed."

46   _____. "Petrified Man." Instructor's Manual, Ten Masters: An Anthology of the Short Story, 3rd edition. New York: Harcourt Brace Jovanovich, pp. 59-60.
"Perception and revelation" are more important than plot as a means of creating character. Welty's presentation of character is enhanced by her precise use of "speech mannerisms."

1972

47   DOLLARHIDE, LOUIS. "One of Eudora Welty's Wisest Books."
      Clarion-Ledger (Jackson), (7 May), E, p. 10.
         The Optimist's Daughter is Welty's "wisest book."
      Stripped of the humor of the New Yorker version and re-
      fracted through the sensibilities of Laurel, it shows the
      ultimate irony and tragedy of life.

48   DORHEIM, JEAN. "Love, Power and Humanity: Eudora Welty Says
      It All." Milwaukee Journal (Wisconsin), (6 August), V, p. 4.
         Welty tells a "compact, beautiful and complex story of
      partial self-discovery." By the end of the novel, Laurel
      has seen through her father's failure to face reality.

49   EVETT, ROBERT. "Surprising Novel from Welty." Review of The
      Optimist's Daughter. Washington Sunday Star (Washington
      D.C.), (14 May), C, p. 5.
         The Optimist's Daughter is a book with not only wit but
      also humor, the humor of life's "utmost gravity." Much of
      Welty's earlier work was too elusive, but The Optimist's
      Daughter is a good beginning for a reader of Welty. It is
      "subtle" but readable. Fay is "one of the bitchiest vil-
      lainesses in American literature."

50   FINGER, LARRY LIVINGSTON. "Elements of the Grotesque in Se-
      lected Works of Welty, Capote, McCullers, and O'Connor."
      DAI, 33 (September-October), 1721-A--1722-A (George Peabody
      College, 1972).
         Welty and O'Connor use the grotesque to show man's "digni-
      ty and his depravity." In Welty's fiction, the grotesques
      have the most "dignity" and the most normal have the most
      depravity.

51   FLANDERS, JANE. "Optimist's Daughter Pits Old Against New."
      Pittsburgh Press (Pennsylvania), (4 June), H, p. 7.
         Welty has a "witty eye" for capturing the speech and
      manners of distinct Southern classes, but her bias in favor
      of the upper classes, "with whom she associates all the
      humane values of civilization," is a serious flaw.

52   FRAZER, JAN. "Book Corner." Review of The Optimist's Daugh-
      ter. County Broadside (Ellsworth, Maine), (21 November).
      See 1972.B53.

53   _____. "Book Review." Review of The Optimist's Daughter.
      Naples Star (Florida), (28 September).
         The Optimist's Daughter is "full of quiet wisdom" about
      human relationships. It presents an "accurate picture" of
      how people react to death.

1972

54   FULLER, EDMUND. "Miss Welty, Mississippi and Meaning." Review of The Optimist's Daughter. Wall Street Journal, 179 (1 June), p. 16.
       In its compression, it reflects greater "implications about living" than many longer works, including Losing Battles. One possible flaw is the character of Fay, who, according to Forster's definition, is a "flat character." But "there are flat people," and Welty presents Fay "convincingly."

55   GAINES, ERVIN J. "A Master at Work." Review of The Optimist's Daughter. Minneapolis Tribune (Minnesota), (21 May), D, p. 8.
       In her attention to details and significant gestures, Welty creates in miniature the great themes of life. Her characters are neither good nor evil; they are merely "enmeshed in life's web." The writing "is a marvel of craftsmanship" and Welty is "one of our great authors."

56   GEISMAR, MAXWELL. "Woman of Culture and Feeling." Review of The Optimist's Daughter. Chicago Sun-Times (Illinois), Showcase, (28 May), V, p. 22.
       Like her earlier work, The Optimist's Daughter is "artfully simple." In plain, "spare prose," Welty depicts a world which is filled with genuine human feeling. The major shortcoming of the book is Welty's failure to question the values of the Southern middle class.

57   GORDON, JOHN. "Eudora Welty Deep in Mississippi." Review of One Time, One Place. Rocky Mountain News, (9 January), p. 13.
       Although the photographs are not remarkable as works of art, they are interesting revelations of the point of view of a very "articulate" writer. By combining the photographs into a single book, Welty--whether she wants to or not--is making "a social document."

58   GOSLINER, KATHY. "Memory Petrified by Sleepwalkers in a Dream." Review of The Optimist's Daughter. Rocky Mountain News, (20 August), Startime, p. 15.
       Lacks "adventure and surprise," but demonstrates "superb craftsmanship." Welty combines the literal truth and the fantastic qualities of a dream.

59   GOVAN, CHRISTINE. "High Point of a Career." Chattanooga Times (Tennessee), (9 July), B, p. 2.
       In form and content, The Optimist's Daughter is Welty's most perfect book. With "insight" and "sympathy," she

(GOVAN, CHRISTINE)
   fits every character and every detail into a perfectly
   developed structure.

60   HAINS, FRANK.   "Eudora Welty Gets Gold Medal from American
        Academy." Clarion-Ledger (Jackson), (21 May), D, p. 14.
        Katherine Anne Porter presented the award in New York
        ceremonies.

61   _____. "Eudora Welty's 'One Place' Receives a Christopher
        Award." Jackson Daily News, (22 February), p. 20.
        According to Father Richard Armstrong, director of the
        Christophers, Welty (and others) received the award for
        using her "'God-given talents to provide high quality
        literature and entertainment for the general public.'"

62   _____. "Miss Welty Doesn't Want to Be 'Anybody's Damn Grand-
        mother.'" Jackson Daily News, (17 August), D, p. 6.
        Hains summarizes Henry Mitchell's interview with Welty
        which appeared in the Washington Post on Sunday, 13 August.
        He includes Welty's comments about being evicted from a
        Jackson restaurant, and her reactions to various letters,
        especially one from a man in Taiwan who wanted Welty to be
        a grandmother to his children.

63   HALL, WADE.   "Eudora Welty: Her Comic Sense as Sure as Ever."
        Review of The Optimist's Daughter. Courier-Journal and
        Times (Louisville, Kentucky), (25 June), F, p. 5.
        Welty combines symbolism and folk patterns in the crea-
        tion of structure, character, and comic technique. The
        result is--like Losing Battles--an example of Welty's "un-
        flagging talent."

64   HALLIDAY, MARK.   "The Craft and Wisdom of Eudora Welty."   Re-
        view of The Optimist's Daughter. Providence Journal
        (Rhode Island), (9 July), H, p. 15.
        Welty's style and construction are "audacious" but cor-
        rect. With "craft and wisdom," she constructs metaphors
        which are often far-fetched but usually insightful and
        tells a story with "relentless perspicacity."

65   HARTLEY, LODWICK.   "Eudora Welty's The Optimist's Daughter."
        Review of The Optimist's Daughter. News and Observer
        (Raleigh, North Carolina), (4 June), IV, p. 6.
        In a "nearly flawless work," Welty presents poetic lan-
        guage of great beauty in which ambiguity is part of the
        design of the whole work. In spite of her vulgarity, Fay
        is never a completely unsympathetic character; nor is the

137

1972

(HARTLEY, LODWICK)
more sophisticated Laurel flawless. Both are part of the
intentional irresolutions of the theme.

66   HICKS, GRANVILLE. "Universal Regionalist." Review of The
Optimist's Daughter. New Leader 55 (7 August), p. 19.
Welty usually writes about upper-class people in the
South (except in that "tour de force," Losing Battles),
and generally accepts upper-class values. But in The Optimist's Daughter, she looks at those values "discriminat-
ingly." It is a rich novel in which the personal crises
of several people unfold. Although the setting is regional, Welty presents a universal theme, "the human condition."

67   HILL, WILLIAM B., S. J. Review of The Optimist's Daughter.
America, 126 (20 May), 549.
Except for the fact that Fay "is a bit over done," the
book is "magnificent." It is disciplined and exact.

68   _____. "The Optimist's Daughter." Best Sellers, (15 May),
pp. 95-96.
Unlike many modern novelists, Welty makes every word
count. Her plots are like Frank Lloyd Wright's "best
architecture"; they are perfectly blended with setting.

69   HOLLENBECK, RALPH. "The Optimist's Daughter." Parade of
Books, (4 June), pp. 2-3.
In perhaps her "most brilliant" achievement, Welty cre-
ates "the old medieval conflict between good and evil."
In representing this conflict, Welty is true to human
psychology.

70   HOLLIDAY, BARBARA. "Some Weltian Insights on Life, Dying and
Love." Review of The Optimist's Daughter. Detroit Free
Press (Michigan), (21 May), C, p. 5.
Welty has captured not only the manners of a Southern
funeral, but also makes a serious comment on understanding
the meaning of life. If Fay's reaction to this meaning
seems too distorted, it is because Welty reveals Fay from
Laurel's point of view.

71   HOLMAN, HUGH C. The Roots of Southern Writing: Essays on the
Literature of the American South. Athens, Georgia: University of Georgia Press, p. 90.
Holman links Welty and Porter as writers who "have used
highly refined and almost poetic, brief art forms to state
their visions of experience."

72   HOWELL, ELMO. "Eudora Welty and the Use of Place in Southern
        Fiction." ArQ, 28 (Autumn), 248-256.
        Welty faces a problem common to most Southern writers:
     being aware of her cultural tradition without becoming
     self-conscious about it. Her use of the Southern setting
     is effective in "A Worn Path," but in Losing Battles, she
     lets her consciousness of place eclipse human values. In-
     stead of people, she reproduces "the texture of life in
     the hill country of North Mississippi."

73   JANEWAY, ELIZABETH. Review of The Optimist's Daughter.
        SatR, 55 (1 July), 60.
        Welty shows "the force and reality of the accidents of
     life" but is too simplistic in her representation of Fay.
     After Faulkner, Fay's type is too easy to attack. If
     Welty had placed greater emphasis on Adele's point of view
     and less on Laurel's, the novel would have given a more
     balanced view of humanity. Adele perceives the all-grasp-
     ing vulgarity of Fay, and yet she can still accept Fay as
     a human being.

74   KEEFE, ROBERT S. Untitled. Washington and Lee University
        News Service, (28 May).
        Announces that Welty will receive an honorary degree from
     Washington and Lee at the June 1 commencement exercises.
     Notes tribute Welty received in Shenandoah.

75   KING, LARRY L. "Surviving a Death in the Family." Review of
        The Optimist's Daughter. Life, 72 (26 May), 25.
        Welty faces "the harsher psychic realities" and presents,
     in a style "like a dream," the serious message that "we
     are all victims of each other." It is a serious book in
     which humor "is grotesque or bizarre."

76   K. R. "Stuff of Life at a Funeral." Review of The Optimist's
        Daughter. New Haven Register (Connecticut), (28 May).
        Although The Optimist's Daughter may appear "to be about
     mundane, unexciting affairs," it "is elegiac in tone" and
     "is both moving and significant."

77   KRIEGMAN, ALAN M. "Arts Media." Washington Post (Washington,
        D.C.), (2 December), B, p. 2.
        Notes that Welty accepted an invitation to the two-day
     symposium on the arts and media at the National Academy of
     Science auditorium.

78   KUEHL, LINDA. Interview with Eudora Welty. Paris Review, 14
        (Fall), 72-97.

1972

(KUEHL, LINDA)
Welty comments about literary likes and acquaintances, the writing and critical reception of Losing Battles, the undesirability of someone writing her biography, her friendship with Faulkner, stories of social concern, the inspiration for "Powerhouse," her first stories, the source for Morgana in The Golden Apples, repeated themes and character types in her fiction, her methods of revising, and her use of metaphor.

79   LANE, GEORGE. "Chinaberry Trees and Garden Party Chat." Review of The Optimist's Daughter. Patriot-Ledger, (16 May), p. 28.
Welty's method of narration is indirect and is sometimes "useful" but "other times perversely coy." Because Fay is a "two-dimensional" character, her "ignorance" and "gracelessness" fail to evoke much interest.

80   LAWSON, ANNA. "Precise Parts of an Art that Entertains, Explains." Roanoke Times (Virginia), (21 May), B, p. 13.
Discusses the central theme of The Optimist's Daughter: "the past must be understood and the fact of the future accepted for Laurel to go on living a meaningful present." This theme is developed through such recurring symbols of time as "clocks and chimes" and by emphasis on vision and seeing.

81   LEIGHTON, BETTY. "Eudora Welty Shows Artistry in Depicting Man's Failings." Review of The Optimist's Daughter. Winston-Salem Journal (North Carolina), (8 July), D, p. 4.
The Optimist's Daughter is a simple yet compressed statement about "the patterns and dreams that constitute the mystery of life." Laurel can invoke memories of the past; Fay cannot.

82   No Entry

83   L. M. J. "The Optimist's Daughter." Review of The Optimist's Daughter. Chattanooga News-Free Press (Tennessee), (1 October).
The Optimist's Daughter is short but "very well written" and may be her best work. She brings "a real life situation to her characters."

84   LUCID, ROBERT F. "Aristocrat of American Letters." Review of
      The Optimist's Daughter. San Francisco Sunday Examiner and
      Chronicle (California), This World, (25 June), p. 39.
         Lucid notes that the aristocratic mystique of Welty in-
      cludes an unwillingness of her admirers to analyze her
      prose style. The character of Fay, however, deserves anal-
      ysis. In her vulgarity, Fay is all we flee from and yet
      she is much more memorable than the aristocratic and sensi-
      tive Laurel.

85   _____. "Nicer Moments of the Fictional Year." San Francisco
      Sunday Examiner and Chronicle (California), This World,
      (31 December), p. 26.
         Lucid does not consider 1972 a great year for American
      fiction, but a "nice" one. One of the "nice" books is
      Welty's The Optimist's Daughter, with its unforgettable
      character, Fay.

86   MANNING, MARGARET. "Survival--Strangest Fantasy." Review of
      The Optimist's Daughter. Boston Evening Globe (Massachu-
      setts), (22 May), p. 20.
         Welty probably will be rated a "minor" writer because she
      avoids "the guttier facts of life." But in her depiction
      of the old Southern values of "honor and value," and in her
      mastery of the craft of fiction, her work will endure. The
      Optimist's Daughter is "lyrical" but "simple."

87   MARX, PAUL. "The Moment the Shutter Snaps." Review of One
      Time, One Place. Nation, 214 (17 January), 92.
         The method of this "beautiful book" reveals a prime qual-
      ity of her fiction. She does not intrude upon her charac-
      ters; she presents them as they are in one point of space
      and time. Welty does not attempt to moralize or give a
      pictorial history of the times.

88   MAY, CHARLES E. "Le Roi Mehaigne in Welty's 'Keela, The Out-
      cast Indian Maiden.'" MFS, 18 (Winter), 559-566.
         The name Le Roi is little king, and, therefore, he has a
      more dominant place in the story than most critics have
      given him. He is a scapegoat figure and is quite aware of
      the role he is playing. He carries away not only the sins
      of Steve, but also those of the entire South.

89   M. D. "The Limits of Love." Review of The Optimist's Daugh-
      ter. Time, 99 (5 June), 88, 90.
         Welty's writing has always had "immense tenderness" but
      "no sentimentality at all" and a sure sense of structure
      and comedy. Losing Battles was a "raucous hymn to rural

1972

(M. D.)
life," but The Optimist's Daughter is a "more inward, con-
templative book than any she has written.

90   MITCHELL, HENRY. "Eudora Welty: Rose-Garden Realist, Story-
teller of the South." Washington Post (Washington, D.C.),
(13 August), L, p. 1.
Mitchell relates a long, rambling interview with Welty
which includes letters from her admirers, comments about
literary acquaintances, and specific observations about
Losing Battles and The Optimist's Daughter. She denies
that Losing Battles is comparable to The Tempest (as suggested by Reynolds Price). She considers Austen her favorite writer and admits that she was not particularly
influenced by Milton. The Optimist's Daughter is her first
directly autobiographical work, with Laurel's mother based
on her own mother and the boys based on her brothers.

91   _____. "Miss Welty Talks at Home." Roanoke Times (Virginia),
(10 September), B, p. 14.
See 1972.B90.

92   MOODY, MINNIE HITE. "Fine Regional Novel Has Universal
Theme." Columbus Dispatch (Ohio), (18 June).
Welty presents not a regional theme, but a universal one:
the necessity for survival. She presents this theme in a
"truly fine book" in which she distinguishes carefully the
"varied cultures which have produced Laurel and Fay."

93   MORTON, KATHRYN. "About Books." Review of The Optimist's
Daughter. Virginian-Pilot (Norfolk, Virginia), (25 June),
C, p. 6.
Notes that as the work of "one of the best, maybe the
very best writer in America today," The Optimist's Daughter
is "tight, whole and simple." It also has great depths and
subtleties that appear with re-readings.

94   MOSS, HOWARD. Review of The Optimist's Daughter. Clarion-
Ledger (Jackson) (28 May), G, p. 11.
See 1972.B95.

95   _____. "Eudora Welty's New Novel about Death and Class." Review of The Optimist's Daughter. New York Times Book Review, (21 May), VII, p. 1, 8.
In The Optimist's Daughter, Welty dramatizes the clash
between two sets of values: those of a refined, sensitive
woman of the upper classes, and those of a vulgar, insensi-
tive, materialistic woman of the lower classes. The

(MOSS, HOWARD)
creation of such extreme opposites could create stereotypes
and sentimentality, but in Welty's hands, it does not. Although Fay is vulgar, she has energy to face the future;
although Laurel has civilization, she has an almost effete
obsession with the past. Thus, Welty neutralizes the ex-
tremes to maintain an equilibrium. The Optimist's Daughter
is "the best book Eudora Welty has ever written."

96 MURRAY, MICHELE. "Eudora Welty Traces a Circle of Empty
Lives." Review of The Optimist's Daughter. National Observer, 11 (10 June), 22.
As in Losing Battles, Welty equates isolation from family
and community with death. But in The Optimist's Daughter,
the central character, Laurel, is so overshadowed by the
vulgar character, Fay, that the serious theme of isolation
is obscured.

97 NEWSOM, THOMAS B. "Local Values of Death." Review of The
Optimist's Daughter. St. Louis Post-Dispatch (Missouri),
(6 August), F, p. 3.
Welty has proved once again that the "South of Faulkner
and Warren" is a viable subject for the modern writer.
Laurel represents the old South and Fay, the new, but Welty
is not too harsh with Fay. Instead of traditional and fad-
ing values, Fay has "a certain strength."

98 NICKELL, TOM. "Welty Sparse Again, and Excellent." San Anto-
nio Express-News (Texas), (8 October), Sunday One, p. 17.
As a "succinct" autobiographical statement, The Optimist's Daughter is "a collection of perceptions for anyone
who appreciates fine writing" and a comment "about the act
of survival."

99 NORRIS, MELINDA. "Eudora Welty Novelette Is Thinner than a
Praline, about as Live as Dixie." Daily World (10 November), p. 7.
Critics have invented "profundities for the terse prose."
In fact, The Optimist's Daughter is an "overinflated novella." The characters are all stereotypes and rather than
projecting irony, they project self-pity. The novel does
not come to terms in any way with real social concerns.

100 PARRILL, WILLIAM. "Welty in Top Form Says Critic of Novel."
Review of The Optimist's Daughter. Nashville Tennessean,
(14 May), F, p. 14.
Losing Battles was somewhat unsatisfactory in its length
and in its evidence of the labor that went into creating

1972

(PARRILL, WILLIAM)
it. But in The Optimist's Daughter, Welty proves that she
can master the form of the short novel. Unlike Losing
Battles, "there is hardly a word extra or a word mis-
placed." The story is "simple" in form but complex in its
presentation of human relationships.

101 POLK, PEGGY. "Delves Deeply into Lives of Characters." Gary
Post-Tribune (Indiana), (28 July).
See 1972.B102.

102 _____. "Echoes of Death." Review of The Optimist's Daughter.
Memphis Scimitar (Tennessee), (28 July).
Few writers express "the deepest currents of her charac-
ters' lives" as well as Welty.

103 REAL, JERE. "Miss Welty Collects Southern Album." Review of
One Time, One Place. Richmond News-Leader (Virginia), (12
April).
The photographs lack "self-conscious artistry and delib-
erate social comment...." Instead, they offer a "very
human vision."

104 ROGERS, W. G. "Miss Welty Writes Fascinating Tale." Youngs-
town Vindicator (Ohio), (21 May).
See 1972.B105.

105 _____. Review of The Optimist's Daughter. Book Service for
Newspapers (edited especially for newspapers every week by
the Saturday Review), (20 May), pp. 1-2.
Like Agee's A Death in the Family, The Optimist's Daughter is a relatively "great novel." It has nothing to do
with current social concerns, and therefore may be "an old
fashioned tale," but "its substance is everlasting to human
nature."

106 RUBIN, LOUIS D., JR. The Writer in the South: Studies in a
Literary Community. Athens, Georgia: University of Georgia Press, p. 115.
Rubin notes that in many of Welty's books, including
The Golden Apples and Losing Battles, the community clashes
with the "private sensibility." The community sees knowledge and consciousness as a threat to its values.

107 RUSS, MARGARET. "Eudora Welty Quietly Tells Tale of Death."
Buffalo Courier-Express (New York), (28 May), p. 18.
The Optimist's Daughter "is a simple, little story,"
but it "makes the ordinary most extraordinary." At its

1972

(RUSS, MARGARET)
center is the struggle between Laurel, who looks deeply
into life and death, and Fay, who sees everything super-
ficially."

108 SANDRAF, NANCY. "New Contemporary Novel." Review of The
Optimist's Daughter. Worcester Telegram (Massachusetts),
(6 August).
Welty's story is "so deceptively simple and clear," that
it is difficult to analyze. Nevertheless, her theme is
universal, and her reputation is well-deserved.

109 SCIAKY, FRANCOISE. "Eye View." Interview with Welty about
The Optimist's Daughter. Women's Wear Daily, (19 June),
p. 8.
Welty comments about her family, writing book reviews,
lecturing, traveling by train, and the character Fay in
The Optimist's Daughter. Fay "'is unfeeling and dense.
She misses out on just about everything.'"

110 _____. "Healthy, Welty and Wise. WWD Interviews Miss Welty."
Jackson Daily News, (26 June), C, p. 2.
See 1972.B109.

111 SHAFFNER, CLAIR. "Southern Upmanship." Review of The Optimist's Daughter. Charlotte Observer (North Carolina), (11
June), D, p. 5.
The Optimist's Daughter is an "excellent" book, far better than the reader might have expected after reading
Losing Battles. With great sympathy, Welty presents
"depth of character and richness of humor."

112 SKAGGS, MERRILL MAGUIRE. The Folk of Southern Fiction.
Athens, Georgia: University of Georgia Press, pp. 234-248.
In discussions of The Robber Bridegroom, Delta Wedding,
The Golden Apples, "Lily Daw and the Three Ladies," "Death
of a Traveling Salesman," "No Place for You My Love," "The
Burning," "Asphodel," "The Whistle," "A Piece of News,"
"Kin," Losing Battles, The Ponder Heart, and "Why I Live
at the P.O.," Skaggs explains how Welty uses conventions of
the nineteenth-century local colorists in very inventive
ways.

113 SMITH, CAROL PORTER. "The Journey Motif in the Collected
Works of Eudora Welty." DAI, 32, 5807-A--5808-A (Univer-
sity of Maryland, 1971).
Smith traces the use of the journey motif throughout
Welty's fiction. She notes specific symbolic qualities of

1972

(SMITH, CAROL PORTER)
the journey in specific works and concludes that Welty
uses the motif "as a conscious artistic choice."

114 SPACKS, PATRICIA MEYER. Review of The Optimist's Daughter.
HudR, 25 (Autumn), 508-510.
Welty's powers are still strong with "Chekovian under-
statement" and "Faulknerian verve." She demonstrates her
observation of detail, her ear for language and her comic
sense. Like her central character, Laurel, she comes "to
terms with actuality without succumbing to it."

115 STAHL, THOMAS H. Review of The Optimist's Daughter. America,
127 (9 September), 160.
The Optimist's Daughter is "more substantial and sadder"
than Welty's earlier work.

116 SUDLER, BARBARA. "Eudora Welty's Sensitive Perception Features 'Optimist's Daughter.'" Denver Post (Colorado), (6
August), pp. 12, 14.
The serio-comic scenes are masterpieces, but the main
characters tend to be too stereotyped. Fay is so "bad"
and Laurel so "good," that the reader is "incredulous."
Nevertheless, Welty "is an accomplished and secure novelist," and The Optimist's Daughter "may be one of 1972's
award winners."

117 TARBOX, RAYMOND. "Eudora Welty's Fiction: The Salvation
Theme." AI, 29 (Spring), 70-91.
Traces R. J. Almansi's "Hypnagogic Phenomenon" (face-
breast equation) through several of Welty's stories. By
showing parallels between passages in the stories and
statements from Almansi, Tarbox finds the "face-breast
equation" in Losing Battles, "A Memory," "Why I Live at
the P.O.," "Clytie," "The Purple Hat," and "Death of a
Traveling Salesman." Characters who are intensely interested in breasts or faces have blended in infancy the
mother's breast with her face. Thus, the characters who
are isolated--as most of Welty's are--seek gratification
through either face or breast fixations.

118 THEROUX, PAUL. "The Details of Death." Review of The Optimist's Daughter. Washington Post (Washington, D.C.) Book
World, 14 May, VI, p. 5.
Its lack of ornament and symbol makes the book seem at
times simple and clumsy, but it is concrete and vigorous
and is "a superb affirmation of life and healing."

146

119   . "The Details of Death." Review of The Optimist's
Daughter. Chicago Tribune (Illinois) Book World, (14 May),
IX, p. 5.
See 1972.B118.

120 THOMAS, LEROY. "An Analysis of the Theme of Alienation in the
Fictional Works of Five Contemporary Southern Writers."
DAI, 33 (July-August), 768-A (Oklahoma State University,
1971).
Thomas relates Welty's fiction to the theme of existen-
tialism found in the works of Sartre, Camus, and Unamuno.

121 THOMAS, PHIL. "Finds Life Links." Review of The Optimist's
Daughter. West Memphis Times (Arkansas), (5 July).
See 1972.B127.

122   . "Heroine Finds Life in Tale for Women." Review of
The Optimist's Daughter. Asbury Park Press (New Jersey),
(12 June).
See 1972.B127.

123   . "Mississippian's New Novel is Concise, Moving Story."
Clarksdale Press Register (Mississippi), (22 July).
See 1972.B127.

124   . "Moving Account of Life." Review of The Optimist's
Daughter. Ellwood City Ledger (Pennsylvania), (14 June).
See 1972.B127.

125   . "Moving Novel." Review of The Optimist's Daughter.
Oakland Tribune (California), (9 July).
See 1972.B127.

126   . (signed L. O.). "Optimist's Daughter Moving Welty
Story." Indianapolis Star (Indiana), (9 July), VIII, p. 10.
See 1972.B127.

127   . "The Optimist's Daughter Novel of the South by Eudora
Welty." Springfield Republican (Massachusetts), (29 October), LT, p. 9.
Welty develops what seems to be a simple plot "in tight,
highly polished sentences . . . ."

128   . Review of The Optimist's Daughter. North Penn Reporter (Lansdale, Pennsylvania), (3 June).
See 1972.B127.

129   . Review of The Optimist's Daughter. Shreveport Times
(Louisiana), (2 July), F, p. 13.
See 1972.B127.

1972

130   THOMAS, SIDNEY. "Novelist Captures Small Town South." Review
       of The Optimist's Daughter. Atlanta Constitution (Geor-
       gia), (4 June), C, p. 8.
          Welty describes the people and manners of Mississippi
       with precision and in "the most sparing of prose." The
       result is "a lovely, cleansing book...."

131   THOMPSON, VICTOR H. "Life's Impact is Oblique: A Study of
       Obscurantism in the Writings of Eudora Welty." DAI, 33
       (September-October), 1745-A (Rutgers University, 1972).
          Demonstrates that Welty's efforts to depict the myster-
       ies of human experience sometimes lead her to obscurantism.
       But in her best fiction, she maintains a balance between
       mystery and obscurity through control of source material,
       point of view and symbolic context.

132   TRAIL, GEORGE Y. "Faulknerian Theme Lacks Faulkner's Sympa-
       thy." Houston Post (Texas), Spotlight, (11 June), p. 19.
          If Welty had presented Laurel's "sensitive righteous-
       ness" ironically, she might have expressed more sympathy
       for Fay and made all the characters more human. As the
       novel stands, however, the case is so "loaded" against Fay,
       that the reader is forced to take her side. Faulkner is
       much more sympathetic and honest than Welty in his treat-
       ment of "the descendants of the carpet baggers."

133   WEEKS, EDWARD. Review of The Optimist's Daughter. Atlantic,
       229 (June), 111-112.
          The Optimist's Daughter contrasts two "breeds of Southern
       culture" which are represented in the novel by Laurel and
       Fay. Laurel looks to the past, but Fay to the future.
       Laurel is sensitive, but Fay is "aggressive" and "crude."

134   WOOD, MICHAEL. "Cunning Time." Review of The Optimist's
       Daughter. New York Review of Books, 18 (29 June), p. 8-9.
          Like Musgrove in The Robber Bridegroom and Uncle Ponder
       in The Ponder Heart, Laurel is unwilling (or unable) to
       survive in a world where most people are cunning and self-
       serving. Fay is the opposite, and her one principle is
       survival. Because the book is told from the point of view
       of Laurel, Fay's avariciousness seems particularly offen-
       sive. But the Fays of the world must be reckoned with.
       The only flaws in an otherwise excellent book are Welty's
       occasional uses of heavy-handed symbolism.

135   YARDLEY, JONATHAN. "About Books." Review of The Optimist's
       Daughter. Greensboro News (North Carolina), (21 May), E,
       p. 3.
          See 1972.B136.

148

136   _____. Review of The Optimist's Daughter. Boston Review of
       the Arts, (July), 57-58.
       Although many critics consider Welty a sentimentalist,
       her work is actually "as tough and complex as a writer
       could" make. Her fiction is the best in America, and The
       Optimist's Daughter is among her best works. In The Opti-
       mist's Daughter, she develops the theme that mankind is
       fated to "blunder" but "she finds real humanity in the er-
       rors her people make, and she views them with humor and
       affection."

1973 A BOOKS

1   HOWARD, ZELMA TURNER. The Rhetoric of Eudora Welty's Short
     Stories. Jackson, Mississippi: University and College
     Press of Mississippi.
         In brief analyses of representative stories, Howard uses
     the methods and terminology of Wayne C. Booth's Rhetoric of
     Fiction. She devotes a chapter to each of the following
     subjects: "Narrative," "Archetype, and Semantics," "Use of
     Rhetoric to Individualize Experience," and "Time as a Rhe-
     torical Device."

1973 B SHORTER WRITINGS

1   ALBRITTON, A. B. "Pulitzer Surprizes the First Lady of South-
     ern Letters." Commercial Appeal (Memphis), 8 May, p. 1.
         Welty notes The Optimist's Daughter is close to her own
     experience and that it is in essence "'a coming to terms
     with loss and grief and a realization of the meaning of
     love and affection.'" She also mentions a forthcoming
     collection of short stories.

2   ANON. "Miss Welty's Collections in Archives." Clarion-Ledger
     Jackson Daily News, (8 April), H, p. 1.
         Notes that the Mississippi Department of Archives and
     History "has the largest collection of Eudora Welty materi-
     al in the world." Also lists some of the holdings and
     gives the scope and nature of the collection.

3   ANON. "Mississippi Pays Tribute to Welty." New York Times,
     (21 April), p. 24.
         Notes the proclamation of May 2 as Eudora Welty Day in
     Mississippi. The celebration will include exhibitions re-
     lating to her work, readings by the author, and perform-
     ances of the stage adaptation of The Ponder Heart.

1973

4   ANON. "'Ponder Heart' Opening Recalls First on B'Way."
    Jackson Daily News, (25 April), D, p. 8.
        Describes the new opening of The Ponder Heart including
    Welty's gift of a Southern ham to Una Merkel who played
    Edna Earle.

5   ANON. "Many Honors for Miss Welty." Clarion-Ledger, Jackson
    Daily News, (29 April), H, p. 1.
        Summarizes the scheduled events for Eudora Welty Day on
    May 2.

6   ANON. "Army Head Resigns." New York Times, (2 May), Notes on
    People, p. 41.
        Notes that May 2 is Eudora Welty Day in Mississippi and
    that Welty will give readings of her works.

7   ANON. "Eudora Welty Honored by Native Mississippi." New York
    Times, (8 May), L, p. 32.
        Mississippi Governor William L. Waller proclaimed "Eudora
    Welty Day." Welty was honored for winning the Pulitzer
    Prize and for the high quality of her writing.

8   ANON. "Handel Concert to Honor Miss Welty." Jackson Daily
    News, (8 May), p. 22.
        Announces that the Southern Academy of Letters, Arts and
    Sciences will present Welty with the Order of the South
    award. The presentation will include "a concert of praise
    to honor Miss Welty by the Cathedral Chamber Society."

9   ANON. "Welty Book Wins Pulitzer for Fiction." Clarion-Ledg-
    er, (8 May), p. 1.
        Notes that Welty--who "has been hailed as a leading ex-
    ponent of the so-called Southern school of letters"--won
    the Pulitzer prize for The Optimist's Daughter. Most of
    the article is dedicated to the winners of other awards.

10 ANON. "Icing on Eudora's Cake." Jackson Daily News, (9 May),
    p. 14.
        Notes that Welty has already won more prestigious prizes
    than the Pulitzer and that--in terms of prizes--she has
    already equalled Faulkner.

11 ANON. "A Surprise for Prize Winner." San Diego Union, (13
    May), E, p. 6.
        Welty gives advice for young writers: "'read.'"

12 ANON. "Eudora Welty Receives Degree." Queens College Close-
    Up, 5 (Summer).

(ANON.)
Summarizes Welty's achievements including her writing
awards and her other honorary degrees from Smith, University of Wisconsin, University of the South, Denison University, and Millsaps College. For being "one of the most
important writers in America today," Welty was awarded an
honorary Doctor of Humanities Degree by Queens College.

13   ANON. "MVCS Prof Writes Study on Miss Welty." Jackson Daily
News, (11 July).
Discusses Zelma Howard's, The Rhetoric of Eudora Welty.
According to Howard, Welty uses a "deceptively simple
style" to present the mysteries and complexities of "man's
inner experiences...." (See 1973.A1).

14   ANON. Mississippi State College for Women Alumnae News, 90
(Fall), 2.
Mentions a Eudora Welty award to be given by Mississippi
Educational T.V. for "outstanding productions for broad-
casting." The subject should be Twentieth Century American
life. Welty will help select the manuscripts.

15   ANON. "Writers Visit Prairie to Extol Its Soul, Willa Cather." New York Times, (30 October), p. 36.
Welty observes that Cather's characters are most notable
for their rebelliousness and that they "gain self-discov-
ery, rather than glory...." Her prairie settings are dynamic rather than static.

16   ANON. "Photographer Welty Captivates N.Y. Crowd." New York
Times, (16 November), C, p. 9.
Describes Welty's presentation of photographs from One
Time, One Place at the Museum of Modern Art. Notes that
Welty made no judgments "about poverty, race or society,"
but instead made "an eloquent statement of human endurance."

17   BALAKIAN, NONA. "A Day of One's Own." New York Times, (27
May), VII, p. 23.
Describes some of the events of the Eudora Welty celebration which extended from May 1-6. Balakian includes comments about the party at Welty's home and the significance
of Welty's writing. Welty has made her home town "a cross-
road of the world."

18   _____. "Welty Transforms Jackson to Crossroads of the World."
Jackson Daily News, (31 May), E, p. 5.
See Balakian, 1973.B17.

19   BARRY, FLO SCOTT. "Don't Leave Home, Eudora." Mississippi
State College for Women Alumnae News, 90 (Fall), 3.
Gives Welty's reaction to receiving the Pulitzer Prize
for The Optimist's Daughter. Also gives her view of critics' dissections of The Robber Bridegroom: "'People ask
if it is Fascism, Communism, or absurd things.'"

1973

20   *BLACKWELL, LOUISE. "Eudora Welty's Roots vs. Yellow Gui-
     tars." Separata da Revisa de Lettres.
     Listed in Mississippi Quarterly annual bibliography.

21   BRADFORD, M. E. "Miss Eudora's Picture Book." MissQ, 26
     (Fall), 659-662.
        The pictures foreshadow Welty's methods as a writer:
     they reflect a spontaneous response to the truths of life.
     Welty sees her subjects with no abstract theories about the
     nature of art and life but only with the sense of "shock
     and sympathy."

22   BROOKS, CLEANTH. "The Past Reexamined: The Optimist's Daugh-
     ter." MissQ, 26 (Fall), 577-587.
        In this "small masterpiece," Welty contrasts Laura's re-
     discovery of the past with Fay's obsession with the pres-
     ent. Like Faulkner's Flem Snopes and Jason Compson, Fay's
     rejection of the past makes her less than human, and
     Laura's rediscovery of the past revives her humanity and
     saves her from Fay.

23   BUCKLEY, WILLIAM F., JR. "The Southern Imagination: An
     Interview with Eudora Welty and Walker Percy." MissQ, 26
     (Fall), 493-516. (Reprint of the Firing Line T.V. program
     conducted by W. F. Buckley, Jr. and taped at WMAA in Jack-
     son, Mississippi on 12 December, 1972).
        Buckley presses the question: what is distinctive about
     Southern Literature? Welty answers that a writer must
     have a thorough knowledge of place, but whether that place
     is North or South, East or West is unimportant. What is
     important is that the writer sees the world from a clearly
     defined viewpoint. In spite of Buckley's directed ques-
     tions, Welty does not admit that ignorance, racism, and
     violence are part of the Southern way.

24   CAPERS, CHARLOTTE. "Eudora Welty Day on May 2 to Highlight
     Arts Festival." Clarion-Ledger Jackson Daily News, (8
     April), H, p. 1.
        Discusses Welty's international fame as well as her local
     reputation. Notes that Welty is as friendly and unpreten-
     tious with neighbors as she is with visiting "literary
     superstars."

25   CARSON, FRANKLIN D. "'The Song of the Wandering Aengus' Allu-
     sions in Eudora Welty's The Golden Apples." NMW, 6
     (Spring), 14-18.
        Yeats' "Song of the Wandering Aengus" is one of the cen-
     tral structural elements in the book. It is significant

(CARSON, FRANKLIN D.)
    not only in "June Recital" where it is quoted but through-
    out the entire collection.

26 CHAMBERS, ELSIE MAY. "'You Are Kidding' Was Response of Eudo-
    ra Welty to Pulitzer News." Clarion-Ledger, (8 May), A,
    p. 1.
        Welty claims that The Optimist's Daughter was the most
    difficult of her books to write because it was the closest
    to her personal experience. She also considers it her
    best book.

27 CLARK, CHARLES C. "The Robber Bridegroom: Realism and Fan-
    tasy on the Natchez Trace." MissQ, 26 (Fall), 625-638.
        The central theme of the novel is the doubleness of all
    things, particularly truth and fantasy, good and evil,
    merchant and robber. Clark develops this thesis in a dis-
    cussion of sources and commentaries about modern culture.

28 CLARK, EMILY. "Miss Eudora Welty Gets Another Honor." Clar-
    ion Ledger, (11 May), A, p. 13.
        Notes that Dean Robert Oliver of St. Andrews Cathedral
    (Jackson), presented Welty with the Order of the South
    Award from the Southern Academy of Letters, Arts and Sci-
    ences. Clark also summarizes Welty's achievements.

29 COOLEY, JOHN R. "Blacks as Primitives in Eudora Welty's
    Fiction." BSUF, 4 (Summer), 20-28.
        Welty's portrayals of blacks are oversimplified and
    therefore do not adequately present the theme of exploita-
    tion of blacks by a white society. In "Keela," Lee Roy
    does not have a very clear sense of the way he had been
    exploited. In "A Worn Path," Phoenix is primarily a some-
    what stereotyped countrified black. Of all her blacks,
    "Powerhouse" comes the closest to being a distinct person-
    ality with a fairly thorough understanding of his position
    in a white society, but Welty fails to distinguish between
    the narrator's point of view and the rather limited point
    of view of the white audience which accepts Powerhouse's
    primitivism as their temporary escape from the civilized
    white society.

30 CORRY, JOHN. "Pulitzers Go to Washington Post, Frankel;
    Frankel, Championship Season." New York Times, (8 May),
    p. 1.
        Notes that Welty--"whose first novel was published in
    1941"--won the prize for fiction.

1973

31 CULBERTSON, JEAN. "Welty's 'Ponder Heart' New Stage's Finest
      Hour." Jackson Daily News, 26 April, F, p. 6.
        Culbertson reviews the New Stage production of The Ponder
      Heart which was performed as part of the Arts Festival.
      She also comments about Frank Hains' editing of the origi-
      nal script to make "a better play out of it."

32 DETWEILER, ROBERT. "Eudora Welty's Blazing Butterfly: The
      Dynamics of Response." Language and Style, 6 (Winter),
      58-71.
        Detweiler analyzes "Old Mr. Marblehall" in terms of
      Frye's "Historical Modes" in Anatomy of Criticism. He re-
      lates the story to "low mimetic tragedy." Of the comic
      ironic forms, it "would come closest to the comedy of man-
      ners." He also applies Wayne C. Booth's Rhetoric of Fic-
      tion to Welty's method of narration.

33 DONLAN, DAN. "'A Worn Path': Immortality of Stereotype."
      EJ (Honolulu, Hawaii), 62 (April), 549-550.
        Phoenix is not a "negative black stereotype." In paral-
      lel with the Phoenix myth, she is "a symbol of immortality."
      Donlan shows parallels between Phoenix's journey and ele-
      ments of the Phoenix myth.

34 DRAKE, ROBERT. "Not Proven." Review of The Optimist's Daugh-
      ter. Modern Age, (Winter), pp. 107-109.
        Because all the characters are "flat," Welty does not
      develop her major theme of "love and separateness." The
      language and characters are mannered and insufficiently
      "rendered." Losing Battles had too much context, but The
      Optimist's Daughter, "seems very spare indeed."

35 EAST, CHARLES. "The Search for Eudora Welty." MissQ, 26
      (Fall), 477-482.
        East traces his own growing awareness of Welty from a
      casual comment by an English teacher to a direct influence
      on his own writings.

36 ENSAF, THUNE, and RUTH PRIGOZY. Short Stories: A Critical
      Anthology. New York: Macmillan Co., p. 408.
        Welty achieves "brilliant comic effects" through "collo-
      quial speech" and universality in spite of her attachment
      to her own locality.

37 FERGUSON, MARY ANNE. Images of Women in Literature. Boston,
      Massachusetts: Houghton Mifflin, pp. 233-234.
        Jenny's multiple rape in "At the Landing" is a result of

(FERGUSON, MARY ANNE)
false values. Because she has been so over-protected, she
has never been able to "distinguish between sex and love."

38 FLEISCHAUER, JOHN F. "The Focus of Mystery: Eudora Welty's
Prose Style." SLJ, 5 (Spring), 64-79.
In her major work, Losing Battles, as in many of her
earlier works, Welty starts with a confusion of images and
finally brings them into focus at single places. The result is the transformation of the ordinary world into a
place of mystery. Welty compounds this mystery by creating
an indefinite point of view. Each character has his own
perspective which is by necessity a limited one. He cannot tell the reader the truth because he does not know it.

39 GROSS, SEYMOUR L. "Eudora Welty's Comic Imagination." The
Comic Imagination in American Literature, ed. Louis D.
Rubin, Jr. New Brunswick, New Jersey: Rutgers University
Press, pp. 319-328.
"Welty's comedy is celebrative not critical." Except in
"Petrified Man," her humor is not primarily social criti-
cism; it is the expression of freedom from a society which
places too much emphasis on control and order. In this
sense, she is part of the "American Transcendentalist com-
ic tradition." In The Robber Bridegroom, The Ponder
Heart, and many of the stories, the truly comic characters
manage to free themselves from overly rigid social forms.

40 HAINS, FRANK. "About Eudora Welty: A New Book and a T.V.
Program Tonight." Jackson Daily News, (29 June), C, p. 4.
Discusses Zelma Turner Howard's book, The Rhetoric of
Eudora Welty and a television tribute to Welty, "Black
Life." The book is more than "timely," and "Black Life"
is a "television adaptation of One Time, One Place.

41 _____. "Eudora Welty Day in Festival, State." Jackson Daily
News, (2 May), A, p. 1.
Gives a first-hand account of the events of Eudora Welty
Day including comments made by Governor William Waller.

42 _____. "Eudora Welty: 'I Learn Through My Roots....and
Those Are the Tools." Jackson Daily News, (9 April), B,
p. 6.
Gives excerpts from Welty's appearance on "Firing Line,"
particularly those that deal with the special condition of
being a Southerner. See 1973.B23.

1973

43   HAINS, FRANK. "Reunion in Natchez: Miss Welty and Uncle
         Ponder Get Together." Clarion-Ledger Jackson Daily News,
         (5 August), B, p. 7.
            Discusses David Wayne's visit to Miss Welty and their
         reminiscing about the Music-Box production of The Ponder
         Heart in which Wayne played Uncle Ponder.

44   HARRELL, DON. "Death in Eudora Welty's 'The Bride of the
         Innisfallen.'" NConL, 3 (September), 2-7.
            By making the American girl the center of consciousness,
         Welty controls and directs the main idea of the story,
         life's journey to death. Although the characters are flat,
         the American girl sees all their diverse experiences as
         leading to one end. It is an end represented impression-
         istically.

45   HASSAN, IHAB HABIB. Contemporary American Literature 1945-
         1972. New York: Frederick Ungar Publishing Co., p. 67.
            Considers Welty "the best" of the Twentieth Century
         women novelists. With concreteness and a sense of "life,
         love, humor, and grotesqueness" she "represents a vanish-
         ing way of Southern life."

46   HOWELL, ELMO. "Eudora Welty and the Poetry of Names: A Note
         on Delta Wedding." Love and Wrestling, Butch and O.K.
         South Central Names Institute Publication 2, Commerce,
         Texas: Names Institute Press, pp. 73-78.
            Like Mark Twain, Welty uses concrete details to create
         a sensuous effect. Among these details are the names of
         characters, places, and things which--unlike Faulkner's--
         evoke a concrete sense of her own region. Although her
         themes are abstract--"love, beauty, civility"--she brings
         these abstractions to earth with her art of naming.

47   KEITH, DON LEE. "Eudora Welty: 'I Worry Over My Stories.'"
         Times-Picayune (New Orleans), (16 September), III, p. 8.
            In a visit with Welty, Keith gathers desultery comments
         about many subjects. He includes Welty's comments about
         her early days in New York before she was an established
         writer, her comments about the stage production of The Pon-
         der Heart (she liked it but barely recognized the novel),
         her desire to write a movie script, her attitude toward the
         novelist as crusader, and her well-mannered impatience with
         critics who reduce her work to clinical exercises.

3   KING, WILLIAM PORTER. "A Thematic Study of the Fiction of Eu-
         dora Welty." DAI, 33, 3652-A--3653-A (George Peabody Col-
         lege, 1972).

(KING, WILLIAM PORTER)
King traces the following themes through Welty's fiction: "the celebration of man," "isolation," the "mystery of Man's relationships," and "the mystery of the universe."

49   KREYLING, MICHAEL. "Myth and History: The Foes of Losing Battles." MissQ, 26 (Fall), 639-649.
The central conflict of the novel is between the myth-making mind and the history-making mind. Both try to come to terms with man's mortality, but the way of the myth-maker is cyclical and ritualistic whereas the way of the history-maker is linear and abstract. Both sides ultimately lose, but in her presentation of the struggle, Welty gives a novel which is universal in scope, "a novel true to the widest range of human life."

50   LANDESS, THOMAS H. "The Function of Taste in the Fiction of Eudora Welty." MissQ, 26 (Fall), 543-557.
Landess defends Welty against the attacks of those critics who insist that she "gratuitously exploits the rude and uninstructed for the malicious delight of a sophisticated readership." Like Austen and James, Welty depicts characters within well-defined social codes and conventions. Characters who consistently display boorish behavior are generally represented less favorably than those who do not. But social code often acts as a backdrop for values which are in some ways more important than the social code.

51   McHANEY, THOMAS L. "Eudora Welty and the Multitudinous Golden Apples." MissQ, 26 (Fall), 589-624.
Uses three major reference works in tracing mythological allusions and patterns in The Golden Apples: G. A. Fraser's The Golden Bough, Bullfinch's Mythology: The Age of Mythology, and the variorum edition of the Poems of W. B. Yeats. Although acknowledging Welty's statement in an interview with Charles T. Bunting that The Golden Apples is not a novel, McHenry finds a sense of completeness in Welty's use of Celtic and Graco-Roman mythology. In all the stories, two major legends seem to clash with each other: the Wandering Aengus who is in perpetual search for beauty and love and Perseus who faces the harsh realities of everyday life. The entire collection of The Golden Apples is a balance of these opposite qualities.

52   McMILLAN, WILLIAM E. "Conflict and Resolution in Welty's Losing Battles." Crit, 15 (First Quarter), 110-124.
The two sides of the central conflict are represented by

1973

(McMILLAN, WILLIAM E.)
Julia Mortimer and Granny Vaughn. Julia tries to integrate
family with the world; Granny tries to preserve family as a
sacred unit of its own. The resolution is the ultimate
triumph of Julia. Her prize pupil, Gloria, has won the
prize Beecham and together they will go off into the world
to create a life of their own.

53   MOORE, CAROL A.   "The Insulation of Illusion and Losing Battles."   MissQ, 26 (Fall), 651-658.
Welty uses the illusion of family tradition and legend
as a defense against an encroaching and hostile world.
Insiders know all the details of the family stories, but
such outsiders as Judge Moody, Gloria, and Julia Mortimer
do not. The outsiders' lack of knowledge of family matters
suggests that they are a threat to family unity. Welty
uses a similar method in Delta Wedding and The Ponder
Heart, but Losing Battles is in some ways inferior. Welty
uses figurative language so extravagantly that she seems to
be using her technical skill for "showing off."

54   MORSMAN, JULIA C.   "Daughter Tries, but Father's Wife
Strange." Douglas County Gazette, Metro, (21 February),
p. 2.
Welty's gifts as a writer may be perceived intellectually
but not felt emotionally.

55   PICKETT, NELL ANN.   "Colloquialism as a Style in the First-
Person Narrator Fiction of Eudora Welty." MissQ, 26
(Fall), 559-576.
Pickett uses numerous examples of imagery, grammar, and
rhythm to demonstrate how Welty recreates "lowland southern
dialect" in portraying first person narrators of many different social strata. The lowland black, for example, uses
speech forms that would not be used by the low class lowland whites, and the high class lowland white has a style
all his own. Pickett's essay gives many examples from
many of Welty's works, and concludes with a detailed analysis of dialect in "Why I Live at the P.O."

56   POLK, NOEL.   "A Eudora Welty Checklist." MissQ, 26 (Fall),
663-693.
A two-part bibliography. The first part is a comprehensive descriptive bibliography of Welty's writings. It includes separate publication of books, contributions to
books and periodicals (including stories, essays, sketches,
criticism, book reviews, poetry, and interviews). The

(POLK, NOEL)
second part of the bibliography is a selective list of secondary materials. It includes all full-length studies,
some reviews, textbook explications, and most dissertations.

57 SEMEL, JAY M. "Eudora Welty's Freak Show: A Pattern in 'Why
I Live at the P.O.'" NConL, 3 (May), 2-3.
The seemingly irrelevant details of sister's narrative
all reinforce the central theme of the story: sister's
jealousy and frustration because Shirley--in the normal
process of human nature--has produced a child. The
"freaks" are all those who are in some way sexually abnormal.

58 SEIDL, FRANCIS. "Eudora Welty's Phoenix." NMW, 6 (Fall), 53-55.
Welty supports the life-in-death symbolism of the name
Phoenix with several complementary symbols. The scarecrow,
which seems like a ghost, is a "death-life symbol" as is
the paradoxical combination of Phoenix's blue eyes and black
hair with the statement that she is "'a hundred years old.'"
Color symbolism also suggests life in death, particularly
red and green.

59 SIMPSON, LEWIS P. "An Introductory Note." MissQ, 26 (Fall),
pp. 475-476.
Simpson describes the honoring of Welty during Mississippi Arts Festival Week. In spite of all the official pres-
ences--including that of the governor--Welty's presence
dominated. She was the story teller--the celebrator of
life. Even though she read sections of Losing Battles soft-
ly, and the people had to strain to hear her, she dominated
the occasion. (See 1973.B60).

60 SKELTON, BILLY. "State Pays Eudora Welty Tribute." Clarion-
Ledger (Jackson), 3 May, A, p. 1.
Skelton gives an eye-witness account of Eudora Welty Day
in Jackson. He includes dialogues between Welty and Jack-
sonians, descriptions of Welty's dress, and Welty's readings from Losing Battles.

61 SLETHANG, GORDON E. "Initiation in Eudora Welty's The Robber
Bridegroom." SHR, 7 (Winter), 77-87.
Rosamond's quote from the ballad "Young Andrew" helps
establish the initiation theme of the novel. The ballad
presents the essentially evil view of abduction and rape,
but in The Robber Bridegroom, this evil is set against the
happier world of the fairy tale. Rosamond's abduction is
at least in part a willing one and in return for lost

1973

(SLETHANG, GORDON E.)
virginity she discovers her humanity. Rosamond thus moves
from a simplistic vision of life to a highly complex one
in which good and evil are inextricably mixed.

62 SMITH, CAROL P. "The Journey Motif in Eudora Welty's The
Robber Bridegroom." SSCRev, pp. 18-32.
Smith demonstrates that all the characters in The Robber
Bridegroom take journeys which have both literal and figurative significance. But because of man's double identi-
ty--one of the main themes of the novel--most of the characters misunderstand the nature of their quests.

63 STANFORD, DONALD D. "Eudora Welty and the Pulitzer Prize."
SoR, 9 (Autumn), xx-xxiii.
The Optimist's Daughter is certainly deserving of the
Pulitzer, but Losing Battles was even more worthy. Welty
should have received the prize in 1971 for Losing Battles.

64 THOMPSON, VICTOR H. "The Natchez Trace in Eudora Welty's
'A Still Moment.'" SLJ, 6 (Fall), 59-69.
Thompson discusses Welty's use of sources in "A Still
Moment." He finds that Welty uses specific passages from
Audubon and Dow, but that she adapts them to the theme of
her story: place dominates character and unifies three
separate beings in a single moment of intense insight.

65 VANDE KIEFT, RUTH M. "The Vision of Eudora Welty." MissQ,
26 (Fall), 517-542.
Vande Kieft demonstrates how Welty controls point of
view in "A Memory," "A Still Moment," The Golden Apples,
Delta Wedding, Losing Battles, and The Optimist's Daughter.
Welty's method of control is best stated by Welty herself
in her introduction to One Time, One Place. Just as photographs capture single moments in a constantly changing
field of vision, so does the writer. He captures word
pictures of scenes which are in constant flux. Although
the narrator gives these pictures subjective interpreta-
tions, the physical details are always as clear as a photograph.

66 WAGES, JACK D. "Names in Eudora Welty's Fiction: An Onoma-
tological Prolegomenon." Love and Wrestling, Butch and
O.K., South Central Names Institute Publication 2, Com-
merce, Texas: Names Institute Press, pp. 65-72.
Discusses the significance of names in "Petrified Man,"
"Why I Live at the P.O.," "Lily Daw and the Three Ladies,"
"Clytie," "A Worn Path," and "Death of A Traveling

(WAGES, JACK D.)
Salesman." In Welty's fiction, names always support theme.
Rondo in "Why I Live at the P.O.," for example suggests the
musical form of repeated themes and thus suggests the repeated patterns of family strife.

67   WELTY, EUDORA. "Some Notes on Time in Fiction." MissQ, 26
(Fall), 483-492.
Time is perhaps even more important than place to the
writer of fiction. Place is definable and objective, but
time is changeable and subjective. (Stream of consciousness fiction is a natural product of the human time sense
and is therefore not as difficult as novels which use a
more objective and arbitrary method of narration.) Welty
illustrates this observation with a brief discussion of
The Sound and the Fury. She also alludes to Henry Green
and to Porter's "The Grave."

68   YARDLEY, JONATHAN. "For Eudora Welty, May Was the Month That
Was." Greensboro News, (3 June), B, p. 3.
Relates insights and information gained while visiting
Welty at her home. Welty tells about her family and about
her emerging writing career. Yardley notes that Welty is
particularly pleased by her local recognition. (She was
well-known nationally before she was known locally.) He
also discusses Welty's style. It is "at once sophisticated
and innocent." And he relates for the first time the
source of "The Wide Net."

1974 A BOOKS - NONE

1974 B SHORTER WRITINGS

1   ALBRITTON, NANCI C. "Eudora Welty Credits 'Luck and Ignorance.'" Rocky Mountain News, Now (12 May), p. 10.
In an interview, Welty reveals some aspects of her methods of writing. She broods over things that bother her and
after a period of time, finds a clue to turn these brood-
ings into a story. She has a trained visual memory; she
composes at the typewriter, and she writes about people
she knows.

2   ANON. "Eudora Welty T.V. Special Tuesday." Clarion-Ledger
(Jackson), (25 August), H, p. 4.
Announces the presentation of two programs about Welty
to appear on Mississippi educational television: "A Season of Dreams," and "One Time, One Place." The first

1974

(ANON.)
   presents through readings and scenes such "favorite characters" as Edna Earle, Ponder, Ruby Fisher, Jamie Lock-
   hart, and William Wallace Jamison. The second features
   Welty "narrating a gallery of the photographs which compose
   her book."

3   ANON. "Honor Planned for Allen Tate." New York Times, (5
   November), p. 31.
      Notes that Welty will attend a symposium at the Univer-
   sity of the South to celebrate Tate's 75th birthday.

4   BOATWRIGHT, JAMES. "Speech and Silence in Losing Battles."
   Shenandoah, 25 (Spring), 3-14.
      Losing Battles is like a play except for the presence of
   a "narrative voice." As in a play, speech and silence are
   in constant interplay with each other. The speech--which
   is almost constant on the part of many characters--is the
   reassurance of family solidarity and community. The silence is the underlying suggestion of separateness and
   isolation. In the midst of the talking characters, the
   silences of Judge Moody, Granny Vaughn, Gloria, and Nathan
   are significant. They are a constant reminder that the in-
   sistent unity of the speakers--like all things in this
   world--is temporary.

5   BOLSTERLI, MARGARET. "Mythic Elements in 'Ladies in Spring.'"
   NMW, 7 (Winter), 69-72.
      "Ladies in Spring" is "an initiation story" in which the
   boy is unknowingly led into the mysteries of the adult
   world of sex and fertility. This world is suggested sym-
   bolically by the fish ("an ancient and universal symbol
   for fertility"). by the transformation of a wasteland into
   a lush countryside, by the color black ("the color tradi-
   tionally associated with rain making"), and by the suggestion that the boy--like his father--will understand the
   mysteries of the adult world.

6   BRYANT, J. A. "Seeing Double in The Golden Apples." SR, 82
   (Spring), 300-315.
      Bryant accepts the thesis of Louis Rubin and others that
   The Golden Apples is a unified work, but finds the unify-
   ing element not so much in the characters as in the theme
   of "seeing double." In their undefined quests, the major
   characters have moments of intense vision when they see the
   world doubly as "a fire in the head" and with a sense of
   poetry "and the mythic consciousness."

7   COLE, HUNTER M.   "Windsor in Spenser and Welty: A Real and
    an Imaginary Landscape." NMW, 7 (Spring), 4-11.
        Cole describes the ruins of Windsor Castle and explains
    how Welty has used details of this specific place in
    "Asphodel." According to Cole, Welty preserves some of the
    details but transforms them into what the original Windsor
    might have looked like. Cole also notes that Windsor--near
    the Old Natchez Trace--is one of Welty's favorite settings.
    She discusses it in "Some Notes on River Country" and had
    her picture taken in front of it for New York Times Book
    Review.

8   DIETRICH, R. F., and ROGER H. SUNDELL. The Art of Fiction.
    2d. edition. New York: Holt, Rinehart & Winston,
    pp. 531-532.
        Welty emphasizes "the eccentricities of neurotic person-
    alities...." (One of her major techniques is "symbolic
    violence.") Also atmosphere is more important than action
    and plot.

9   HAINS, FRANK. "Eudora Welty's Robber Bridegroom." Jackson
    Daily News, (4 November), C, p. 4.
        Hains discusses the musical comedy version of The Robber
    Bridegroom which was to appear in St. Clement's Workshop
    directed by Gerald Freedman and produced by Stuart Ostrow.

10 HELTERMAN, JEFFREY. "Gorgons in Mississippi." NMW, 7
    (Spring), 12-20.
        Helterman traces parallels between the gorgon myths and
    "Petrified Man." The three women in the beauty shop paral-
    lel the three Gorgons in their scorn for love and in their
    desire to castrate their husbands. Billy Boy is "likened
    to Perseus" in his wearing of the caps, in his apparent
    invisibility, and in his symbolic recovery of the phallis
    (when he takes the peanuts).

11 HOLLENBAUGH, CAROL. "Ruby Fisher and her Demon-Lover." NMW,
    7 (Fall), 63-67.
        Ruby Fisher's fantasies are distinctly sexual. She is
    extremely conscious of her body throughout the story, and
    even the rain and thunder contribute to her yearning for
    sexual fulfillment. In scorning the newspaper clipping,
    however, Clyde also scorns the physical desires of his
    wife and fails to become the "demon-lover."

12 LOEWEN, JAMES W., et al. Mississippi: Conflict and Change.
    New York: Pantheon (Random House), pp. 233-234.
        Gives a brief biographical sketch and notes Welty's

1974

    (LOEWEN, JAMES W., et al)
        dedication to Mississippi as both a place to live and as a
        source for her fiction. Though her situations are "local,"
        her "themes" are universal.

13   McDONALD, W. U., JR. "Eudora Welty Manuscripts: A Supple-
        mentary Annotated Finding List." Bulletin of Bibliography,
        31 (July/September), 95-98, 126.
          Updates the Finding List of 1963 (Bulletin of Bibliogra-
        phy, 24 [September/December, 1963, 44-46]). Includes mate-
        rial about Losing Battles, The Wide Net, The New Yorker,
        and The Optimist's Daughter. The list is divided into four
        parts: published fiction, published non-fiction, unpub-
        lished writings, and letters. McDonald cites important
        variants in manuscript versions of the fiction and states
        the subject matter of the letters.

14   SIERICHS, BILL. "Baptist T.V. Wins Welty American a Medal."
        Clarion-Ledger (Jackson), (10 November), A, p. 3.
          Dr. Margaret Walker, Professor of English at Jackson
        State, comments about Welty, Faulkner, and Wright who share
        the themes of "race, violence, and decadence."

15   SIMMONS, MONTY. "Eudora Welty Discusses Her Ideas About
        Writing." World-News (Roanoke), (20 February), p. 10.
          While being honored at Hollins College, Welty makes nu-
        merous comments about the art of writing which Simmons
        quotes directly. She includes observations about charac-
        terization in Losing Battles, the relationship between fic-
        tion and film, and Welty's attitude toward the feminist
        movement in literature.

16   _____. "Young Writer Talks with Eudora Welty." Books,
        Roanoke Times, (24 February), C, p. 4.
          Welty interviewed while being honored at Hollins College.
        Simmons talks at length about her own experiences in read-
        ing Welty. She notes Welty's "power of characterization
        and evocation of mood" and considers Welty "a writer to be
        reckoned with."

17   STANFORD, DONALD E. "Eudora Welty and the Pulitzer Prize."
        SoR, (January), xx-xxiii.
          Stanford is delighted that Welty won the prize for The
        Optimist's Daughter which is "vintage Welty" but he ques-
        tions the wisdom of the Pulitzer Prize Committee for not
        giving her the award sooner. A Curtain of Green was a
        possibility, and Losing Battles should have been a certain-
        ty.

18 STONE, WILLIAM B. "Eudora Welty's Hydrodynamic Powerhouse."
    SSF, 11 (Winter), 93-96.
       Stone demonstrates how Welty uses water imagery to
    achieve structural unity and to reveal the tragic depths
    of her central character, Powerhouse. Water has universal
    connotations of "harsh reality and death," connotations
    which are particularly associated with black people.
    Whether Powerhouse is in concert, or in the World Cafe, or
    fantasizing about Uranus Knockwood, he is associated with
    water imagery.

19 TAPLEY, PHILIP ALLEN. "The Portrayal of Women in Selected
    Short Stories by Eudora Welty." DAI, 35 (February),
    5429-A--5430-A.
       In analyses of twenty-one stories, Tapley traces three
    distinct patterns of women characters in Welty's fiction:
    girls initiated into womanhood, women living in isolation,
    and women who find fulfillment in the home with children.
    All three types are complex and realistic. Welty avoids
    sentimentality, stereotypes, and a feminist stand.

20 WELTY, EUDORA. "The Feast Itself." New York Times, (5 De-
    cember), p. 47 (adapted from speech given before the Gov-
    ernor's conference on the arts in Jackson).
       If the artist aims for excellence rather than for the
    masses, he will create an art which can give all people
    "a quickened imagination."

21 _____. "Is Phoenix Jackson's Grandson Really Dead?" Critical
    Inquiry, 1 (September), 219-221.
       Welty answers the question which she claims is the most
    frequently asked about "A Worn Path." It does not matter
    whether or not he is dead. The important point of the
    story is the journey itself and Phoenix's indominable hope.

22 YARDLEY, JONATHAN. "A Quiet Lady in the Limelight." Miami
    Herald, (17 February), pp. 1, 5.
       Yardley knows Welty well and comments about details of
    her private life (her reading and writing habits, her in-
    terest and involvement in civil rights, her afternoon
    bourbon).

1975

1975 A BOOKS - NONE

1975 B SHORTER WRITINGS

1 HEMBREE, CHARLES WILLIAM. "Narrative Technique in the Fiction
of Eudora Welty." DAI, 35 (March), 6139-A--6140-A (University of Oklahoma, 1974).
Hembree analyses Welty's method of narration in A Curtain
of Green, The Ponder Heart, The Golden Apples, and Losing
Battles. He also discusses The Robber Bridegroom, Delta
Wedding, and The Optimist's Daughter.

2 HINTON, JANE LEE. "Out of All Times of Trouble: The Family
in the Fiction of Eudora Welty." DAI, 35 (June), 7906-A
(Vanderbilt University).
In much of Welty's fiction, the sense of family is the
central organizing principle. In its desire for unity and
changelessness in the presence of dissolution and mutabil-
ity, the family is Welty's "most significant metaphor for
all human relationships."

3 THORSBY, LINDA. "Author Describes Historical Tale." Clarion-Ledger (Jackson), (8 March), p. 22.
Welty tells the Mississippi Historical Society about The
Robber Bridegroom. She explains how she used historical
people, places, and incidents to create a work of the
imagination.

4 WELTY, EUDORA. "In Memorium." Clarion-Ledger Jackson Daily
News, (27 July), H, p. 14.
Welty gives a tribute to Frank Hains who was a life-long
supporter of the arts in Jackson and whose "dramatic productions of my stories are among the proudest and happiest
events of my working life."

Index

Blackwell, Louise, 1965.B4;
    1966.**B3**; 1973.B20
B. O., 1966.B3
Boardman, Anne Cawley, 1970.B16
Boatner, Maxine Tull, 1970.B17,
    1972.B24
Boatwright, James, 1970.B18,
    1972.B25, 1974.B4
Bode, Winston, 1963.B3
Bogan, Louise, 1941.B12
Bolsterli, Margaret, 1974.B5
Bookhart, Mary Alice, 1949.B11;
    1956.B9
Booth, Wayne C., 1967.B7
Boozer, William, 1972.B26
Bornhauser, Fred, 1955.B19
Bowen, Elizabeth, 1947.B3;
    1954.B16, 1962.B2
Boylan, Mildred, 1971.B7
Boyle, Kay, 1941.B13
Bradbury, John M., 1958.B4;
    1963.B4
Bradford, M. E., 1971.B8;
    1973.B21
Bradham, Jo Allen, 1964.B10
Bradley, Van Allen, 1970.B19
Brady, Charles A., 1970.B20
Brantley, Frederick, 1942.B12
Braverman, Millicent, 1972.B27
Breit, Harvey, 1949.B12
Bresler, Riva T., 1955.B20
Brickell, Herschel, 1941.B4,
    B14; 1942.B13; 1943.B11;
    1947.B4; 1949.B13;
    1951.B2
The Bride of the Innisfallen,
    1955.B1-B13, B15-B46, B48,
    B50-B51, B53, B55-B58,
    B60-B71, B72-B76, B78-B81;
    1969.B12
Brodley, Van Allen, 1970.B21
Brooks, Cleanth, 1959.B3, B4
    1971.B9; 1973.B22
Brooks, John, 1951.B3
Brown, Ashley, 1969.B3
Broyard, Anatole, 1972.B28
Bryant, J. A., Jr., 1968.A1;
    1974.B6
Buckley, William F., Jr.,
    1973.B23

Bullock, Florence Haxton
    1946.B17
Bunting, Charles T., 1972.B29
Burger, Nash K., 1969.B4
"The Burning", 1951.B2, 1957.B6,
    1969.B10
Burns, Landon C., Jr., 1970.B22;
    1971.B10
Burns, Roberta, 1967.B8
Buswell, Mary Catherine, 1961.B5;
    1972.B30
Butcher, Fanny, 1954.B17
Butler, M., 1946.B18
Caldwell, David S., 1970.B23
Callaway, John, 1972.B32
Campbell, Harry Modean, 1954.B18
Canfield, Dorothy, 1946.B19
Cannon, Lee E., 1949.B14
Capers, Charlotte, 1946.B20;
    1966.B4; 1973.B24
Carr, Arthur J., 1942.B14
Carson, Franklin D., 1973.B25
Carter, Thomas H., 1955.B21
Chambers, Elsie May, 1973.B26
Chapman, John, 1954.B19
Cheney, Francis Neel, 1971.B12;
    1972.B33
Cheney, Winifred Green, 1970.B24
Chodorov, Jerome, 1956.B12
Chriss, Nick, 1954.B20
Clark, Betty Gail, 1972.B34
Clark, Charles C., 1973.B27
Clark, Eleanor, 1949.B15
Clark, Emily, 1973.B28
Clarke, Clorinda, 1949.B16
Clarke, George Herbert, 1943.B12
Clayton, Robert, 1970.B25
Clemons, Walter, 1970.B26;
    1971.B13; 1972.B35
Clerman, Harold, 1956.B10
"Clytie", 1966.B6
Cochran, Robert W., 1968.B5
Cockshutt, Rod, 1971.B14
Cole, Hunter M., 1974.B7
Cole, McKelva, 1963.B5
Collins, L. A., 1946.B21
Comic Sense, 1954.B12, B16, B29,
    B34, B46, B48; 1955.B8;
    1963.B10; 1964.B2;
    1970.B15-B16, B25, B46;
    1973.B39

Index

INDEX